# Yoshida Shigeru
# and
# His Time

# Yoshida Shigeru and His Time

Okazaki Hisahiko

Translated by Noda Makito

Japan Publishing Industry Foundation for Culture

TRANSLATION NOTE

All Japanese names appearing in this book are written with surname first and given name last. In addition, all Japanese words and names have been romanized in accordance with the Hepburn system, and macrons have been applied to indicate long vowels wherever deemed appropriate.

*Yoshida Shigeru and his Time*
Okazaki Hisahiko. Translated by Noda Makito
Published by Japan Publishing Industry Foundation for Culture (JPIC)
3-12-3 Kanda-Jinbocho, Chiyoda-ku, Tokyo 101-0051, Japan
First English edition: March 2019
© Okazaki Hisahiko, Okazaki Akiko, 2003.
English translation © The Japan Institute of International Affairs (JIIA)
This book is the result of a collaborative effort between The Japan Institute of International Affairs (JIIA) and Japan Publishing Industry Foundation for Culture (JPIC)
Originally published in Japanese under the titles of *Yoshida Shigeru to sono jidai* by PHP Institute, Inc. in 2003.
Jacket & cover design: Miki Kazuhiko, Ampersand Works
All rights reserved.

Printed in Japan
ISBN 978-4-86658-070-8
http://www.jpic.or.jp/

# CONTENTS

CHAPTER

1

# How Japan-the-Loser Was Treated

*—Unconditional Surrender: The Winners Take All—*

## U.S. Occupation Policies

On August 15, 1945, Japan accepted the Potsdam Declaration and surrendered to the Allies.

It meant a close to a half-century of history for the Empire of Japan since the days of the First Sino-Japanese and Russo-Japanese Wars. Ending the war required the extraordinary insights by national leaders, including Prime Minister Suzuki Kantarō and Emperor Shōwa, as I wrote in the final chapter of the previous volume of this series, *Shigemitsu/Tōgō to Sono Jidai* (Shigemitsu, Tōgō, and Their Time).

Japan had ceased to be an actor that could decide its own destiny. By that time, Japan had no other option than to entrust its fate to the hands of the victors.

One may wonder, then, how the Allies, including the United States, intended to treat Japan. According to diplomatic historian Iokibe Makoto,

> The Suzuki Kantarō cabinet and the Harry Truman administration, two governments born in April 1945 on opposite sides of the Pacific [the Suzuki cabinet formed on April 7; Truman succeeded Franklin

Roosevelt, who passed away on April 12], put an end to the war by fundamentally changing the policies of their respective predecessors [the Tōjō Hideki and Koiso Kuniaki cabinets in the case of Suzuki and the Franklin D. Roosevelt administration in the case of Truman].

In both countries, there were powerful elements not only in the governments but also among citizens that strongly opposed these policy changes. Examples are the advocates of an unconditional surrender by Japan in the United States and those in Japan who resisted such surrender to the bitter end.

While both President Truman and Prime Minister Suzuki paid due consideration to the voices of these elements, and to some extent appeared to have succumbed to those elements, in the end they succeeded in realizing an early peace, through policy changes, while successfully preventing a schism in their respective nations. It was the Potsdam Declaration that enabled this narrow compromise. The Potsdam Declaration was a fragile compromise for the U.S. government as it was under fire from domestic criticism that it was being too accommodating. The same can be said about the Japanese side . . .

This quote is from the conclusion of Iokibe's 500-page masterpiece *Beikoku no Nippon Senryō Seisaku* (U.S. Occupation Policy toward Japan). Ever since I started writing about the complete history of modern Japanese diplomacy, I have concentrated on grasping the major flow of history, relying solely on secondary source materials without trying to spend all of my time in a thorough search for the minute details that might be contained in the primary sources. I was allowed to enjoy this luxury because Japanese scholars are without exception peerlessly accurate in describing the events regardless of their ideological convictions. Particularly, I find Iokibe's works to be the most exhaustive in their analysis and, above all, highly objective. Thus, I beg the readers' indulgence for the frequent quotes from Iokibe's works in the rest of this chapter.

In the foreword to *Beikoku no Nippon Senryō Seisaku*, Iokibe uses elegant literary expressions to explain how he reached the above conclusion. He writes:

When I finally gained a full view of the process through which U.S. occupation policies were formed, what came to my mind was its surprising analogy to how a classical symphony is developed. I realized that the shocking theme—the unconditional surrender that would incapacitate Japan and Germany almost eternally—formed the main melody played repeatedly by the top leadership of the United States (President Roosevelt). I also realized that a second melody, totally different from the main melody, had subtly begun at the same time by the lower echelon at the State Department. The second melody reflected the proposal from the State Department's Japan specialists that the United States should sympathize with the domestic situation in Japan and help it rehabilitate into the postwar international community. . . . In short, the U.S. occupation policies for Japan had a succinct structure composed of the simultaneous development of two incompatible themes and their subsequent integration.

This is an excellent paradigm and it should allow us to explain everything accurately.

The term "unconditional surrender" was first used officially in the joint press statement by U.S. President Franklin Roosevelt and British Prime Minister Winston Churchill at the Casablanca Conference in January 1943.

What does this unconditional surrender entail? Traditionally wars ended by way of a certain process: cessation of hostilities, conclusion of a treaty of armistice, peace treaty negotiations, conclusion of a peace treaty, and ratification of the treaty. During this time, the government of the defeated country remained active and became the party to negotiate toward armistice and peace. In the case of an unconditional surrender, there is no treaty of armistice, nor any peace treaty negotiations. The defeated is simply occupied by the victor. Government functions are transferred to the hands of the victor, who is allowed to determine conditions for peace arbitrarily.

Admittedly, it would be useless to criticize the unconditional surrender as a deviation from conventional international laws. That is, if we define international laws as rules to govern relations between and among states, then an unconditional surrender can be perceived as a complete subjugation of the defeated by the victor. In this case, no international law can be applied because the nation-state of the defeated ceases to function.

One of the reasons behind the use of an unconditional surrender was the escalation of the scale of war in the 20th century: Wars began to call for all-out efforts by the entire nation. As such, in order to secure national support for waging a war, governments needed to convince their citizens that they were the good guys and the enemies were the evil ones. In the case of the United States, its unique democratic nature further reinforces this inclination. As George Kennan once said, "Democracy fights in anger." In sum, when a good guy fights an evil, the good guy has to fight until it achieves a complete victory over the evil, making a compromise between the two practically impossible. This is the justification for an unconditional surrender.

Another factor behind Roosevelt's demand for Japan's unconditional surrender was his leftist leanings, which made him harsh on Japan and Germany yet tolerant toward the Soviet Union. In fact, after the press conference, Roosevelt was heard to say, "Stalin should welcome this policy."

Roosevelt's consideration for the Soviet Union could be in part explained from a standpoint of realpolitik needs—i.e., a need to prevent the Soviet Union from retiring from battle as it had done during World War I. When the formation of the second front in Europe that the Soviet Union had demanded was not progressing promptly and when the Soviets were reluctant to comply with the U.S. request to use Soviet airbases in Siberia for air raids on Japan, Roosevelt did have a reason to please the Soviets.

However, Roosevelt's decision regarding the unconditional surrender can be attributed more to his Marxist complex. The record of a dialogue between President Roosevelt and Archbishop Francis Spellman (later cardinal) in September 1943 strongly hints at Roosevelt's pro-Soviet inclination. It was confirmed that a number of Roosevelt's aides and close friends were later found to be Communists, including Alger Hiss, who took part in the Yalta Conference of February 1945.

As shown by the case of Japan's Ozaki Hotsumi, these highly intellectual Communists deeply understood the Comintern's intricate strategies and took well-calculated actions in order to carry them out.

The Soviet strategy was straightforward. The Soviets wanted Japan not to advance north toward the Soviet Union but rather clash with Britain and the United States first. Once it brought Japan into a war with the United States, the Soviet Union hoped to make the United States agree to the expansion of the Soviet sphere of influence. Subsequently, in light of

Churchill, Roosevelt, and Stalin in Yalta in February 1945

the most prominent obstacles that Germany and Japan posed to its western and eastern advances, the Soviet Union wanted to keep the two countries as weak as possible and for as long as possible. Communist strategies, no matter how mysterious they may have appeared under the cloak of absolute secrecy, were actually as simple as that when analyzed in real politics.

The Yalta Agreement was such a top secret that even President Truman, to his surprise, learned of its content for the first time when he opened President Roosevelt's safe after his death. The Agreement had widely adopted Soviet demands.

The Agreement recognized Soviet possession of the Kuril Islands in addition to the recovery of the territories Russia had lost as the result of the Russo-Japanese War. Even though Japan specialists in the U.S. State Department were fully aware of the historical background of Japan's possession of the islands, Roosevelt promised cession of the Kuril Islands to Stalin against the advice of U.S. Ambassador to the Soviet Union W. Averell Harriman and without consulting the State Department.

Moreover, Roosevelt even promised Stalin the regaining of concessions that the Russian Empire had possessed in Manchuria before the Russo-Japanese War, even though China at that time was fighting a war on the same side as the United States. Theodore Roosevelt earlier had refused to do this, but Franklin Roosevelt even promised Stalin that the United States would try to persuade Chiang Kai-shek on this humiliating concession.

To be sure, the argument for the Soviet Union's participation in the war so as to minimize American casualties before Japan's surrender was convincing. As a matter of fact, however, the Kwangtung Army had been substantially weakened by that time because its main body had been transferred to Southeast Asia, mainland China, and Okinawa. Unaware of this development, Roosevelt might have overestimated the Kwangtung Army's potential.

Nevertheless, what Roosevelt did was such a one-sided compromise that the above reasoning alone cannot justify it. Therefore, it seems undeniable that the pro-Soviet sentiment of Roosevelt and some of his aides or even political maneuvering on the part of the Comintern via Communist Party members serving as Roosevelt's aides was behind the president's actions.

However, it might be unfair to blame Roosevelt alone. After all, those were the days when the horrible realities of Soviet Communism were mostly unknown to outsiders, and the dream of societal revolution or the Marxist complex evident since the 1920s still remained persistent among intellectuals.

Even among the Japanese military, quite a number of officers adored Soviet Communism more than the corrupted capitalism. Toward the end of the Greater East Asia War, some officers even insisted on requesting Soviet assistance to continue the war against the United States.

One can comprehend the situation in Japan in those days from a report that Prime Minister Konoe wrote to the Emperor in April 1945. In this report, Konoe secretly appealed for an early termination of the war on the grounds that further continuation of the war might lead to a Communist revolution in Japan. Konoe pointed to "clandestine maneuvers of the leftist element that has, behind the scenes, tried to fan . . . pro-Soviet sentiment among the Japanese people as a flip side of the rise of hostile feelings against Britain and the United States." Konoe was particularly apprehensive of the reformist movement within the military. Remembering that "[those reformist elements] openly declared at the time of the Manchurian Incident that the true purpose of the Incident was to facilitate domestic reforms, . . . it is obvious today that it was a deliberate plan by these elements to start the Manchurian Incident and the Second Sino-Japanese War first and, eventually, lead the country to the Greater East Asia War."

Furthermore, Konoe stated that, "Even though the reformist elements within the military do not necessarily pursue a Communist revolution, I believe it would be safe to say that ignorant and simple military officers are being manipulated by several bureaucrats and private conspirators who harbor an intention to deliberately draw Japan to an eventual Communist revolution." And he wrote, "This is a conclusion that I humbly have come to after pondering on my past associations over several decades with a multitude of people from the military, bureaucrats, and rightists and leftists."

Reflecting critically on his past attempts at securing the nation's unity by "forestalling the military," Konoe said,

> When Your Imperial Majesty instructed me to form a cabinet twice, I tried to accomplish a cabinet of national unity both times by accommodating as many demands from the reformists as possible in order to avoid frictions within Japan. It was to my greatest regret that I foolishly failed to detect the hidden intentions of those reformists entirely due to a lack of insight on my part. I feel deeply responsible for my failure and humbly beg Your Imperial Majesty's pardon.

In light of his persistent efforts to forestall the military, this was a bitter confession on the part of Konoe that he had been manipulated by the military's maneuvering and puppeteered by the Comintern through the likes of Ozaki Hotsumi.

Underestimation of the Communists' strategy was an error that both Konoe and Roosevelt, who belonged to the same generation, committed. Had Roosevelt acknowledged that Japan's participation in the war would cause irreparable losses for the U.S. citizens, Roosevelt too might have similarly recalled the remorseful past, affirming that some of his close aides were in fact Communists.

The difference between the United States and Japan, then, was that the former had enough leeway to allow that degree of trial and error.

To use Iokibe's expression, in the background of the main melody, which was played by Roosevelt, who wanted to force an unconditional surrender on Japan, was a second melody played by the Japan experts in the U.S. Department of State. Former U.S. Ambassador to Japan Joseph Grew played a particularly significant role.

After returning home from Japan as part of the exchange of personnel between the two warring countries, Grew toured around the United States to deliver speeches to enlighten Americans on their enemy country, Japan. In 1944, Grew agreed to be appointed Assistant Secretary of State for Far Eastern Affairs, paying no heed to his demotion as a bureaucrat that this appointment entailed. When he was momentarily promoted to Undersecretary of State, he left his former position to another Japan expert, Joseph William Ballantine.

According to Iokibe,

> Thus, a comprehensive line up of Japan experts was completed in the State Department in the late 1944–early 1945 period. The shift encompassed the policy planning level (George Hubbard Blakeslee and Hugh Borton), the policy formulation level (Ballantine and Eugene Dooman), and the policy decision-making level (Grew). It was an unprecedented, highly unusual development in the State Department where the relative weight of Japan issues and the Japan experts was extremely low under normal circumstances.

It was around the time of the German surrender in May 1945 that Grew learned of the secret Yalta agreements for the first time.

As soon as Grew became aware of the secret agreements, he wrote a memorandum that included such questions as "Is the Soviet Union's participation in the war so absolutely necessary?" and "Can the Yalta agreements be reviewed?" Receiving this memorandum, Secretary of War Henry Stimson wrote in his journal how happy he was that "an opportunity to review [the Yalta agreements] was given." Stimson also had been quite apprehensive about Roosevelt's arbitrary actions.

A governmental conference was convened immediately to review the secret Yalta agreements. However, the perception that Soviet participation in the war was absolutely necessary to minimize American casualties prevailed. It was also judged premature to resume renegotiations with the Soviet Union on the conditions of the Yalta agreements before the top secret production of an atomic bomb.

Grew said to Dooman, "We have absolutely no time to spare." Probably, he meant that the United States had no other choice than to hasten

Japan's surrender in order to prevent the Soviet Union from joining the war. And this meant that the United States had to prepare and present conditions for surrender that were acceptable to Japan.

All the while, Grew had known that the Allies had to guarantee maintenance of the status quo of the Emperor to make Japan agree with termination of the war and that the only way that could end the war was an imperial edict issued by the Emperor.

By the end of the war with Japan, American interrogators of Japanese prisoners-of-war began to believe in the simple conclusion that "the Japanese warriors would lay down their weapons with the imperial order."

What followed then was a bout between the overwhelming majority who advocated President Roosevelt's good and evil dualism and believed in the thorough annihilation of Japan, on the one hand, and those who supported promoting the realistic compromise proposal submitted by the Japan specialists, on the other.

Grew proposed that the United States officially demand Japan surrender on the condition that the Allies would not depose the Emperor. Although his proposal faced fierce opposition from Assistant Secretary of State for Economic Affairs Dean Acheson and others at the conference in the State Department, Grew adjourned the meeting and brought the proposal directly to President Truman by virtue of his authority as the Acting Secretary of State.

Although Truman found his proposal a "sound one," holding Grew's experiences in Japan in high esteem, he nevertheless left the decision to a conference participated in by the U.S. Army and Navy.

Having served the republican administration as Secretary of State before the four terms of the Roosevelt administration, Secretary of War Stimson, being almost eighty years old at that time, was the patriarch of the Truman administration. Stimson participated in the government as a nonpartisan contributor. He was proficient at Japan policy and someone who had once pinned his hopes on Shidehara Kijūrō at the time of the Manchurian Incident.

After fully endorsing Grew's proposal, Stimson said, "I have one complaint." Having said that, he added a very favorable comment about Japan, saying, "[Grew's proposal] failed to acknowledge Japan's ability to produce progressive leaders such as Shidehara, Wakatsuki Reijirō, and

Hamaguchi Osachi, who are on a par with leading statesmen of the West."

On this incident, Iokibe gave the following observation:

> At the very moment when Japan, an enemy to the United States, was about to fall, old Stimson referred to the names of internationalists that Japan had produced during Taishō Democracy. Obviously, he had not forgotten about them. In the history of Japan, there is a discontinuation between Taishō Democracy and the post–World War II democracy. In this case, adept Japan specialists in the United States played the role of bridging these two democracies together.

Stimson's comment was held in high esteem at the conference, where nobody opposed Grew's proposal. Only General George Marshall intervened, saying that although he supported the proposal in principle, the United States could not issue a presidential announcement immediately due to "military reasons." Presumably Marshall was alluding to the production of the atomic bombs. Consequently, the presidential announcement was postponed.

It is not hard to imagine how mortified Grew must have felt at the postponement of his proposal after having come that far. One may wonder what would have happened if the U.S. presidential announcement had been issued promptly as proposed by Grew. By that time, it is said that Minister of Navy Yonai Mitsumasa had told people around him that he would not disapprove of an early surrender by Japan as long as the Emperor system was allowed to survive. Had a supreme war leaders' conference been convened and had Prime Minister Suzuki decided to request an imperial decision at this point, the war would have been stopped and the citizens of Hiroshima and Nagasaki as well as Japanese residents in Manchuria would not have suffered from such atrocious tragedies. While it can be imagined that the military might have opposed a surrender much more strongly before the atomic bombs and before the Soviet's participation in the war, the U.S. presidential announcement on the Emperor system would have been much more acceptable to the Japanese than the Potsdam Declaration.

In the end, Japan surrendered, but at the price of the Potsdam Declaration, the atomic bombs, and Soviet participation in the war. While the Potsdam Declaration may have been a setback from the presidential announcement that Grew had drafted, it was undoubtedly a mitigation of the unconditional surrender that Roosevelt had originally demanded. As Iokibe pointed out in the paragraph quoted at the outset of this chapter, the declaration was indeed a narrow compromise for both the United States and Japan given their respective domestic conditions. The Japanese government's decision to accept the Potsdam Declaration was a courageous act. Yoshida Shigeru described this decision as "an unprecedentedly gallant acceptance of defeat on our part." Japan's surrender was, thus, the fruit of utmost efforts on both sides.

The draft of the Potsdam Declaration was presented to the British government before the document was formally issued. While endorsing the declaration in general, the British government made three minor but nevertheless very important modifications.

First, the British government requested that the document be addressed to "Japan" or "the Japanese government" instead of "the citizens of Japan." Second, the British government proposed that the declaration directly and clearly specify that primary responsibility for the democratization of postwar Japan would be in the hands of the Japanese government. Third, the scope of the occupation by the Allies was changed from "Japanese territory" to "points in Japanese territory." It is believed that the advice of Sir George Bailey Sansom, a great expert on Japan, was behind these modifications. Coincidentally, both Grew and Sansom, American and British experts on Japan respectively, contributed respectively to setting more appropriate conditions for Japan's surrender.

I believe that area study is a paramount form in academics. While political science or economics focuses on only one aspect of human society, area study aims to hold a comprehensive view of a country, including its history, tradition, culture, politics, society, and economy. Especially in the realm of international politics, decision-makers are liable to make all kinds of errors and misjudgments if they fail to follow the advice from area specialists because decision-makers themselves are not experts on the region/country. Had Britain and the United States acted upon the advice of Grew and Sansom, the war could have ended much earlier. Furthermore, mismanagement caused by the subsequent occupation might also have been alleviated.

The plan drawn up by leading Japan specialists stipulated that it was only the Japanese military that would surrender unconditionally and that the post-war democratization would be undertaken by the Japanese government under the emperor. That is what one reads in the Potsdam Declaration even today.

In the face of victory-drunk and highly vengeful Allies officials, however, the Potsdam Declaration became just a piece of paper once Japan surrendered. Particularly after Grew retired as if to say that his mission had been accomplished with Japan's surrender, nobody paid attention to the wording of the Potsdam Declaration.

For one thing, there was the European precedent of Germany. In the case of Germany, its entire territory was conquered militarily and the German government no longer existed. This situation put the entire country under the military administration of the occupation forces. In case of Japan, in contrast, it was the Japanese government that accepted the Potsdam Declaration and the occupation forces on its territory. But an ordinary American could not be expected to make such a fine distinction.

Incidentally, the alliance with Germany brought a number of unnecessary blows to Japan, most notably the comparison of the Nanjing Incident to the Holocaust. The Holocaust was a premeditated ethnic cleansing, having no direct relation with the war, and it deserves to be condemned even long after the event. The Nanjing Incident, on the other hand, was, by definition, damage done to non-combatants during a state of war. And whether its scope has been exaggerated or not still remains open to question. In this sense, what happened in Nanjing should be viewed from the same perspective as the atomic bombs on Hiroshima and Nagasaki, the air raids on Tokyo and Dresden, and the brutal conduct of Soviet soldiers in Berlin and Manchuria.

In the earlier days of the occupation, the Japanese side resisted to the excessive and unnecessary occupation authority.

On September 2, 1945, when the Japanese instrument of surrender was signed on board the *USS Missouri,* the U.S. side presented the Japanese government with the following three astonishing proclamations that were scheduled to be issued the next day. First, all authority of the Japanese government would be exercised under the Supreme Commander for the Allied Powers; second, noncompliance with orders of the General Headquarters would be punished, at maximum, by death by the court of the occupation forces; and third, military currency issued by the occupation forces would be circulated together with yen issued by the Bank of Japan.

Appalled to hear this, the Ministry of Foreign Affairs successfully dissuaded the occupation forces from issuing these proclamations. At the background of this success was, of course, Japan's remarkably disciplined acceptance of the Potsdam Declaration and the orderly reception of the occupation forces.

But this was the extent to which Japan was able to resist. On September 6, the U.S. government issued a document which Iokibe noted as "the most uncivilized of all the documents to General Douglas MacArthur that the U.S. government produced in relation to Japan's defeat and its occupation." The document stated, ". . . Our relations do not rest on a contractual basis, but on an unconditioned surrender. . . Control of Japan shall be exercised through the Japanese Government to the extent that such an arrangement produces satisfactory results. . ."

This document is believed to be the result of advice to President Truman from newly appointed Acting Secretary of State Dean Acheson. He was a Japan policy hardliner who, upon hearing of the cancellation of the September 2 proclamations, tried to dissuade the administration from adopting further accommodative policies toward Japan.

In a nutshell, international politics is a power game. The moment Japan surrendered and disarmed itself, it no longer had any bargaining power no matter how it was treated. Had it been before the disarmament, Japan might have been able to argue against harsh demands from the United States, threatening the latter with a possible defiance from the lower echelons of the military and with obstruction to occupation administration. But as things stood, it became meaningless to complain that under the terms of the Potsdam Declaration it was only the military that had accepted an unconditional surrender. The only choice left for Japan was to win the goodwill of the occupation forces with its sincerity or flattery and hope that the occupation forces would evidence civilized conduct. This became the basic structure of the seven-year long occupation.

## Tragedy in Manchuria

Theoretically, the tragedy that took place in Manchuria shared the same roots as the occupation of mainland Japan. The only difference was the conduct of the occupation forces. In the case of Manchuria, they were by no means civilized.

From the Japanese viewpoint, the Soviet invasion of Manchuria was carried out abruptly. It took place while the Soviet-Japanese Neutrality Pact was still valid and the Japanese side had no knowing of the Yalta secret agreements that included the Soviet commitment to join the war. After all, the Soviet Union's participation in the war was such a top-secret document that even Truman had been unaware of it until he became the president of the United States.

In the first half of 1945, when the entire Eurasian continent became a scene of carnage, destruction, and starvation, Manchuria was actually the only sanctuary left unaffected. There were even some Japanese who evacuated to Manchuria because their homeland was suffering from frequent air raids and shortages of food. It was this sanctuary that the Soviet troops invaded out of the blue.

On August 15, the Imperial Rescript on the Termination of the War was read out by the Emperor on radio, followed by the Imperial Headquarters' instructions on the cessation of hostilities and the transfer of weapons to the Allies on August 16. On August 19, Lieutenant General Hata Hikosaburō, the Kwangtung Army's Chief of Staff, and Lieutenant Colonel Sejima Ryūzō, Staff Officer, as well as Miyagawa Funao, Japanese Consul-General at Harbin, reported to Aleksandr Vasilevsky, Commander-in-Chief of Soviet forces in the Far East, and signed the armistice agreement. Unfortunately, this armistice agreement failed to be communicated throughout the entire army in Manchuria due to communications failure in various locations, resulting in a few more days of fierce battles in places.

On August 19, Soviet troops advanced to Manchurian cities including Hsinking, Manchukuo's capital city, by air and abducted the commander of the Second Area Army, the main-force unit of the Kwangtung Army, crippling its chain of command. Disarmed, the Japanese troops in Manchuria were deprived of their means to resist. In retrospect, the Imperial Japanese Army should have handed over their weapons only after completing the evacuation of the Japanese residents in Manchuria, particularly women and children. Furthermore, the army should have negotiated a ceasefire on the condition of disarmament at the port of Dalian. By all accounts, the Japanese troops still had the strength to do so at the time. Having no experience of defeat, however, the Japanese military must have been totally unable to foresee the cruel fate that awaited after it gave up its weapons. As a matter of fact, Lieutenant General Hata strongly requested the Soviet side "respect the honor of the Imperial Japanese Army and take full measures to protect the Japanese residents." Obtaining ready consent from the Soviet side, Hata ordered the full disarmament of his troops. After the troops were disarmed, however, the Soviet side did not even pay the slightest heed to this promise.

The Soviet side did not allow officers and soldiers of the Kwangtung Army to return home, which was a violation of both the Potsdam Declaration and international law. Japanese troops were reorganized into work battalions and mobilized to remove the industrial facilities in Manchuria and ship them to the Soviet Union. Subsequently, they were taken captive in the Soviet territory as forced laborers. According to Japanese Ministry of Welfare (present-day Ministry of Health, Labor, and Welfare) statistics, 575,000 Japanese were detained by the Soviet Union, and the term of detention extended to eleven years at the longest. Some 500,000 detainees died from cruel treatment and malnutrition. Furthermore, among 1.55 million civilian Japanese residents of Manchuria, 176,000 lost their lives.

The Japanese did not have much experience of being the defeated. When the Mongols invaded Tsushima Island in the 13th century, islanders hid themselves deep in the mountains. It is recorded that they killed crying children so as not to be found. Women captured by the Mongols were nailed through their hands and hung in the bows of Mongolian ships. The defeat in the Greater East Asia War was the first such nationwide affliction since this 13th century experience.

While a number of personal accounts of the tragedies that befell the Japanese residents in Manchuria exist—some of which I have personally collected—I cannot find it in my heart to introduce them. I am afraid that the book may turn into a bizarre historic collection of human cruelty. In any event, it seems safe to say that the Japanese residents became the subject of all forms of unimaginable cruelty, abuses, and sexual assaults.

As a result of the dissolution of the Soviet Union in 1991, we now hear from Russians themselves a variety of honest testimonies about what really happened in those days. One common theme repeatedly heard in these testimonies is the claim that, in those days, Russians themselves had been subject to similar treatment. In other words, Russians themselves were also the victims of the inhumane characters of the Communist regime. In short, losers are at the mercy of the victor, and subject to practically any treatment, depending on the sense of morality of the victor.

Let me introduce a tanka that Tōgō Shigenori composed after the end of the Greater East Asia War while he was imprisoned as a war criminal:

> Listen carefully, my children
> Thou shalt not fight, but
> Never forget that you must win when you have to fight

The tragedy in Manchuria was the first of its kind that the Japanese people had experienced. Many anecdotes exist. One of them is a tale that the Kwangtung Army officers and soldiers ran away first, abandoning the Japanese residents.

To introduce some of the facts that refute this tale, the 124th Division engaged in a head-on battle with the enemy in eastern Manchuria, endured ferocious charges from the main-force unit of the Soviet troops for five days, and ceased fire only after it had successfully completed the evacuation of some 30,000 Japanese residents of Mudanjiang. The 107th Division in western Manchuria also put up a good fight and assisted the Japanese residents to evacuate safely. When the Soviet troops refused to postpone their advance until Japanese residents were safely evacuated, the Mongolia Garrison Army stationed in Inner Mongolia fought the invading Soviet troops and succeeded in evacuating all 40,000 Japanese residents in Zhangjiagang in exchange for its own heavy casualties.

It is undeniable that there were cases in which the Japanese residents suffered from the ravages of war, particularly among those who had been isolated from communications with the outside. Individual experiences varied depending on each person's circumstances.

In any event, in light of the Japanese mentality in those days, it is utterly unthinkable that the Japanese military would neglect the lives and safety of the Japanese residents.

Shōwa-Heisei historical novelist Shiba Ryōtarō denounced the inhumanity of the Japanese military, quoting an army officer who presumably ordered the tanks to advance, running over and killing the Japanese evacuees who filled the roads. I find it hard to believe that a responsible military officer could issue such an order. Even if he had, Japanese soldiers under his command could not possibly have complied with the order which would mean running over Japanese civilians.

I would not hesitate to credit the historical contributions that Shiba made as a writer. After all, in the midst of the time when Japanese had to perceive everything in the prewar days since the Meiji Restoration as evil, Shiba insisted that Japan had been right and heroic at the time of the First Sino-Japanese and Russo-Japanese Wars. It was as if Shiba was trying to help the Japanese breathe by pointing out where they could stick their noses and mouths out above the mud. Perhaps in an attempt to emphasize the righteousness of Japan during these two wars, Shiba rode the tide of the prevailing opinions on Japan's history, particularly concerning the Japanese military in the Shōwa period.

## Smooth Withdrawal from Mainland China

The situation in mainland China was in stark contrast to Manchuria.

While there were a few cases of sporadic violence during the confusion immediately after the war, 1.1 million Japanese troops and 500,000 Japanese residents returned to Japan in an orderly fashion.

Unlike the situations in mainland Japan proper and Manchuria, the Japanese military in China was able to retain its arms, which allowed the Japanese troops to fulfill their duty to protect the Japanese residents. This smooth withdrawal of the Japanese residents from China resulted in part from the policy of Chiang Kai-shek, who had studied in Japan beginning in 1907 and served for two years in the Imperial Japanese Army from 1909-1911, which allowed the Japanese military to retain arms until the last minute.

Fully aware of Japan's acceptance of the Potsdam Declaration, the Nationalist government in Chongqing demanded on August 14 that General Okamura Yasuji, Commander-in-Chief of Japan's China Expeditionary Army, surrender to Commander-in-Chief of the Chinese Army He Yingqin. In the dead of night on the same day, Chiang confined himself in his room and wrote a draft for his radio speech on his "requite anger with virtue" (以德報怨) policy. Chiang wrote each and every word in this speech by himself. Even his usual speechwriter, Ch'en Pu-lei, was surprised to hear this speech over the radio. In this speech, Chiang said,

Our resistance won us victory today . . . We must remember that "not to blame the people for old errors" (不念旧恶) has been the Chinese people's highest and noblest traditional virtue . . . We must bear in mind that if we respond to violence with violence and react to an enemy's misguided sense of superiority with contempt, hatred will reproduce hatred, perpetuating a conflict . . .

Chinese civilization, with its 5,000-year history, is truly magnificent. Chiang asked the people to learn a lesson from what ancient China's Boyi and Shuqi had lamented, "With violence he replaces violence unsure of his wrongdoing." Hearing this, many Japanese were once again reminded that the Japanese were no match for the Chinese.

Indeed, the order from Chiang Kai-shek was faithfully carried out by the rank and file of the Chinese troops. Moreover, Shanghai's newspapers, which were resumed by the end of August, unanimously editorialized the importance of Sino-Japanese friendship. Being wise people, the Chinese must have understood the strategic significance of this posture toward Japan.

In fact, this policy was in line with the conventional policy of the Nationalist government.

Initially, Chiang Kai-shek's strategy was to annihilate the Communist Party of China first and then confront Japan. However, Chiang had to change his priorities and fight the Japanese for eight years because of the outbreak of the Xi'an Incident and the Marco Polo Bridge Incident. From the viewpoint of Chiang, who was a great strategist, it was easy to predict that Japan would be defeated as soon as it started a war against the United States. Thus, his main strategic focus was on how to beat the Communist forces after the end of war with Japan. The reports from the U.S. side during the war complained that the Nationalist government did not actively engage in the fight against Japan and that the Nationalists retained their weapons and ammunition provided by the United States for a future battle with the Communists.

Judging from the equally lethargic battle between the Communist forces and Japan toward the end of the Second Sino-Japanese War, it appears that the Communists also retained their weapons and ammunition for the coming showdown with the Nationalist forces.

Facing the imminent termination of the war, the utmost concern for

Chiang Kai-shek, therefore, was to make sure that occupied territories, weapons, and ammunition of the Japanese troops were handed over to his Nationalist government instead of to the Communist forces. In order to realize this, Chiang needed the orderly cooperation of the Japanese troops. For this reason, the Japanese troops in mainland China were allowed to maintain their organization, live unconfined with weapons for self-defense, put the Japanese civilian residents under their protection, and, eventually, return home on board transport ships provided by the U.S. military by the summer of 1946.

Meanwhile, at the request of the Nationalist government, the Japanese troops were mobilized to resist the Communists' advances. Even after the summer of 1946, some Japanese troops stayed behind in China to join the anti-Communist military operations or to provide technical advice.

Chiang Kai-shek's policy toward Japan in anticipation of a showdown with the Communists was, thus, impeccable. He could not have his own way, however, in Manchuria, which the Soviet troops had invaded.

From the beginning, the greatest concern for Chiang Kai-shek after defeating Japan had been the Nationalist government's relations with the Soviet Union. It may be unnecessary to go into details of this issue because it had nothing to do with Japan after its surrender. But, simply put, the situation was closely related to the concessions in Manchuria that Roosevelt had ceded to the Soviet Union during the Yalta conference without any prior consultation with Chiang. In the end, Chiang had to recognize the Yalta agreements on the condition that the parties to the agreements acknowledged the legitimacy of the Nationalist government in China. However, the huge stock of Japanese weapons and ammunition in Manchuria was in fact handed over to the Communist troops, forcing the Nationalists to initially lose hold of Manchuria. Subsequently, the Nationalist troops, in which traditional warlord culture had been preserved, were soon proven to be no match for the Communists' revolutionary army, resulting in their eventual defeat in the final showdown with the Communists in mainland China.

Another factor that facilitated the smooth withdrawal of the Japanese troops from mainland China appeared to be the cordial relations they maintained with the local people.

As I touched upon earlier in the chapter on the Nanjing Incident in *Shige-*

*mitsu/Tōgō to Sono Jidai*, there were admittedly cases of undisciplined conduct among Japanese troops at the time of the occupation of Nanjing.

Other than that, however, the Japanese troops in China generally remained strictly disciplined. In Beijing, which was among the first cities that the Japanese troops occupied, city elders even proposed raising a statue of the commander of these highly disciplined warriors, whose behavior was in stark contrast to the brutal and barbaric Western soldiers at the time of the Boxer Rebellion. In the case of Luoyang and Guilin, both of which were occupied by Japanese troops toward the end of the war, their cultural heritages and the people's livelihood were so thoroughly protected that some in these cities today still remain grateful for how the Japanese conducted themselves. General Okamura Yasuji, Commander-in-Chief of the China Expeditionary Army, upheld the occupation policy of "compassionate treatment of the local people": he ordered his soldiers to recite the three prohibitions of 1941, "thou shalt not burn, rape, or kill," every day.

Incidentally, the genesis of the so-called Three Alls Policy, for which the Japanese military has been accused, was propaganda initiated by the Chinese Communist's organ, *Kaihō Nippō* (Liberation News), in its December 1941 issue to ridicule Okamura's three prohibitions. *Kaiho Nippo* claimed that, although Japan's occupation of China was executed as a civil, rather than a military, operation, it would resort to the "Three Lights Policy (3光作戦)" as soon as its current attempts proved futile. Ironically, this claim of the *Kaihō Nippō* proves that at the time of writing Japan had not launched the "Three Alls Policy."

Meanwhile, as the Second Sino-Japanese War became part of the Greater East Asia War, the reconstruction of Asia based on a collegial relationship with China became one of Japan's major war objectives, both in name and substance, as a result of Foreign Minister Shigemitsu Mamoru's new China policy.

*Shūsen Hishi* (Unknown History of the End of the War), by Meiji-Shōwa bureaucrat and statesman Shimomura Kainan, introduced an episode of an Imperial Japanese Army unit stationed in Henan. As the story goes, the local people continued to live side by side with the Japanese troops even after Japan's defeat:

Until April 1946, a very idyllic nine months passed in which there was no knowing where the war was, who won the war, and who lost the war. Whenever local farmers slaughtered a pig or wrung a chicken, they offered the meat and local wine to the Japanese troops, and began a feast with this toast: "We want no more war. It's best to be good friends from now on. Cheers!" . . . I do not think that this scene was repeated everywhere else in China, but this is nevertheless a true story. I find here a magnanimous (continental) ambiance that is quite different from the insular atmosphere which was prevalent in Japan.

There also are rumors that some local people even regretted the departure of the Japanese troops. Given the situation in those days, this comes as no surprise. For local people who had just learned how to come to terms with the Japanese occupation, there was no knowing what kind of a warlord or bandit would take over next. Also in many of the localities that came under Communist rule, residents above middle class were massacred. It was, therefore, no wonder that local people were worried about the future after the withdrawal of the Japanese troops.

This reality must be a part of the historical truth. Those good impressions that the Japanese people had left in some parts of China, however, were wiped out from the Chinese people's memory by the Communist regime, which used hatred as an engine of the revolution in contrast to the more enlightened approach of Chiang. Moreover, in recent years, the Chinese government's campaign to fuel people's hatred toward the Japanese has been escalated. The campaign includes erecting monuments in various places commemorating the brutal acts by the Japanese military during the war, some exaggerated and others not true at all.

Had the Japanese military perpetrated all possible atrocities and become the object of the Chinese people's deep resentment, as campaigns by the Chinese government and the masochistic view of history in postwar Japan suggest, the Chinese people would have surely retaliated on a significant scale after Japan's defeat. Subsequent history shows that such was not the case.

In any event, it is a historical fact that more than one million Japanese, both military and civilian, were able to return home safely to Japan without any major incident, thanks to the magnanimous strategic thinking of Chiang Kai-shek and the generally cordial relations that the Japanese troops had maintained with the local people. The warm episodes provide a soothing sense of peace and relief in an otherwise gruesome spectacle caused by the horrors of war.

CHAPTER

# 2

# Prince Higashikuni Cabinet and General MacArthur

*—Any Humiliation Is Worth Enduring*
*to Maintain the Imperial System—*

## Problem Child with a Promising Future

The Emperor Shōwa read out the Imperial Rescript on the Termination of the War on the radio at noon on August 15, 1945 (20th Year of Shōwa). Until the recorded speech was actually broadcast, it encountered a number of obstructions by those who insisted on the continuation of the war. For instance, the commander of the Imperial Guard Division was assassinated, and there was a covert plan to steal the phonograph record of the speech. Japan faced multiple dangers until the last minute as it took each and every step toward surrender.

After the broadcast of the Emperor's speech, the Suzuki Kantarō cabinet resigned at 3:30 p.m., as if to say it had accomplished its mission.

During the consultation among Kido Kōichi, Lord Keeper of the Privy Seal, and others on who should succeed Suzuki, there was a consensus that, in light of alarming signals from the Imperial Japanese Army and Navy, a mere subject of the Emperor could not manage the cabinet. Eventually, Prince Higashikuni Naruhiko (東久邇宮稔彦) was appointed prime minister and former Prime Minister Konoe Fumimaro his advisor.

At first, Prince Higashikuni declined the nomination. Aside from the principle that a member of the Imperial family should not be involved in politics, the political situation at that time did not augur any success for anyone. Persuaded that this appointment was Emperor Shōwa's wish and that, in light of restless movements among some members of the Imperial Guard and others, no other statesman would be able to handle the situation, Prince Higashikuni finally accepted the nomination, adding that he did not know whether he would succeed or not. His remarks may sound a little irresponsible in today's context, but this was the traditional Oriental way of declaring one's determination. What Prince Higashikuni said should be interpreted as, "I may not succeed, and I do not care what happens to me should I fail. I shall just do my very best." Zhuge Liang (諸 葛孔明), ancient China's great strategist in the Three Kingdoms period, expressed a similar determination in his famous letter, *Chu Shi Biao*, which he wrote before he led a nearly hopeless northern expedition to the kingdom of Wei. In any case, citing his inexperience in politics, Prince Higashikuni requested the assistance of Konoe.

It was indeed beyond doubt that at the time there was nobody except the Imperial family who could control the military. And among the many members of the Imperial family, it was widely agreed that the only person who could be relied on at this critical juncture was Prince Higashikuni.

Prince Higashikuni was the type of person who persisted in his belief from early in his life. His early days were full of hardships. His father, Prince Kuninomiya Asahiko, had been a leading figure in the *Sonnō Jōi* (尊王攘夷) (Revere the emperor, expel the barbarians) movement at the twilight of the shogunate but was forced to lead an unfortunate life in his final years as he became alienated from the mainstream of the Meiji government after the death of Emperor Kōmei. Meanwhile, Prince Higashikuni was separated from his parents and adopted by a farming family, with whom he spent his childhood as a farmer's child. This alone distinguished him from the weak other Court nobles.

As Prince Higashikuni entered Gakushūin and advanced to the Imperial Japanese Army Cadet School and the Imperial Japanese Army Academy, a regular educational path for peers in those days, he became increasingly frustrated with the "discrimination based on the assumption that Court nobles cannot endure rigorous training." He went through intensive training, and also threatened to leave the Imperial family twice for trifling reasons. The manly conduct explains well why Prince Higashikuni became highly respected as a military man in later days. Moreover, judging from the fact that he was allowed to marry Emperor Meiji's ninth daughter, Princess Toshiko, upon graduation from the Army War College, it appears that, despite having been a troublesome youth from time to time, Prince Higashikuni was looked upon as a court noble with a promising future.

After arriving in France in 1920, Prince Higashikuni graduated from the *école spéciale militaire de Saint-Cyr* in 1923. After that he entered the *école polytechnique* in Paris where he studied sociology, political science, economics, and diplomatic history. Through his personal hobby of painting, he became close to Claude Monet, who later introduced him to Georges Clemenceau.

Clemenceau was a distinguished French statesman with astonishing foresight. In the first half of the 1920s, the world witnessed the rise of the issue of racial discrimination and a naval armament race. The possibility of a war between the United States and Japan became the subject of discussion. At one time, when Prince Higashikuni asked Clemenceau his view on the possibility of a U.S.-Japan war, Clemenceau replied,

> It is a matter of course. The United States will have to eliminate Japan's influence in order to expand its own influence in Asia and the Pacific. The United States once hammered Germany during World War I. Therefore, the Americans will most likely target Japan. But the United States would not be foolish enough to commence a war against Japan. Instead, it will torment Japan through diplomacy. Being unskillful in diplomacy and short-tempered, Japan, when pressured hard, will without a doubt be provoked to start a war itself. The United States will use its foreign policy to make sure that Japan does so. Once a war does break out, Japan will be no match for the United States, with the U.S. superior military power and production capabilities. Japan's defeat will be inevitable. Therefore, whatever it takes, Japan should endure all provocations and never start a war with the United States.

Subsequent history developed as exactly as Clemenceau had predicted, making his observation look almost like a prophesy. Generally speaking, the French are capable of analyzing things with coolheaded logic detached from emotion, ideology, and morals. In light of the emotional confrontation over the racial issue and the opposing views on the naval armament race between the United States and Japan, Clemenceau's observation was truly one of the logically constructed scenarios.

In 1941 (16th Year of Shōwa), Prince Higashikuni informed Prime Minister Tōjō Hideki of Clemenceau's analysis in an attempt to dissuade Tōjō from waging a war with the United States. Betting on Japan's chance of winning the war, however, Tōjō did not listen.

After returning home from France, Prince Higashikuni maintained liberal ideas and an outlook that was highly compatible with that of Prince Saionji Kinmochi, who had developed a similar philosophical belief in his youth. In his military career, Prince Higashikuni served as commander of the Imperial Japanese Army's glorious 2nd Division, which carried a reputation as the strongest unit in the Japanese army during the Russo-Japanese War and the Manchurian Incident. Prince Higashikuni was later promoted to commander of the 2nd Army stationed in north China. In 1939, Prince Higashikuni was promoted to major general of the Imperial Japanese Army.

When Tōjō recommended Prince Higashikuni succeed the outgoing Prime Minister Konoe to Lord Privy Seal Kido Kōichi before the beginning of the Greater East Asia War, Kido opposed the idea. Kido at that time believed that the Imperial family should not be involved in making such an important decision for the nation as war. That is, should the war go wrong, the Imperial family could become a target of the Japanese people's resentment. Thus, it appears that Kido believed that "An Imperial family member should not form a cabinet unless the state is absolutely determined to pursue the policy of peace."

While Kido made several critical misjudgments in the run-up to the Greater East Asia War by going along with Konoe, who had been his friend since Gakushūin days, Kido's good judgment on Tōjō's recommendation was truly commendable. As Lord Privy Seal, it was Kido's duty to protect the Imperial family. In later days, one can see the consistency in Kido's thinking when he recommended Prince Higashikuni as prime minister to restore peace in Japan after the defeat.

# First Hurdle toward Peaceful Surrender

Prime Minister Higashikuni also asked Ogata Taketora (緒方竹虎) for his cooperation on Japan's peaceful surrender. Ogata was originally a journalist who became vice-president of the *Asahi Shimbun*. He later turned politician, serving in various posts including President of the Intelligence Bureau. He was also Prince Higashikuni's horse-riding mate and comrade in seeking to engineer peace with China during the Greater East Asia War.

Meanwhile, Ogata played an active role as Chief Secretary of the Higashikuni cabinet in the selection of cabinet members and secretaries: the cabinet was called a "de facto Ogata cabinet." The cabinet was also called an "*Asahi Shimbun* cabinet" because it recruited a lot of competent people from this daily newspaper.

Although Ogata was temporarily purged from public service after the end of the war, Yoshida Shigeru was so impressed with Ogata that he tried to appoint Ogata to important positions as soon as he was allowed to make a comeback. Ogata was a magnificent man with a deep-thinking and modest personality, and few speak ill of him even today.

In the meantime, Foreign Minister Tōgō Shigenori resigned because he had been foreign minister at the start of the war, and Arita Hachirō declined the nomination for foreign minister for health reasons. In the end, Shigemitsu Mamoru became foreign minister.

Immediately after the formation of his cabinet, Prime Minister Higashikuni made a radio speech on August 17 in which he appealed to the nation:

> The message that His Imperial Majesty bestowed on us and the Imperial Rescript on the Termination of the War request the citizens of Japan to control and contain the military so as to survive the current critical situation.

The primary mission of the Higashikuni cabinet was, thus, to restrain the military, carry out the stipulations of the Potsdam Declaration, and accept the occupation forces peacefully.

Not surprisingly, both Higashikuni and Ogata expected an outburst by the frustrated military. Ogata wrote,

> When the Imperial Japanese Army and Navy, with their 70-year

history, were about to perish in front of our eyes, shouldn't we expect some rebels to appear like the Shōgitai, or League to Demonstrate Righteousness, at the end of the shogunate? At the risk of contradicting my official position, I must confess that I had expected a demonstration of that kind of chivalry from the military. And I wanted Prime Minister Prince Higashikuni to calm the rebels down.

By the time Higashikuni and Ogata formed the cabinet, however, the major course of events had already been settled. It might have made sense for the rebels to obstruct the radio broadcast of the Imperial Rescript on the Termination of the War. Once the Imperial Rescript was delivered, however, there was absolutely no means to change the flow of the tide. The predictions of Grew and other Japan specialists in the United States were proven to be correct.

Meanwhile, there were additional plots to assault government leaders deemed responsible for accepting Japan's defeat and to block the landing of the occupation forces. However, everyone knew that such acts would be useless in terms of changing the general flow of the tide. And, in fact, these plots were not intended to change the course. The plots were nothing but an expression of the people's uncontrollable emotions. Even if the plots had succeeded, they would not have led the rebels anywhere other than the path to suicide.

For instance, twelve members of the patriotic group Sonjō Dōshikai, assaulted Lord Keeper of the Privy Seal Kido Kōichi. Failing to accomplish their goal to assassinate him, they holed up in the Atagoyama Shrine and committed suicide on August 22, surrounded by police forces. Before killing themselves, they announced, "We will go down together with our motherland." On August 23, twelve members of Meirōkai, another patriotic group, committed suicide together in front of the Imperial Palace.

They were followed by fourteen members of Daitōjuku, which even today is considered to be an orthodox rightwing society. These members honorably disemboweled themselves in accordance with the traditional rites on August 25. Acting head of the society, Kageyama Shōhei, left a death poem which reads, "Ferocious heart anxious about the motherland / might be becalmed at its extreme / when rising to the seats of the gods."

These suicides were actions driven by a feeling of hopelessness. The only thing one could do was to follow his country to the grave to protect the honor of the country and individual suicides, terrorist uprisings, and rebellions would not have been able to change the course of events, and there was no way of stopping the imminent arrival of the U.S. occupation forces or preventing "barbarians" from landing on the Emperor's land.

Atsugi airbase in the suburbs of Tokyo, where the occupation forces were expected to land, was a major stronghold of the Imperial Japanese Navy. Some officers blustered that they would hurl their bodies into Douglas MacArthur's airplane, while others repeatedly flew over Tokyo to express their valor. Some cheered members of the Sonjō Dōshikai who had holed up in Atagoyama.

Nevertheless, even at Atsugi airbase, the Imperial Japanese Army and Navy troops complied with the order to transfer the few dozen remaining aircraft to nearby Kumagaya airfield, where they were disarmed. The Army troops responded to Prime Minister Higashikuni, who concurrently served as minister of war and who had issued the orders. Likewise, the Navy troops were persuaded by Prince Takamatsu, who was dispatched by the Emperor. As these cases clearly illustrate, the Emperor's authority and the Japanese people's loyalty to the Emperor proved highly effective in settling situations at the end of the Greater East Asia War.

Shortly after the above incident at Atsugi airbase on August 24, the Japanese side hastily prepared to receive the occupation forces. Preparations were completed in time for the arrival of the U.S. advance party on August 28 and of MacArthur himself on August 30. MacArthur landed at Atsugi unarmed, with his famous corn cob pipe in his mouth: this became a symbol of the bloodless occupation accomplished by U.S. forces. Thus, with the help of the authority of the Imperial Family and the common sense judgment shared among the Japanese at large that further resistance would be futile, Japan was able to clear the first hurdle toward a peaceful surrender.

## Shigemitsu Mamoru's Persuasion

The signing of the Japanese Instrument of Surrender took place on September 2 onboard the *USS Missouri,* anchored in Tokyo Bay.

Because surrender was perceived to be the first national disgrace in the history of Japan, nobody wished to be a signee. In the end, it was decided that Foreign Minister Shigemitsu Mamoru would officially represent the

Japanese government.

Shigemitsu's resolution was well represented in the tanka poem he composed on the morning of the signing ceremony:

> It is my sincere hope
> That this country of the Emperor will recover again
> And I will be denounced by my posterity

Both Foreign Minister Shigemitsu and his predecessor, Tōgō Shigenori, were well-cultured gentlemen who were capable of using tanka to express their feelings. While Tōgō's tanka were sharp and more artistic, Shigemitsu's tended to be more prosaic and, therefore, mundane. Nevertheless, the above appears to reflect Shigemitsu's mindset at that time quite accurately.

The decadent state of Japanese minds in subsequent days was, however, beyond Shigemitsu's imagination. On October 20, 1945, Shigemitsu wrote in his *Zoku Shigemitsu Shuki* (Sequel to the Shigemitsu Diary):

> Nowadays, all the leaders in Japan, whether in officialdom or in the private sector, are bustling around to pay tribute to MacArthur. Besides, it appears that top government leaders actually regret not having attended the signing of the Japanese Instrument of Surrender. I am simply baffled by the change in their attitudes between yesterday and today.

Shigemitsu attributed these changes in attitude to people's fear of being accused of being war criminals. And he observed,

> [Every approach to MacArthur] was an act of detestable flattery. It was unbearable for me. And this is by no means a phenomenon confined to the top government leadership; it is also rampant among ordinary citizens.

Shigemitsu also stated, "Many of these behaviors remind me of the situation in the beginning of the Meiji Restoration," and deplored the Japanese people's change of heart—how they ingratiated themselves with the new authority, just as people had done when the power had been shifted from the shogunate to the Imperial court. He concluded his observation with the lament, "Have the Japanese people degraded themselves into third- or fourth-class citizens without independence of mind?"

Immediately following the signing onboard the *USS Missouri*, draft proclamations were presented to the Japanese government from the Supreme Commander for the Allied Powers (GHQ). As I wrote in the first chapter of this book, these draft proclamations contained such measures as depriving Japan of judicial power and imposing a military currency issued by the Occupation Forces on the Japanese economy. Simply put, the proclamations demanded similar measures as those imposed on Germany instead of introducing indirect rule based on the spirit of the Potsdam Declaration.

On the evening of September 2, Okazaki Katsuo, director of the Central Liaison Office, rushed to Yokohama and somehow succeeded in dissuading GHQ from issuing the proclamations. The next day, Foreign Minister Shigemitsu successfully requested a meeting with General MacArthur. In this meeting, MacArthur said to Shigemitsu, "In short, as far as this issue is concerned, it is entirely up to how the Japanese government and people behave." Basically, MacArthur did not insist on the type of occupation, whether it was military administration or indirect rule, as long as the occupation was successfully carried out. Now that the Japanese military had been disarmed, Japan was not in a position to make claims regarding the wordings of the Potsdam Declaration. Fully aware that it had the last trump card—i.e., that it could use whatever power it possessed when necessary—GHQ agreed to give indirect rule a try.

In any event, Shigemitsu scored big at the beginning of the occupation. But Japan soon realized the harsh realities of defeat and occupation. Shigemitsu earned GHQ's displeasure after he boasted of his accomplishment in a subsequent press conference.

I suspect it was not a simple case of Shigemitsu hurting the pride of the occupation forces. At that time, the occupation forces were faced with the need to carry out a dual-front operation. It was their duty to accomplish the trouble-free occupation of Japan, on the one hand, and to demonstrate an authoritative posture as the victor in the eyes of domestic audiences in the United States and other allied countries, on the other. From that viewpoint, Shigemitsu's conduct was totally uncalled for, and it could have spoiled the compromises that GHQ had made for his benefit. The United

States began to take a much tougher stance toward Japan thereafter.

However, it may have been futile to expect Shigemitsu to be more considerate as one of the defeated Japanese. After all, Shigemitsu had developed his career as a proud diplomat of the Empire of Japan.

It is more appropriate, instead, to deem Shigemitsu's behavior as the last mettle of a Japanese and give it due credit.

On September 11, when U.S. military police tried to apprehend Tōjō Hideki, the former prime minister attempted suicide by shooting himself. He failed and was taken into custody. Shigemitsu visited Yokohama to personally lodge a protest with Lieutenant General Richard Sutherland, MacArthur's chief of staff, over the arrest. As a result, it was decided that subsequent arrests of war criminals would be carried out by the Japanese government under GHQ's command, instead of directly by the Occupation Forces.

Subsequently, the cabinet decided that the first 39 individuals designated as war criminals, including all the cabinet members at the start of the war, should be treated with special courtesy. The cabinet also decided to request GHQ to allow war criminals to be tried by the Japanese authority. In Shigemitsu's view, the request was an attempt to protect Japan's sovereignty, whether GHQ approved it or not. Shigemitsu's position was supported by Minister of Justice Iwata Chūzō, who quoted a number of samurai anecdotes in which an enemy's extradition requests for individuals were answered by severed heads.

Emperor Shōwa objected to the request that war criminals be tried at the hands of the Japanese, saying, "We do not find it in our heart to execute under our name our ministers whom we had trusted until yesterday." A few decades after the end of the war, when the inclusion of the so-called Class-A war criminals in the list of war dead honored by Yasukuni Shrine became an issue, it was rumored that Emperor Shōwa had objected to the enshrinement of Class-A criminals. It is obvious, however, that the Emperor had no intention to treat his ministers, who had remained loyal until the end, as war criminals.

When Shigemitsu visited the Imperial Palace to reiterate his intentions, the Emperor inquired about the prospect of negotiating with GHQ. Shigemitsu replied, "There is hardly any chance for us to succeed, but I nevertheless wish to pursue this argument for the reason that I have just submitted to Your Imperial Majesty." The Emperor responded, "We understand it well."

As Shigemitsu predicted, this negotiation with GHQ proved futile. Then came the International Military Tribunal for the Far East.

## Emperor Pays a Visit to MacArthur

According to Yoshida's *Kaiso 10-nen* (literally, 10-Year Reminiscences, but published in English as *The Yoshida Memoirs*), Emperor Shōwa had expressed his wish to meet MacArthur immediately after MacArthur arrived in Japan. Perhaps the Emperor might have refrained from pushing his request in consideration of Shigemitsu's policy to limit the Japanese channel of negotiation with GHQ to the Central Liaison Office.

When Foreign Minister Yoshida, successor to Shigemitsu who had resigned in mid-September, conveyed the Emperor's wish to MacArthur, MacArthur agreed with the idea, saying, "Although I cannot visit the Imperial Palace myself, I would be happy to meet the Emperor if he can come visit me."

In his 1964 memoirs, *Reminiscences*, MacArthur said,

> Shortly after my arrival in Tokyo, I was urged by members of my staff to summon the Emperor to my headquarters as a show of power. I brushed the suggestions aside. "To do so," I explained, "would be to outrage the feelings of the Japanese people and make a martyr of the Emperor in their eyes. No, I shall wait, and in time the Emperor will voluntarily come to see me. In this case, the patience of the East rather than the haste of the West will best serve our purpose."

It appeared that the stances of both sides matched one another after the resignation of Shigemitsu as foreign minister.

Initially, MacArthur admitted, "I had an uneasy feeling [Hirohito] might plead his own cause against indictment as a war criminal." When, however, the Emperor said, "I come to you . . . to offer myself to the judgment of the powers you represent as the one to bear sole responsibility for every political and military decision made and action taken by my people in the

The Emperor and the General

conduct of war," MacArthur recalled that:

> A tremendous impression swept over me. This courageous assump-
> tion of a responsibility implicit with death, a responsibility clearly
> belied by facts of which I was fully aware, moved me to the very mar-
> row of my bones. He was an Emperor by inherent birth, but in that
> instant I knew I faced the First Gentleman of Japan in his own right.

Emperor Shōwa still remains the object of the Japanese people's rever-
ence and love a quarter century after his death. In the Oriental tradition,
an emperor's imperial virtues must be unconditionally praised. During
the Greater East Asia War, moreover, emperor worship, which had been
around since the Meiji era, was imposed on the Japanese people more
coercively, using the propaganda machinery that was common around
the world in those days. This makes it difficult to discern between true
national sentiment toward the Emperor and manipulated sentiment.

Various personal anecdotes of Emperor Shōwa, however, give one the
impression that he must have been equipped with special virtues. Having
learned kingcraft from outstanding tutors of the time since his early childhood, personally attended to each and every critical juncture in Japan's
modern history in the 20th century, and deepened and sharpened his
insights through these experiences, it was in fact no wonder that Emperor
Shōwa had developed such outstanding personality and wisdom.

Emperor Shōwa's mindset at the time of Japan's defeat can be witnessed in two imperial tanka poems:

Dsiregarding whatever eventualities may
Consequently happen to my own person,
I have decided to stop the War,
Being unbearable any longer to see
My subjects suffer untold deaths
Caused by the prolonged hostilities.

And

Unbearable any more to see my subjets
Suffer untold deaths and miseries
Caused by the incessant bombings,
Have I decided to stop the War.
Disregarding all the eventualities that may happen
To my own person.
(Translated by SHIMOJIMA Muraji)

Poems reflect the integrity of the composer. Those who are familiar with the composer's works can detect the true feelings of the composer. We can safely assume that the above two tanka were expressions of Emperor Shōwa's genuine feelings. Toward the end of the war, the fierceness of the air raids by American bombers on Japan was beyond description. The longer surrender was delayed even by one day, the greater damage the Japanese civilians would suffer. The Emperor wished to stop the war and the suffering of his people at any cost.

When MacArthur received the Emperor at GHQ, the Commander-in- Chief of the Occupation Forces addressed the Emperor as "Sir," a word by which he had perhaps never addressed anyone after he became a general. It was reported that MacArthur was courteous and polite when he saw off his guest.

Newspapers carrying the photo taken during this meeting were banned by Japan's Home Ministry. This invited strong protest from the GHQ.

Now that we all know the background of the meeting and the attitude of MacArthur toward the Emperor, this picture of the two does not cause any particular repulsion among the Japanese today. In those days, however, this was the most shocking scene for the Japanese who had had a fixed notion that anyone must maintain a certain physical distance from the Emperor to show respect. A picture of an American military man in an open-necked uniform standing shoulder to shoulder with the Emperor in full regalia as if he were the Emperor's equal was beyond their imagining. As such, the photo brought the Japanese back to reality that Japan had lost the war. The Home Ministry's opposition toward the photo and banning of its release was understandable, while GHQ's anger at the Home Ministry's conduct was equally justifiede. This episode reveals that the Japanese had not yet come to terms with being occupied.

While this incident became one of the triggers for GHQ to take a tougher stance toward Japan, which shortened the life of the Higashikuni cabinet, allow me to expand on it in the next chapter. In the rest of this chapter, I wish to discuss MacArthur's personality and his policy toward Japan, particularly his attitude toward the emperor system in Japan.

## Bonner Fellers' Views on the Emperor System

Simply put, Douglas MacArthur was not only the elite among the military elites but also the top elite in American society.

Throughout his four years at West Point, United States Military Academy, MacArthur remained at the top of his class. Behind his academic achievements were tremendous efforts by his mother, Mary "Pinky" MacArthur. After helping MacArthur pass the Academy's entrance examination by tutoring him in mathematics, English, and history, Pinky continued to stay at a hotel near the Academy, away from her husband, to be with MacArthur for at least half an hour every evening.

For the record, Pinky was not the only mother at the academy who took care of her son like this. A grandson of General Ulysses Grant, a Union Army general during the Civil War and future president, was MacArthur's classmate, and his mother, too, stayed at the same hotel as Pinky. Grant's grandson ended up second in his class, behind MacArthur.

A mother's power is truly magnificent. It is beyond any doubt that there would have been no MacArthur to talk about had it not been for his mother's contribution.

Today's conventional wisdom has it that this kind of over-education would produce a distorted personality. Admittedly, MacArthur had noticeable defects in his personality that could be attributable to his background.

One of MacArthur's personality defects was revealed in his relations with women. Tall and good looking with a bright future, MacArthur had no reason to be unpopular with women. In collaboration with his mother, however, he succeeded in evading marriage traps one after another, failing to learn how to develop ordinary affectionate relations with women. As a result, MacArthur kept repeating loveless relationships with women until he was close to sixty years old. MacArthur overcame this personal defect completely when he married his second wife, Jean, around the time that Pinky died of an illness.

MacArthur was 57 years old when he married Jean, who was 18 years younger, and they had a son. It was said that Jean "worshiped her husband like God." She was a perfect partner in the MacArthurs' social life. The husband loved and fully trusted his wife, who allowed him to concentrate on his duties without any worry about family affairs. It is believed that MacArthur's accomplishments during the occupation owed much to his wife's support.

MacArthur's cordial relations were not confined to his marriage. His relations with his subordinates also remained excellent throughout the occupation period. The ideal relations for a person of MacArthur's disposition are those in which subordinates unconditionally revere the leader as a great man, trust him fully, obey his orders faithfully, and dedicate themselves to him. Both Major General Charles Willoughby, Chief of Intelligence, and Major General Courtney Whitney, Chief of the Government Section, were such subordinates who worked in unison under MacArthur's command.

Another personality defect of MacArthur was his habit of amplifying and dramatizing his experiences in his memory, indulging in a fantasy that he had lived in a higher dimension than ordinary persons. This is why the credibility of MacArthur's memoirs is always in question.

Nevertheless, personality distortions of this degree are found in any historical figure. While some people, driven by a persecution complex of the conquered, tattled irresponsibility about MacArthur's character, it had no bearing on the general flow of history. Instead, we should pay due respect to MacArthur's thorough execution of policies he believed in, his perfect command over his subordinates during policy implementations, and his firm but skillful elimination of outside interference.

It was Brigadier General Bonner Fellers, psychological warfare director during the Greater East Asia War, who designed the principles of MacArthur's Japan strategies during the occupation period. Fellers had been a long-time Japan expert who had already written a treatise on the psychology of Japanese soldiers when he was a captain in the U.S. Army ten years before the occupation. He was a cousin of Gwen Terasaki, wife of Terasaki Hidenari, who served the Emperor as a general affairs official in the Imperial Household after the war. Throughout the occupation period, Fellers communicated with the Imperial Court via Terasaki.

In the summer of 1944, one year before the occupation, Fellers put together his thoughts on the necessary measures regarding the emperor system of Japan. The major thrust of his plan was to drive a wedge between the Emperor and his royal vassals and the military clique. This became GHQ's basic principle after the psychological strategy conference in Manila in the spring of 1945. Subsequently, the U.S. military reflected this principle in its propaganda and transmitted a message on radio that stated, "The military clique neglected their sacred duties to the Emperor and brought these ravages to Japan."

In early October 1945, Fellers wrote a lengthy but coherent treatise on policy toward the Emperor. In a nutshell, Fellers said:

> The Emperor is the living symbol of the race in whom lies the virtues of their ancestors . . . Loyalty to him is absolute. . . To try him as a war criminal would not only be blasphemous but a denial of spiritual freedom.
>
> It is a fundamantal American concept that the people of any nation have the inherent right to choose their own government. Were the Japanese given this oppotunity, they would choose the Emperor as the symbolic head state. . .
>
> If the Emperor were tried for war crimes the governmental structure would collapse and a general uprising would be inevitable. The people will umcomplainingly stand any othe humiliation. Athough they are disarmed, there would be chaos and bloodshed. It would necessitate a large expeditiory force with many thousands of public offcials. The period of occupation would be prolonged and we would have alienated the Japanese.

In efect, he argued that in order to accomplish the peaceful occupation of Japan, promote its reconstruction, and prevent a Commuinis revolution, the U.S. must collect evidence to prove that the Emperor was not responsible for the war. If sufficient evidence cannot be found, the U.S. should take active measures to avoid the trial of the Emperor.

This is a superb analysis. The history of the occupation of Japan was, simply put, that of how the Japanese people would endure the "any other humiliation" in order to protect the emperor system. It was only after the rulings at the International Military Tribunal for the Far East were finalized toward the end of 1948 that the Emperor's position became secure. Until then, the Japanese government had to obey all the instructions from GHQ, whether it be the purging of designated people from public service or the drafting of a new constitution, as if the Emperor had, so to speak, been taken hostage. Even after 1948, the Emperor's situation provided little room for any optimism until the signing of the peace treaty in 1951.

MacArthur remained thoroughly faithful to the measures proposed by Fellers. It was, in John Dower's expression, a "daunting challenge" for MacArthur in those days. Back in the United States, a Gallup poll revealed that 70 percent of respondents demanded severe punishment for the Emperor. On September 18, the U.S. Senate passed a resolution that supported severe punishment for the Emperor. This was followed by the Joint Chiefs of Staff's order to collect evidence of the Emperor's war responsibility. It was also predicted that Australia, the Philippines, and the Soviet Union would insist on the abolition of the emperor system at the Far Eastern Commission when it was launched.

MacArthur pursued and successfully accomplished his "daunting challenge," with his authority and manipulations. His dedication was simply remarkable.

Behind MacArthur's efforts were political situations in Washington, D.C., that Japan had nothing to do with.

An issue of Britain's *The Economist* in January 1946 carried an analysis of the occupation of Japan. Even today, editorials in *The Economist* are famous for their detached and objective analysis full of "British phlegm." In this issue, *The Economist* editorialized that "MacArthur is also an element of the power struggle in the United States. Even if he himself is not considering running in the 1948 presidential election, there are many who are considering it on his behalf."

An April 1946 Gallup survey showed that respondents chose MacArthur as the most admirable person in the world over Dwight Eisenhower,

Harry Truman, Winston Churchill, and Thomas Dewey. (It was Dewey who later became the Republican presidential candidate, not MacArthur.)

*The Economist* continued to say,

> Clearly his career will be tested during this period of being the highest authority in Japan. He cannot afford to make a mistake. Equally, he cannot afford to bring about confusion that results in miserable living conditions or starvation, either. His career must not be damaged at any cost. Thus, MacArthur is facing a pragmatic challenge of finding an administrative organization that can prevent Japan from falling.

The editorial further stated, "The only available means for MacArthur is to make use of the existing administrative organization of Japan."

U.S. occupation policy for Japan had undergone a series of transitions—from Roosevelt's emotional unconditional surrender argument, to the Potsdam Declaration's "unconditional surrender applicable only to the military" advocated by such Japan specialists as Joseph Grew and George Sansom, and then to the post-disarmament "unconditional surrender."

As it turned out, however, occupation policy ended up taking the form of de facto indirect rule, due to the absolute need for a successful occupation, and to MacArthur's ability to eliminate all resistance. It should be hastily added, however, that this "indirect rule" was made possible with the threat of GHQ's readiness to switch to direct rule any time by taking the Emperor hostage. Indeed, GHQ actually resorted to the use of power, de facto direct rule, at the time of the Purge in 1946.

American newspapers also began to support MacArthur's occupation policy. Even the weekly *The Nation*, which had been most critical of MacArthur, became a MacArthur supporter after the issuance of Edict No. 109 on the Purge in January 1946. The opinion poll taken in the same month by the weekly showed that 71 percent of respondents were satisfied with how the occupation of Japan was being carried out, exceeding the 60.7 percent who said the same thing about the German occupation.

By securing the support of American public opinion, the true power in the 20th century world, MacArthur was able to confidently and authoritatively fend off the voices demanding the punishment of Japan that persisted in the United States and which represented the majority view of the Far Eastern Commission.

# CHAPTER
# 3

# Resurrection of Freedom and Democracy

*—Shidehara's Devotion to Reconstruct and Reform
Japan on Its Own Initiative—*

## Freedom of Speech, Freedom of Association

In January 2000, ten months before the U.S. presidential election, Republican nominee George W. Bush made a keynote speech on diplomacy. He concluded the speech with the following words.

> We once defeated Japan in a war. But, after the victory, we delivered much-needed food among the Japanese people, drafted their constitution, encouraged the formation of labor unions, and enfranchised Japanese women. What the Japanese received from the United States was, therefore, not the retaliation that they had feared, but mercy.

This is the American historical view that has remained unchanged for more than fifty years since the end of the war. Or, rather, it might be said that this is the view that has been firmly established in the minds of Americans over the past half century. The historical view of the victor is bound to be like this.

Japan's prewar view of its history was similar to the above American view, as Japan had remained invincible before World War II. Only the historical events that made people feel proud of their country were passed on. This was done in the form of brief anecdotes that were easy even for elementary school pupils to understand. In the telling of an anecdote, the darker side was eliminated. Admittedly, this was tantamount to tracing back history as if one was walking through the pages of a picture book. Still, the stories made the Japanese people intoxicated with the greatness of their country. This pride made them learn how to behave as a great nation, which, in turn, added greatness to the country, in the same sense that the United States is currently a great nation proud of its own history.

Many stories of the heroes that have been passed on from generation to generation also appear to be equally simplistic. Nevertheless, these stories became valuable assets to subsequent generations as they showed how noble and great it would be to act in the same way.

It is an undeniable fact that human history is, after all, a history of the winners. The aim of my attempt to write a modern history of Japan's diplomacy is, however, to explore the truth of history. For this purpose, I suggest that we trace the processes of the postwar reforms in Japan in detail.

To begin with, the primary mission of Prince Higashikuni Naruhiko's cabinet was to control the Japanese military and peacefully accept the occupation forces. The cabinet successfully accomplished this.

But Prime Minister Higashikuni harbored his own personal philosophy and policies above and beyond this primary mission, as was evident when they were revealed during his inaugural speech broadcast on radio on August 17 immediately after the formation of his cabinet. The first half of the speech stressed the need for citizens to obey the imperial order and to peacefully accept the surrender in an orderly fashion. In the second half of the speech, Prime Minister Higashikuni said:

> [In order to succeed in reconstructing the country,] it is essential that the Japanese people cherish active and lively aspirations for the country's reconstruction. Because this calls for lively public discussions, I intend to promote lively public discussions and the freedom to form political associations.

Higashikuni raised the banner of constructing a new Japan by referring to freedom of speech and freedom of association above anything else. These two freedoms were singled out in the speech. Here surfaced the liberalism that Higashikuni had learned in France in his younger days. Here also was the resurrection of the liberalism that had been tolerated as a social philosophy during the days of Taishō Democracy.

The ensuing cabinet meeting on August 18 mandated all of its ministers to immediately implement the "release of all political prisoners" and "freedom of speech and association." This was followed by a total ban on the political activities of the Imperial Japanese Army's military police corps, which had been in charge of the wartime control of speeches and political activities.

Prime Minister Higashikuni remained a staunch believer in these policies. When he met MacArthur on September 29, for instance, Higashikuni declared that he would have all the political prisoners, including the Communists, released. While MacArthur and his chief of staff General Richard Sutherland questioned the prudence of such action, Higashikuni said, "It is better to let [the radical thinkers] speak their minds."

The Higashikuni cabinet, however, stepped down before actually implementing the liberalization policies it had announced. The reason was its preoccupation with its primary missions, i.e. the peaceful reception of the occupation forces, disarmament of the Japanese military, demobilization, and emergency war damage restorations. Higashikuni himself once reminisced that things did not proceed as he had planned, saying, "I repeatedly urged the minister of justice to carry out the Decree of Amnesty promptly. But bureaucratic red tape got in the way . . . I was also told that the release of political prisoners should await the completion of demobilization . . ."

Had Higashikuni's liberalization policies, which were well beyond the original intention of GHQ, been actually carried out without GHQ's sanction, the policies would have contributed to correcting the current distorted historical view that all the liberties Japan enjoys today were bestowed by the United States.

Another reason behind the delay in implementing Higashikuni's liberalization policy was the resistance from his cabinet members. Even though Prime Minister Higashikuni himself was liberal and broadminded, other cabinet members, in particular the home minister, were not mentally prepared to go along with Higashikuni.

Moreover, the Japanese cabinet in those days was still under the framework of the Meiji Constitution, which, for the purpose of preserving the prerogative of the Emperor, did not grant the prime minister the authority to dismiss cabinet ministers. The result was that a prime minister had weak control over the cabinet members. This was one of the greatest deficiencies of the Meiji Constitution.

The Home Ministry, for its part, had no intention of easing its restrictions on freedom of speech. It had banned the distribution of the daily *Asahi, Mainichi,* and *Yomiuri* newspapers that had carried the photo of MacArthur standing shoulder to shoulder with Emperor Shōwa. As a result, GHQ overruled the ban and ordered the distribution of the photo. The Home Ministry, however, continued to show resistance, both implicitly and explicitly, infuriating GHQ.

On October 4, GHQ suddenly announced the dismissal of 4,000 officials of the Home Ministry and the Police Bureau, including the home minister. This action was more of an expression of GHQ's dissatisfaction with Home Ministry bureaucrats who continued to resist Prime Minister Higashikuni's liberalization attempt than criticism of the administration of the Higashikuni cabinet as a whole. Nevertheless, the abrupt dismissal of one of Higashikuni's own cabinet members greatly offended Higashikuni's pride.

## Shidehara Kijūrō's Remedial Measures

When Prime Minister Higashikuni asked for his opinion, Ogata Taketora said,

> Because we are under occupation and have accepted an unconditional surrender, we cannot overtly refuse the GHQ's order. But if we simply accept the order, the authority of the Japanese government will disappear completely . . . Therefore, as a passive expression of our disagreement with the order, the Higashikuni cabinet should step down.

Prime Minister Higashikuni immediately agreed with Ogata's proposal and resigned. With this action, Higashikuni chose to protect his pride. As shown in the later part of the chapter, this was the last collective expression of the Japanese government's resistance to GHQ orders.

Upon the resignation of the Higashikuni cabinet, Lord Keeper of the Privy Seal Kido Kōichi decided to recommend Yoshida Shigeru as the next prime minister. When Kido approached Yoshida, however, Yoshida suggested that Shidehara Kijūrō should form the next cabinet.

After this conversation, Yoshida visited General Sutherland at GHQ to inform him that Shidehara had been appointed to form the cabinet to succeed Higashikuni. During this visit, Yoshida obtained Sutherland's confirmation that GHQ had no intention of interfering with Japan's domestic politics.

Yoshida handled this negotiation quite skillfully, revealing his talent as a professional diplomat. Having deliberately informed GHQ beforehand of Shidehara's appointment as a fait accompli to stress that the power over personnel was in the hands of the Japanese government, Yoshida subsequently made GHQ endorse the appointment. When he visited Sutherland, Yoshida said he came to ask for GHQ's *Agrément*, the approval of a diplomatic representative by the state to which he is to be accredited. While fully acknowledging GHQ's capability to veto the appointment, Yoshida stood firm in his conviction that Japan would never compromise its prerogative to appoint its prime minister.

Although Shidehara initially declined the nomination citing his advanced age and inexperience as a politician, he was eventually persuaded by the Emperor to accept it.

As a matter of fact, Shidehara had written "Shūsen Zengosaku" (Remedial Measures to Ride Out Immediate Postwar Days) in early October, a little before the appointment, and handed it to Foreign Minister Yoshida. The writing was a compilation of his views on Japan's future that he had sent to his friends in letters.

Shidehara's intention must have been to offer advice to Foreign Minister Yoshida and the Higashikuni cabinet as a whole. Shidehara's ideas were concentrated in this document as follows :

(1) We must win the confidence of the Allies.
Should the public order be lost, resulting in casualties among the Japanese as well as foreigners, or should the Japanese government fail to carry out its public commitments, resorting to all kinds of plotting and scheming, the Allies would impose more stringent control over our sovereighnty, thereby protracting the period of occupation.

(2) We must engrave a sense of defeat into the Japanese people's minds. If the Japanese people become engrossed in pleasing the Allies merely to make their life easier or if they resort to temporary measures, forgetting the humiliation of the defeat, Japan will lose its chance to rebuild itself.

(3) Japan must take full advantage of the opportunities afforded by the international situations and aim to establish situations favorable to Japan. No two nations can be eternal friends or eternal foes in international affairs. Japan should constantly follow the trends of the major powers in the world so that it can seize the opportunities.

(4) The Japanese government must explore why and how Japan was defeated and open its findings to the public.

What was in Shidehara's mind was the historical example of Leon Gambetta, who paved the way for the future of France by crawling back from the ashes of defeat in the Franco-Prussian War. This episode revealed Shidehara's heartfelt wish for the recovery of the Empire of Japan. Despite such derogatory charges as calling him a weak-kneed diplomat and a traitor, Shidehara was a true patriot who never ceased to love and worry about his country.

Due to the prolonged occupation, infringement on the freedom of speech, and the spread of leftist distorted reporting and education in subsequent days, however, two of Shidehara's four proposals were deeply buried and forgotten. These include the second proposal on engraving humiliation of defeat in people's minds and making them learn a lesson from the defeat, and the fourth proposal on exploring the causes of Japan's defeat.

Instead, Japan's reconstruction was based on the more realistic policies advocated in the first and third proposals and was pursued in collaboration with the occupation forces, further aided by the rise of the Cold War. While these measures met the minimum conditions for Japan's survival, they completely neglected the spiritual reconstruction of the Japanese, which was very much in Shidehara's mind. As a result, Japan has had to pay a high price for over half a century.

The Shidehara cabinet was formed on October 9. This cabinet can be

The Shidehara Cabinet
(Copyright © KYODO NEWS IMAGES INC.)

regarded as the one composed of the best people in the history of Japan's constitutional government.

When selecting his cabinet members, Shidehara did not need to pay due attention to political parties. No existing parties or party politicians could foresee what would happen in the next election. Also, the military had lost all of its influence. Furthermore, nobody knew whether it would be beneficial to assume a responsible position when no one could predict the future course of events. For these reasons, Shidehara had no other choice than to appoint those who would not hesitate to sacrifice themselves for national affairs. As it happened, all of them belonged to an era of the good old days, building their characters and completing their education during the Taishō Democracy before the arrival of the age of militarism in Japan.

The cabinet meeting that was called immediately after the investiture of the Shidehara cabinet on October 9 decided to tackle eight issues that required immediate attention.

Among those eight issues, the second through the fifth were related to immediate postwar measures including food shortages, reconstruction, unemployment, war casualty relief, and repatriation of military and civilian personnel. But it was the democratization of Japan that the Shidehara cabinet deemed the most urgent issue—the first issue that Japan had to tackle among the myriad of postwar imperatives. In order to promote democratization in Japan, Japan needed to hold a democratic election, which called for the amendment of election laws.

It was Home Minister Horikiri Zenjirō and Vice Minister Saka Chiaki who were put in charge of election reforms. Horikiri was a Home Ministry official who had studied election systems after WWI in Germany, which was under the Weimar Constitution. Meanwhile, Saka, who was one year junior to Horikiri, was engaged in the actual enforcement of a law establishing universal suffrage in 1928. For these two who had experienced the Weimar democracy and the Taishō Democracy, post–World War II democracy in Japan was not a new, unexpected development; it was rather a second coming of their own time.

As a matter of fact, Prime Minister Higashikuni had already announced the following political reform programs in his speech at the September 4 extraordinary Diet session: "In order to carry out a fundamental reform of the election system in Japan, we must first lower the voting age and give women the right to vote . . . abolish the House of Peers and institute a senate or a house of councilors." Unfortunately, the Higashikuni government had not been endowed with a bureaucratic organization that was capable of carrying out these programs. Implementation of these programs had to await the birth of the Shidehara cabinet.

The Shidehara cabinet immediately endorsed the reform of the election system on October 9 with the full consent of cabinet members. This was followed by the first MacArthur-Shidehara meeting, which took place that very afternoon at 5:00.

The dialogue between MacArthur and Shidehara is compiled in a detailed document and is still kept at the Ministry of Foreign Affairs. This making of verbatim records was Shidehara's business style as a veteran diplomat. Glancing at this MacArthur-Shidehara verbatim document, one could tell how highly unusual it was for there to be no records of the later three-hour meeting in which Shidehara was supposed to have proposed the renunciation of wars. I would like to touch on these points later in this chapter.

During this October 9 meeting, MacArthur read out a paper that had been prepared beforehand. It was the first time GHQ gave specific instructions aside from the more abstract guiding principles it had issued previously.

MacArthur's instructions consisted of (1) women's suffrage, (2) promotion of labor unions, (3) liberalization of school education, (4) abolition of secret police, and (5) democratization of the economic system.

After reading out the five instructions, MacArthur said to Shidehara, "Although I do not think we are being unreasonable, do not hesitate to say so if any of these instructions seem too harsh." While GHQ later began to impose harsh demands one after another, MacArthur's attitude at that time was still quite sensible and honorable.

In response, Shidehara replied, "While I will have to take these instructions back to consult with my cabinet members, I am quite relieved to find that nothing seems impossible at this moment." When he continued to explain that women's suffrage had already been endorsed at the cabinet meeting and that preparations for democratic elections were under way, MacArthur interrupted and said, "Those are excellent ideas. Please carry them out along those lines."

Subsequently, Shidehara touched on the labor union law and told MacArthur that its adoption had already been discussed at a cabinet meeting he had attended more than ten years earlier. Although it had failed to be carried out due to certain circumstances, Shidehara assured MacArthur that this time nothing seemed to get in the way of its implementation.

Shidehara also foresaw no problem in carrying out the liberal school education as it had been decided by the cabinet and added that abolition of secret interrogation would be a matter of course.

The fifth instruction on democratization of the economic system, however, aroused controversy. Shidehara asked MacArthur what exactly he had in mind. MacArthur replied that perhaps something akin to an antitrust law might have been envisaged, though the details of the instruction were also unclear to him. It was this fifth instruction that became a point of contention for a long time to come as it led to dissolution of the zaibatsu.

In the end, Shidehara said to MacArthur, "The Japanese government has absolutely no intention to wiggle out of any commitmant once made." He told MacArthur that he could count on the Shidehara cabinet no matter what kind of impression MacArthur might have had in his relations with Japanese in the past.

In a nutshell, Shidehara stressed to MacArthur that he should trust the faithfulness of the Japanese.

## The World's Most Outstanding Gentlemen

Before World War II, there was an established perception in the world that the Japanese were worthy of respect.

If I may be allowed to introduce my personal experiences, I happened to be the first Japanese student to be accepted by Cambridge University after World War II. It was a time when Britons still held that prewar perception of the Japanese.

One afternoon, I made an appointment to have a chat along the River Cam with a British student whom I had become acquainted with at a party. On the day of the promise, however, it happened to rain heavily, a situation quite unusual in the British weather. So when I headed for the appointed place, I was half suspicious whether my friend would show up. Yet there he was, waiting for me with an umbrella by the river. His first words to me were, "It's beautiful weather, isn't it?" When I asked him why he had come in this pouring rain, he said, "Oh, I wouldn't have come under normal circumstances. But I heard that the Japanese never fail to keep a promise." It was, therefore, a competition of pride between British and Japanese gentlemen.

Even in more recent years, a member of the U.S. east coast establishment who had served many administrations as a cabinet member said to me, "I heard that Japanese are the world's most outstanding gentlemen. . . ." Perhaps he was holding on to the impressions he had acquired from an old book or what he had heard from his elders in his youth. This perception of the Japanese seems to have lingered at the back of the minds of the Western intellectuals in the olden days.

Shidehara's hope to promote the democratization of Japan on the basis of mutual trust between gentlemen was later shattered miserably by the trend among the American public that branded the Japanese as a barbaric and inferior race that could be reformed only with the whip of the occupation forces.

Shidehara, however, was full of confidence. During the conversation with MacArthur, Shidehara freely expressed his thinking, and said,

> I take it that your intention is to democratize and liberalize Japan. When I was a cabinet member a dozen or so years ago, there was a trend in Japan to move toward democratization and liberalization. However, the eruption of the Manchurian Incident totally reversed the trend. Today, all the factors that could abruptly reverse the trend toward these goals have been eliminated. Therefore, it should not be

difficult for Japan today, to move forward toward the direction it had pursued over a decade earlier.

Meanwhile, Shidehara did not forget to put the brakes on GHQ's democratization policy. He said,

> Democracy takes many forms and shapes, including the American style, the British style, and even the Soviet style. If Japan is expected to establish democracy that is exactly the same as the American, it would be hard to come by. If, on the other hand, democracy here means politics which respects and reflects the people's wishes, Japan will achieve it before long because the spirit of democracy had already sprouted more than ten years ago in Japan. For democracy to succeed in Japan, it will have to be a democracy that fits well with Japan's past environment.

Before the conclusion of the dialogue, MacArthur responded to Shidehara's remark and said,

> I have heard the same story about the days when you were a cabinet member. And I am sure that, had there not been an interruption in those days, Japan would not have had to face what it does today. In this sense, I very much wish for the success of the new Japanese government.

Later, MacArthur wrote in his memoirs,

> Shidehara completely agreed with our instructions and he immediately started acting vigorously. I knew it would have been unwise to impose instructions on the Japanese in the form of a coercive order, because that could lead to dissatisfaction among them. These things [that GHQ's instructions advocated] should be pursued on Japan's own initiative when the Japanese people really desire them.

Subsequently, the Shidehara cabinet steadily carried out these reforms as MacArthur had expected.

The amendment of the election law, including the extension of suffrage to women, was decided at the November 13 cabinet meeting. It passed both houses of the Diet on December 15. The English translation of the new election law was submitted to GHQ on December 24.

There were diverging views within the GHQ Government Section concerning this law. As it turned out, MacArthur approved the law as written, saying that the Japanese people were entitled to conduct elections according to a law they themselves had made. It shows that, up until this point, MacArthur's basic instructions were respected.

The labor union law was created utilizing the experiences of repeated legislation attempts in the Taishō to early Shōwa period. The law passed both houses on December 18. This law was so highly progressive that GHQ found no reason to interfere.

Needless to say, these reform attempts met various forms of resistance within the Japanese government. Nevertheless, the Shidehara cabinet managed to advance political reforms, successfully controlling the opposition from inside without resorting to GHQ's authority.

It would be a meaningless and miserable task to verify whether it was GHQ or the Japanese government that took the initiative in each reform attempt during the occupation. It would only expose the inferiority complex of a defeated nation.

This is because most of these reforms would have been implemented sooner or later no matter who the prime minister was and whether or not there were occupation forces in Japan. It was only natural to liquidate all of its wartime regimes when peace was restored. Also, in light of the trends of the major powers in the world at that time, a country with the cultural level and past political experience as Japan would undoubtedly have accomplished such reforms as women's suffrage sooner or later.

Today, Japanese people whose personal memories only go back to the days of the militarism after the 1930s may believe that the occupation would have been the only way to liberate Japan from the harsh militarism.

But it should be recalled that, during the Taishō Democracy days, Japan became so anti-militaristic that soldiers hesitated to wear their uniforms in public—a phenomenon also seen after World War II—and were refused, in some cases, being allowed to ride in a rickshaw. Given this history, it would have been only natural for Japan after such a crushing defeat to experience a period in which everything that was related to the war and the military was denied and condemned.

Article 10 of the Potsdam Declaration stipulates that "the Japanese government shall remove all obstacles to the revival and strengthening of democratic tendencies among the Japanese people." It is believed that this particular sentence was constructed by Sir George Bailey Sansom, a historian and long-time Japan expert in the British Foreign Service. A historian's memory is longer than a common man's, and, indeed, Sansom added the spirit of the revival of the Taishō Democracy to the goals of the occupation of Japan.

Meanwhile, John Dower and several others stressed the significance of the Japanese public support for the U.S. reform proposals despite resistance on the part of the Japanese government. In my opinion, this view is half correct but half wrong. It is correct to say that the U.S.-initiated reforms were supported by the Japanese people, because that was indeed the general trend of the time in Japan. Resistance on the part of the Japanese government, however, was merely a result of bureaucratic inertia or repulsion to GHQ's high-handedness. Even unattended, the general trends of the time would have taken Japan toward all of those reforms.

In the case of women's suffrage, it was the Japanese government that not only took the initiative but also actually implemented it. In light of the sequence of adoption of women's suffrage in other similarly civilized countries in those days, the reform in Japan would have been a matter of time.

As for the freedom of speech and the freedom of association, which are the fundamental principles behind the promotion of labor unions and liberal education, postwar Japanese governments had already implemented some basic policies on these issues. The policies were initiated by the Higashikuni cabinet and were passed on to the Shidehara cabinet.

Preparations for land reform, which followed these reforms, had also been started under Agriculture Minister Matsumura Kenzō. Many still believe that, among all the postwar reforms in Japan, at least the land reform would not have been possible had it not been for the authority of GHQ. The fact of the matter was that the land reform act that completely banned absentee landlords and limited land ownership of a farming landlord to 5 hectares would have been passed by the Diet anyway, albeit with some possible twists and turns.

To be sure, it was GHQ, or, more accurately, the Far Eastern Commission, whose members included the Soviet Union, that demanded more radical reforms in Japan and made the Japanese government limit land ownership of a farming landlord to 1 hectare instead of 5. In fact, the impact on Japanese society of preserving a class living on rentier income was rather limited, because of a failure to free land from forestry landlords and residential landowners.

Meanwhile, GHQ-initiated reforms that lacked inevitability based on Japanese history and society did not succeed. These include reform of the municipal police system and the dissolution of zaibatsu.

On November 1, in the midst of reform attempts, Shigemitsu Mamoru wrote in his diary, "GHQ tends to coerce Japan to implement reforms as a part of GHQ-initiated democratization even though the GHQ reforms remain just the same as the new policies initiated by the Japanese government and welcomed by the Japanese people." It is highly commendable that Shigemitsu had already discerned GHQ's true intention even though the demand was not so blatant at this stage.

Shigemitsu's observations subsequently became realities one after another. This fact, coupled with GHQ's restrictions on free speech as well as distorted education and biased reporting, ended up becoming the basis for the historic view of the Japanese in general and the postwar historic view that would stay for half a century after the war.

Particularly disturbing is a popular belief among the Japanese postwar generations that the new constitution of Japan contributed to the freedom that we all enjoy today. This belief is both logically and historically wrong. All of the reforms and liberalizations, including women's suffrage, labor unions, and land reform, had been decided and implemented under the Meiji Constitution before the promulgation of the new constitution. There was absolutely not a single case in which articles in the Meiji Constitution became obstacles to those reforms and liberalizations. In other words, the Meiji Constitution had had enough capacity to promote the reforms and liberalizations when and if the current of the times and people's mindsets changed. And this was the perception that Shidehara had had of the Meiji Constitution from the beginning, which was a perfectly correct interpretation of the law.

While another chapter should be devoted to the issue of the constitution, it would not be an exaggeration to say that the only reforms that required a new constitution were Article 9 and the prime minister's authority to dismiss any of his cabinet members. The latter was a clear and plain improvement.

Because nobody opposed the strengthening of the prime minister's authority, we can safely say that today's constitutional controversy in Japan is exclusively about Article 9. If there is any other salient issue related to the constitution, it should have to do with the question of Japan's dignity as a nation-state. The question is this: Is it really appropriate for Japan to eternally cherish the constitution that was imposed by foreign powers during the occupation and which was basically nothing more than a translation of a text written in a foreign language?

## Emperor Shōwa's Humanity Declaration

Having devoted everything he had to the reconstruction and reform of Japan for almost three months since being appointed prime minister in early October 1945, Shidehara fell ill toward the end of the year. The last reform he launched was Emperor Shōwa's Humanity Declaration.

On January 1, 1946 (21st Year of Shōwa), an imperial rescript was issued by Emperor Shōwa that denied his divinity. This was the so-called Humanity Declaration.

It is believed that the genesis of this declaration was neither an order from GHQ nor a spontaneous initiative on the part of Emperor Shōwa. The declaration is believed to have stemmed from a conversation between Colonel Harold Henderson, former professor of Japanese studies at Columbia University and an advisor to the U.S. occupation forces, and Reginald Blyth, a British scholar on Zen Buddhism. The duo came up with an idea that, in order to advance Japan's democratization and peace, a new Imperial Rescript on Education (教育勅語) was called for to deny Japan's supra-nationalism and deification of the emperor.

Since Blyth at that time was teaching at Gakūshuin, an educational institution for the children born to families of the nobility, he was able to convey this idea to the Imperial Court, from which he learned that Emperor Shōwa was supportive of it. Subsequently, a draft declaration prepared by the two was secretly submitted to Yoshida Shigeru.

It was Prime Minister Shidehara himself who took on the task for the Japanese side. When Shidehara inquired the emperor's view on this issue, Emperor Shōwa denounced the deification of the emperor, quoting the case of Emperor Gomizunoo in the 17th century who was unable to receive medical treatment because nobody was allowed to touch the emperor. After Shidehara, in response, shared his own view that the military had ruined the country by abusing the spirit of the deification of the emperor, it was decided that an imperial rescript should be issued on New Year's Day 1946.

Although December 25 was a national holiday (in commemoration of the demise of Emperor Taishō), Shidehara locked himself in alone at the prime minister's official residence to edit the draft declaration. Because the message was initially envisaged to be directed toward the outside world, Shidehara took half a day to write an English draft. Then he translated the draft into Japanese.

Reading the draft declaration, Emperor Shōwa said, "This will do." But he expressed his hope to insert the Charter Oath (五箇条の御誓文, also called the Imperial Oath of Five Articles) of Emperor Meiji. This insertion was intended to emphasize that democracy had been a part of Japan's own tradition since the time of the Meiji Restoration and was not something that had been forcibly imposed on Japan from the outside.

As a result, the imperial rescript became a proclamation of the basic principles of the new Japan rather than a mere humanity declaration of the emperor. Quoting the Charter Oath at the outset, the declaration said, "The proclamation [of the Charter Oath] is so evident in significance and so high in ideals that we have nothing to add."

In the first year of Meiji, after the fall of the shogunate system, there was a brief period in Japan when the Japanese public held out much hope for the new era. There was also a sense of expectation that the democracy declared by the Charter Oath was going to be accomplished in no time.

The newly established *Shūgiin* (集議院, a legislative body in the early Meiji period), however, turned out to be dominated by conservatives, just as Russia's Fifth Duma that immediately followed the fall of the Soviet Union in 1993 and the National Parliament that Mustafa Kemal Ataturk established to modernize Turkey in 1920. Members indulged in unrealistic discussions that went nowhere. And, in no time, they resulted in the formation of an arena of despotism by the *han*-cliques. As a result, it took 20 some additional years for Japan to establish the Imperial Diet.

Once the war regime was totally demolished, it was only natural, in my view, for the Japanese to cherish the sweet memories of this brief but fresh period in the beginning of Meiji.

From the viewpoint of such children of the Taishō Democracy as Emperor Shōwa and Shidehara Kijūrō, it was the Charter Oath, promulgation of the Meiji Constitution, establishment of the Imperial Diet, and the Taishō Democracy that was the orthodox, formal flow of Japan's modern history. On the other hand, despotism by the han-clique (1871–90) and the days of militarism (1932–45) were the unorthodox, dark side of history that was to be overcome sooner or later. Indeed, the very first words that Emperor Shōwa gave to the Higashikuni cabinet immediately after the war were "Respect the [Meiji] constitution." From these words, one can detect Emperor Shōwa's deep resentment against the military that had abused the spirit of the Meiji Constitution. He must have wished to start everything all over again, going back to the spirit of the Charter Oath at the time of the Meiji Restoration.

To Americans in general who were not familiar with Japan's history, including journalist Mark Gayn, the quotation of the Charter Oath itself was a sign of retrogression to the detestable Meiji period, a notion I intend to touch on in the next chapter.

Thus, the Humanity Declaration upheld the principle of Japan's democracy at the outset by quoting the Charter Oath. Then followed descriptions of the distress and challenges the Japanese people were currently facing. Next came the following declaration:

We stand by the people and We wish always to share with them in their moments of joys and sorrows. The ties between Us and Our people have always stood upon mutual trust and affection. They do not depend upon mere legends and myths. They are not predicated on the false conception that the Emperor is divine, and that the Japanese people are superior to other races and fated to rule the world.

The above quoted portion of the imperial rescript is the so-called Humanity Declaration by Emperor Shōwa. It was, however, the spirit of the Charter Oath that Emperor Shōwa wished to reflect in this rescript. MacArthur, too, expressed his admiration for Emperor Meiji's accomplishments when he read the draft rescript. MacArthur later released an announcement concerning this rescript in which he declared, "The Emperor led the democratization of the Japanese people." The imperial rescript had a great effect in mitigating subsequent criticism of Emperor Shōwa, both domestically and internationally.

## Reforms Must Be Implemented by the Hand of the Victor

Reconstructing Japan by resurrecting the democracy of the good old Japan that the Taishō Democracy had once accomplished and by constructing a new Japan under the occupation on the basis of U.S. leaders' respect and understanding of Japan's history, national character, and quality of Japan's leaders was the dream that Shidehara had pursued with confidence. This dream, however, was doomed.

After spending half a day completing the Humanity Declaration in the postwar, poorly heated prime minister's residence in the cold of December, Shidehara fell ill the next day. He was diagnosed with acute pneumonia, a life-threatening condition for an old man.

On January 4, 1946, after surviving the first three days of the New Year, Shidehara suddenly received notice that GHQ had issued orders known as the Purge.

This purge was the strongest weapon that GHQ mustered to manipulate and subjugate Japan's postwar politics.

After the first edict on January 4—Edict No. 109—a series of edicts were issued. The second one was issued in 1947. While the edicts were formally implemented under the name of the Japanese government, GHQ oftentimes pushed through its will mainly for political reasons. In doing so, GHQ ignored the carefully deliberated proposals of the Japanese. As a result, these experiences fostered a sense of powerlessness among the Japanese politicians and bureaucrats. That is to say, to the Japanese it looked as though Japan's politics were in the hands of GHQ, which in turn contributed to the strengthening of GHQ's authority in the eyes of the Japanese. I shall touch on this issue in subsequent chapters.

Edict No. 109 was a basic document outlining the criteria for subsequent purges. Aside from category A (war criminals) and category B (career military men), whose purge was inevitable, the list encompassed a vast range of individuals including category G (militarists and supra-nationalists other than categories A and B) whose definition was arbitrary and subject to GHQ's discretion.

Reading the edict, Emperor Shōwa expressed his apprehension, and said, "This is a very severe and cruel instruction. If this is carried out word for word, all the officials and other individuals who have faithfully served their country will be deprived of their livelihood."

I do not have the heart to describe the miseries that awaited those who were deprived not only of their social status but also of their sources of livelihood and their families by the Purge.

One of the major motivations behind the purge at that time was the need to postpone the imminent free election. The first postwar general election had been scheduled for January 1946. However, if the general election had been implemented exactly as planned under the progressive election law initiated by the Shidehara cabinet, politicians who had been in power during the prewar and war days might have been elected to represent the will of the Japanese people. In order to forestall this outcome, GHQ also ordered the postponement of the general election until mid-March.

Mark Gayn left the following observations in his *Nippon Nikki* (Japan Diary: 1945–1948) on the first postwar general election,:

> The largest political party is *Shimpotō* (Progressive Party), whose backbone consists of 270 former member of the so-called Tōjō Diet. This party only a few months ago happily worked with the Japanese Army. The second largest party is the *Jiyūtō* (Liberal Party), which is as illiberal as the *Shimpotō is* unprogressive.

The screening of candidates for the *Shimpotō* lasted until March 9. Only 14 out of 274 candidates were found to be qualified.

The most outright interference in an election is for the government side to decide who is qualified to run and to have the authority to screen candidates beforehand. If this actually takes place, voters have no chance to elect the representatives of their choice.

It was, without doubt, possible for the Diet to carry out Shidehara's reforms even without the Purge. Nevertheless, it would have been no good, from the U.S. viewpoint, if the reforms had been pursued at the hands of conservative Japanese leaders themselves.

It all boils down to the ego and greed of the winner—American public opinion and the U.S. government—to seek the pleasure of victory. In order to fully enjoy a sense of victory, the United States initially needed the Japanese people to experience a thorough sense of humiliation, and make them realize that reforms would be granted as a favor. This was exactly what Shigemitsu had predicted two months earlier.

To be sure, the decision whether to implement the purge was hotly debated even within GHQ. Career military men such as Major General Charles Willoughby, MacArthur's chief of intelligence, insisted on "limiting the purge to Japan's top leaders in order to prevent a Communist revolution." However, Charles Kades, deputy chief of GHQ's Government Section, and his supporters got their way in the end with the help of some instructions from Washington.

On this issue, Kades was often heard saying, "This is a good measure to facilitate generational change and reinvigorate Japan."

I must say he did not know when to stop meddling with another country's affairs. According to his logic, all the countries in the world would be reinvigorated by dismissing all people at a certain age. Nevertheless, MacArthur later started using this logic himself occasionally, and today even some Japanese historians quote this monologue of Kades to emphasize the positive aspects of the Purge. This is a typical example of the way to influence people's thinking as a whole: that is, endlessly repeating a cause and forbidding all counterarguments by imposing controls on free speech.

As a matter of fact, the Purge had a harmful influence on Japan. The very generation of Japanese who had received high-level education during the peacetime in the Meiji through early Showa periods, who were well exposed to foreign countries, and who had been in responsible positions during the transition from the Taishō Democracy to the era of militarism were dismissed. Instead, those who had only been in mediocre positions during the era of militarism with precious little overseas experience, or their succeeding generations who had received the military education which suppressed personal qualities, assumed leadership positions for a long time in postwar Japan.

As exemplified by the moral decay among the Russians after Joseph Stalin and Lavrentiy Beria purged all of the revolutionary generations who had cherished ardent passion for the idealism of the Lenin era, it is obvious that overdoing things causes more harm than good.

There was a case in which a head of one of the zaibatsus, an outstanding businessman and a graduate of Harvard University, had to tread a thorny path of life. After serving the country as a second-class private during the war, he was about to reconstruct his company but was purged by GHQ. All of his excellent employees he had long nurtured were also purged, forcing him to appoint a local branch manager with only a mediocre reputation as president of his company. This became a source of his long-standing resentment.

It is not hard to imagine that the Japanese leaders of the good old days with rich overseas experiences would have tried to pass on their experiences to the new, postwar generations, skipping the militarism generations, if things had been left to the natural flow of time. In this way, history and the tradition of Japan would have been passed on to the next generations in an appropriate manner.

It was regrettable that, by that time, the U.S. government had lost all of its old Japan experts. Japan experts such as Joseph Grew had already resigned as if to say, "My mission is over." But, had these Japan specialists not resigned when Japan surrendered, and had they chosen to participate in the management of postwar Japan, Japan's history and tradition and the Japanese people's pride would not have been damaged as much as they were.

CHAPTER

# 4

# Psychology and Logic of the Victors

*—Occupation Policy Divided: A Thorough Reform*
*of Japan, or an Anti-Soviet Strategy?—*

## Some in Japan Maintained Their Self-Respect

Although my purpose is to write about the history modern of Japan, I need to spend a few pages to review the American views on Japan in those days.

This is necessary because, at that time, Japan was no longer the sovereign master of its own fate.

Having been deprived of its military force, Japan had no means by which to resist the occupation forces. As a result, the United States no longer had to worry about "the Japanese resistance [against the demilitarization of Japan] that would have required an occupation force of one million to counter it, as had been feared at the beginning of the occupation. Besides, the occupation forces were equipped with coercive measures.

While the most direct instrument for shutting out opposition is to control the freedom of speech, I'd like to elaborate on that in a separate chapter.

The most effective measure taken during the earlier days of the occupation was the Purge, which was applied not only to public officials but also to teachers and businessmen. When one is purged, one is deprived of the social status from which one can be heard.

It also had the effect of threatening people with the fear of losing their means of livelihood. And behind this fear was the starvation that plagued

Japan immediately after the defeat in the war. Even a lion can be tamed when it is starved. It was extremely difficult for people responsible for protecting their families from starvation to sacrifice their families' welfare in order to maintain their own self-respect and pride. The rapid decline of self-respect among the Japanese in the immediate postwar days was due to this economic destitution.

Lee Teng-hui, the former president of Taiwan, was studying at Kyoto University at the time of Japan's defeat. He reminisced that he was amazed to witness the rapid moral decay among the Japanese in such a brief period of time before his return to Taiwan.

There were, of course, people who never lost their self-respect. It is believed that as many as 350 former members of the Imperial Japanese Army and Navy killed themselves, refusing to accept the defeat of Japan. Even among survivors, there were a few who maintained their pride until the very end.

Let me introduce one episode. This is about the friendship between Vice-Admiral Kusaka Ryūnosuke of the Imperial Japanese Navy and U.S. Admiral Arleigh Burke as cited by novelist Agawa Hiroyuki.

Arleigh Burke was a prominent figure in the U.S. Navy, a brave naval officer who had commanded a destroyer squadron in the Pacific during the war and who was later promoted to Chief of Naval Operations and Admiral. During the occupation of Japan, Burke was told by his men that Vice-Admiral Kusaka, his former archrival in naval battles in the Solomon Sea, had been purged by GHQ. In order to survive, Vice-Admiral Kusaka worked as a railroad worker with a pickax in his hand and Mrs. Kusaka sold flowers on the street. When asked if he felt like sending some gift to Kusaka, Burke at first spatted out, "Let him starve for all I care." On second thought, Burke decided to send a box of supplies including canned food to his old rival.

A few days later, a silvered-haired old man barged into Burke's office, yelling something incomprehensible. Instinctively, Burke took out his gun and prepared himself for an assault. He learned via the interpreter that it was Kusaka who came to reject Burke's gifts. Kusaka left with the parting shot, "It is humiliating to receive such a gift. I want no charity, particularly not from an American." Later, Burke reflected that he himself would have done exactly the same as Kusaka had he been in Kusaka's shoes.

Subsequently, after a few ego battles, Burke and Kusaka became close friends. Through this friendship, Burke began to understand the Imperial Japanese Navy well and later played an important role as a founding father of the Japan Maritime Self-Defense Force. Burke received a decoration from the Emperor for his contribution. When he passed away, it was only this Japanese medal among countless decorations he had earned throughout his life that he allowed his family to decorate his remains with at the burial.

I personally learned from people of my father's generation around me that not a small number of Japanese retained their self-respect. While Vice-Admiral Kusaka was fortunate to have his case revisited by the writer Agawa half a century after the end of the war, hundreds and thousands of others were not so lucky. No matter how hard they must have strived to maintain their self-respect, their efforts became unknown even to their own children and grandchildren due to the prolonged occupation of Japan and control on the freedom of speech imposed by GHQ.

This was why I initially hesitated to name this book "Yoshida Shigeru and His Times" until the last minute. Actually, it would have been a more accurate description of the realities to title it "MacArthur and His Times."

What, then, did the Americans want to do about Japan? Let us pursue this question through the testimonies of the Americans.

The occupation policy of the United States is often described in terms of a conflict of views between Charles Kades of GHQ's Government Section, and Charles Willoughby, MacArthur's Chief of Intelligence. Henry Kissinger analyzed this conflict as friction between a crusader-like idealism that sought to spread the gospel of American values throughout the world, on the one hand, and realism based on power politics, on the other. It is quite an accurate description of the situation in those days.

At this point, let me introduce Mark Gayn's *Japan Diary*, a work typical of the former view, and George Kennan's policy discussion, which reflects the view of the latter. Additionally, I would like to introduce Helen Mears to represent the views of Japan specialists at the time. Although she had no influence on the occupation policy, Mears' view reflected the conscience of an American when prominent Japan specialists such as Joseph Grew and George Sansom had already ceased to be influential.

Mark Gayn had been recognized as a reporter with sufficient knowledge about the Far East even before World War II. *Japan Diary* was a record of his one-year stay in Japan after his arrival in a completely demolished Tokyo in December 1945.

One characteristic common to people like Gayn was a total lack of knowledge of Japan's past history. The only thing they had was a vague preconception of the country that perhaps had been nurtured by the wartime propaganda.

On Emperor Shōwa's quotation of the Charter Oath in his Humanitarian Declaration, Gayn writes,

> Emperor Meiji has become the pillar and symbol of militant nationalism in Japan, and whatever the verbiage of some of his proclamations, a popular government was never practiced in his 45-year reign, nor was it intended to function. Under under Emperor Meiji, Japan fought China and Russia, seized Formosa, violated and annexed Korea, and establishd "special rights" in Manchuria.

Sadly, a man's memory is deplorably short. To Gayn's generation, the only image of Japan's past was that of the age of militarism or that of the Meiji-Taishō eras which had been fabricated during the rise of militarism.

In 1945, Henry Stimson was already 78 years old. He had hoped that Japan would restore the era of Hamaguchi Osachi, Wakatsuki Reijirō, and Shidehara Kijūrō after the defeat. Shidehara himself was 73 years old. McArthur and Grew were both 65 years old and they had known the Russo-Japanese War first-hand. MacArthur and Grew contemplated the resurrection of the Taishō Democracy. Except for a few Japan specialists, any generation younger than those men had absolutely no knowledge of the Taishō Democracy or the strenuous efforts made by the advocates of the Freedom and People's Rights movement.

American historian John Dower, who has written voluminous works on Japan during the occupation, said, "While there were some early signs of democracy in prewar Japan, it was far from a democratic country." I feel urged to hastily add, though, that Dower's definition of "democracy" here was a highly leftist one. Likewise, to Dower's mind, the buds of democracy were nipped by the "reverse course" caused by the Korean War before a powerful social democratic force could emerge to complete a two-party system and the accomplishment of full democracy.

Following this logic, now that the Social Democratic Party has greatly declined in power, even today's Japan cannot be regarded as a democratic country. If this implies that postwar Japan is basically no different from prewar Japan in terms of democracy, it is indeed quite a fair assessment in its own right. As can be detected from this, Dower has an inclination to be radically liberal. For instance, while criticizing Japan for refusing to apologize for its inhumane conduct during World War II, he also denounces U.S. conduct in Vietnam.

Kades went even further and openly said, "I have absolutely no knowledge of Japan's history or culture. All I know is Japan's invasion of China and Southeast Asia and its cruel conduct."

When one ignores the country's history and culture, its reform can be boundlessly fundamental. For example, Kades said, "Japanese leaders are trying to nip branches that are sick. But we are convinced that the same sickness will return unless its roots are cut off."

In a similar fashion, Gayn said,

Japan today is *not* like the United States. She is still an unreformed aggressor nation, in which the agencies and instruments of jingoism remain virtually intact. This for us should still be the season of wrecking, before we can embark on our building projects. Too soon, too many Americans here have forgotten that we did not go to war merely to avenge, the sinking of some of our superannuated battleships at Pearl Harbor, but—to a much greater degree—to reshape Japan, so that she would not war again.

The above quote shows that Gayn had totally forgotten not only the history of Japan but also the entire background under which Japan had entered into war. Gayn became convinced that it was an American mission to completely remake Japan and that that had been the aim of the war.

What kind of Japan, then, did Gayn want to build? To summarize what he wrote on this subject, rebuilding Japan entailed purging all Japanese who had collaborated with Japan's war efforts—meaning, in my view, 99 percent of the Japanese who had naturally acted out of their sense of a citizen's duty—from positions of responsibility, and creating a completely new Japan based on the rejection of all Japanese traditions since Meiji. The only criterion to be applied was whether something had been accomplished in making a Japan that resembled the United States.

I imagine young Japanese readers today would be amazed by Gayn's unbelievably simplistic views and might even be enraged by his self-righteousness and arrogance. Nevertheless, when Gayn's diary was translated into Japanese and published as *Nippon Nikki* in 1951, it became an instant bestseller, winning the sympathy of progressive men of culture in Japan. This fact alone makes it clear that there is no need to point out the commonality between the distorted leftist thinking in postwar Japan and the likes of Mark Gayn.

## Realism vs. Idealism

Nevertheless, it is a virtue of the United States to have a system of "checks and balances" that works effectively there in all walks of life.

In fact, from the viewpoint of those who were actually engaged in the occupation administration, the administration of occupied Japan would have become paralyzed had advice from the likes of Gayn been followed.

When Gayn toured the Kansai area, he learned that seven out of fourteen chiefs of the district police stations in a prefecture had been with the Special High Police (Tokkō Keisatsu or 特高警察) during the war. When Gayn found out that the police authority had made those seven chiefs resign before the issuing of GHQ's purge order so that it could reappoint them later, Gayn harshly criticized this.

The Special High Police had been in charge of the investigation and control of "political groups and ideologies deemed to be a threat to public order" and, as such, its officers were required to be highly educated and intelligent enough to understand both Marxism and the rightwing philosophies. Therefore, it was a position to which outstanding Home Ministry bureaucrats with bright future prospects would be appointed at least once. Had these outstanding police officers been purged just because they had once been appointed to the Special High Police, the police administration immediately after the war would have been shattered. Japanese society could not have been sustained if the police organization had been so weakened, especially when only the police had the capacity to maintain peace and order in Japan now that the military had been dissolved. Gayn criticized this trick of the Japanese police, saying, "Japanese did not surrender blindly. As soon as her rulers decided to give in, they put Japan's entire, closely knit, efficient machinery of government to the job of circumventing the pledges they were uttering to the victors"

Having said that, Gayn then directed his criticism at the occupation authority rather than the former Japanese leaders for its deliberate negligence of these Japanese tricks due to "higher political considerations."

From the viewpoint of the occupation administration authority, it was merely natural and realistic to turn a blind eye to a mere district police chief level issue, as the authority needed to ensure smooth administration.

Also, although there was no open confrontation yet around 1946, it became obvious to anyone with a little bit of foresight that a direct confrontation with the Communist bloc was imminent. The strife between realism on an international level, called the Cold War, and idealism as represented by Kades and Gayn became the central theme of subsequent occupation administration. The situation can be summarized as the gradual predominance of realism over idealism as the Cold War advanced.

Although U.S. policy subsequently made a complete turn in later days, the constitutional regime had already become deeply embedded in Japan from the first half of the occupation in various areas, including legal systems as well as labor-management power relations in schools and the publishing industry, thanks to coercive control over the freedom of speech and the threat of the Purge during the first half of the occupation period.

Consequently, public opinion in Japan became completely divided into two camps: one that upheld pacifism as declared by the constitution, unable to cope with changes in the international environment and U.S. policies, and the other that opted to strengthen the U.S.-Japan alliance. This schism in public opinion characterized Japan's history during the half-century long Cold War.

At this point, let me trace back the thinking of George Kennan, a leading ideologue in U.S. policies during the earlier days of the Cold War era, by revisiting chapter 16 of his *Memoirs*.

In mid-1947, Kennan became the founding Director of Policy Planning Staff. In those days, GHQ prided itself as the sole authority of the occupation administration of Japan. As such, GHQ initially had no intention of listening to the argument of a mere State Department official and, moreover, a theorist who was not even an area specialist at that and who knew nothing about reality according to the military. Nevertheless, Kennan succeeded in building mutual trust with MacArthur when Kennan visited Japan in 1948.

George Kennan

To revisit Kennan's thinking in these few years:

> In large part these directives [of GHQ] had been evolved in the final phases of the war. They reflected at many points the love for pretentious generality, the evangelical liberalism, the self-righteous punitive enthusiasm, the pro-Soviet illusions, and the unreal hopes for great-power collaboration in the postwar period which . . . had pervaded the wartime policies of the Allied powers.[1]

In terms of the American assessment of the international situation in general, Kennan emphasized the importance of Japan, saying, "Americans . . . tended to exaggerate China's real importance and to underrate that of Japan," and "if at any time in the postwar period the Soviet leaders had been confronted with a choice between control over China and control over Japan, they would unhesitatingly have chosen the latter."[2]
He continued:

> We Americans could feel fairly secure in the presence of a truly friendly Japan and a nominally hostile China—nothing very bad could happen to us from this combination; but the dangers to our security of a nominally friendly China and a truly hostile Japan had already been demonstrated in the Pacific war.[3]

This was a coolheaded analysis in light of the difference in industrial capabilities between Japan and China as well as Japan's geopolitical

---

1   George Kennan, *Memoirs: 1925–1950* (Boston: Little, Brown & Co., 1967), p. 372.
2   Ibid., pp. 374–375.
3   Ibid., p. 375.

importance in those days.

These views formed the basis for Kennan's criticism of the American occupation policy. He said, "Most serious of all, as I saw it, was the situation created by the wholesale "purging" of people in government, in education, and in business. . . ."[4] and

> to the ordinary Japanese, as I later wrote in my report to the government, ". . . the operation of the purge must be thoroughly bewildering. I doubt, in fact, whether many persons in SCAP [Supreme Commander for the Allied Powers] . . . could explain its history, scope, procedures and purpose. . . ."
>
> The indiscriminate purging of whole categories of individuals, sickeningly similar to totalitarian practices, was in conflict with the civil rights provisions of the new constitution that we ourselves had imposed upon the Japanese. It had had the effect of barring from civil life many people who could not be regarded on any reasonable standards as exponents of militarism and whose only crime had been to serve their country faithfully in time of war. Important elements of Japanese society essential to its constructive development were being driven underground . . .
>
> Obviously, such conditions would constitute, in the event that the occupation should be suddenly removed, a high degree of vulnerability to Communist pressures. Yet nothing had been done to provide the Japanese with any adequate means of looking to their own internal security. . . . This whole establishment [police] was armed, for the most part, only with pistols, and of these there was less than one weapon to every four men. There was no counterintelligence force. Although Japan was an island country, no maritime police force had been created. And there was, of course, no Japanese armed force to back up any of these units in case of emergency. It was difficult to imagine a setup more favorable and inviting from the standpoint of the prospects for a Communist takeover. The Japanese Communists at the same time were being given a free field for political activity

---

4    Ibid., p. 388.

and were increasing their strength rapidly.[5]

This must have been how it was. Indeed, the Communist bloc countries as well as leftist demagogues and public school education dominated by the Japan Teachers' Union under communist influence continued to launch a propaganda offensive under the guise of a "movement for the defense of the Constitution" and an "antiwar movement." These movements were promoted so that the Communists could take full advantage of the most opportune stage for the eventual seizure of power.

After Kennan came back from Japan, he submitted a report to the Secretary of State that contained the following policy proposals:

> The regime of control by SCAP over the Japanese government should . . . be relaxed. The Japanese should be encouraged to develop independent responsibility . . . The emphasis should shift from reform to economic recovery. The purges should be tempered, tapered off, and terminated at an early date.[6]

Subsequently, after experiencing the escalation of the Cold War and the Korean War, U.S. policy was changed as Kennan had suggested.

Kennan arrived in Japan in March 1948, At that time, the prosecutors were making their closing arguments at the International Military Tribunal for the Far East. Kennan found the Military Tribunal to be a political judgment rather than a legal contest and declared it a psychologically unsound trial based on wrong ideas. It should not be regarded as a mere coincidence that some GHQ officials were anti-communist realists who shared Kennan's view. These included Major General Charles Willoughby, who labeled the Military Tribunal "the worst hypocrisy in history," and Brigadier General Elliott Thorpe, who characterized the Tribunal as "a blood feud." While Willoughby and Thorpe criticized the legal and moral injustice of the Military Tribunal, Kennan, a strategist, went further and pointed out that the tribunal was totally uncalled for and meaningless in

---

5    Ibid., pp. 389–390.
6    Ibid., p. 391.

light of the international situation where confrontation with the Soviet Union seemed imminent.

Subsequently the international situation took the course Kennan and Willoughby had predicted. The International Military Tribunal and the Purge that GHQ had carried out proved to be uncomfortable historical facts for both the Japanese and American peoples, which they still do not know how to interpret even today. The fact that these historical facts make people uncomfortable means that the history would have been much more clear-cut had it not been for the International Military Tribunal.

## Treating Enemies and Friends Equally

In 1995, exactly a half century after the defeat of Japan, Helen Mears' *Mirror for Americans, Japan* was translated into Japanese and published. Publication of this book in Japanese had been banned during the occupation period and its original had also long been out of print. Its translator, Itō Nobushi, was so moved by this book that he could not stop crying when he read it.

Helen Mears was a scholar on the Far East from the prewar days. During the occupation, she stayed in Japan as a member of an advisory organization to GHQ's supreme commander on labor policies. It was in 1948 that Mears published this book.

Unfortunately, Mears and her book had almost no influence on the U.S. government's occupation policy. Literally, her views were quite different from either of the two major trends in the occupation policy, i.e. one that called for a thorough reform of Japan and the other that called for strategic thinking in anticipation of confrontation with the Soviet Union.

Mears' book was rather a record of self-reflection by an American intellectual and was filled with her intellectual integrity. It was more of a work of historical philosophy.

As an orientalist, Mears began to question the manner of the occupation administration as soon as she was stationed in Tokyo. It was only natural as a specialist on the Far East.

Other members of the committee that she belonged to were experts in economics, law, and other professional fields. She wrote:

They were, personally, serious and civilized—competent in their own fields in America. Few of the Americans, however, had so much as read a book about Japan . . .

. . . Their attitude was that (a) there were certain basic economic principles which were universally true, and if you knew these and knew how to tackle a job, you could solve any economic problem, whether you knew anything about the specific situation or not; and (b) we were, in any event, not interested in what Japan had been, since our job was to turn Japan into what we wanted it to be. One of the members carried with him slim volumes of Aristotle and Machiavelli, which—during the flight out—he had browsed in from time to time getting a firm grasp on basic principles.

Such attitudes were disturbing . . . Assuming that Americans were, in fact, capable of "reforming" Japanese society to make Japan what "we wanted it to be," it would surely be necessary not only to know precisely, in concrete terms, just what we did want it to be, but also to know what it had been. A scientist in a laboratory would clearly not begin an experiment using chemicals of whose nature he was unaware, or, beginning with unknown materials, he would certainly be prepared for a perhaps fatal explosion.[7]

I have always regarded area studies as a supreme form of scholarship. To be a genuine specialist on an area, you will have to be knowledgeable of everything of the region including its language, history, philosophy, culture, tradition, politics, economy, and society. The area studies specialist is required to possess an accumulation of deep knowledge, comprehensive understanding, and capacity for judgment that are way above and beyond what mere political scientists or economists possess.

For instance, what is required of an economic expert who is going to be stationed in Indonesia is not to study the most recent economic theories at Harvard but to acquire minimum knowledge of the history and politics of Indonesia.

Whenever one wishes to discuss the situation in a foreign country, be it about its politics or economy, it is imperative that the person solicit the

---

7    H. Mears. *Mirror for Americans, Japan* (Boston: Houghton Mifflin. 1948), pp. 38–39.

views of the country specialists at any cost. It is an essential process to connect theoretical and schematic simplifications—a pitfall specialists in peculiar fields are bound to fall into—to the realities. Confucius once said, "Study without reflection, then you would be lost; reflection without study, then you would be in danger."

It was quite understandable for Mears, a Far East specialist, to be apprehensive about and horrified by what other expert members of the advisory committee were doing.

As soon as the Potsdam Declaration, a product of laborious work by such Japan specialists as Joseph Grew and George Sansom, left their hands, Japan's surrender by contract was replaced with an unconditional surrender that allowed the occupation forces to do whatever they pleased. That was what horrified Mears.

As soon as Mears arrived in Japan, she became aware of this transformation. She said,

> Whatever else our Occupation is, it clearly cannot be called a military operation against the military power of Japan in defense of the United States. If the objective of our war with Japan was to destroy its war machine, its war-production and war-producing potential, and to punish the people for not having prevented the rise of these, we could have omitted the Occupation altogether, for it is certain that these objectives were accomplished before we went into the islands. As an outcome of the war itself, Japan was "put in a position where it cannot renew aggressive war."[8]

This was a natural reaction for someone who had known the prewar Japan like Mears when she saw the devastation of postwar Japan up close. She continued:

> The reasons given officially are that it was and is necessary in order to insure that Japan doesn't "try it again." It is claimed that the Occupation must continue until ". . . the present economic and social

---

8    Ibid., p.110.

system . . . which makes for a will to war will be changed so that that will to war will not continue . . ."[9]

From this point on, Mears dug deep into the very essence of the issue, i.e., were Japan's past economic and social institutions to be blamed for the war and, if so, how were they fundamentally different from those of the winners, the United States and Britain? These were indeed the main themes of Mears' book, which was a thorough and conscientious review of Japan's history along these themes.

Around the time Mears had just arrived in Tokyo for duty, the issue of the emperor system of Japan in itself still remained to be solved. According to her, "The idea that Shinto and 'the Institution of Emperor' were inherently warmaking was also incorporated in our post-war policies for Japan."[10]

But she rejected this idea, and said:

> The importance of Shinto and Emperor worship in Japan is the fact that they both represent cultural and religious traditions that are emotionally important to the Japanese in the same way that their own cultural and religious traditions are to any people. In a time of crisis, any tradition—if it is a genuine one—can be used to unify a people . . .[11]

And

> When, following World War II, the British Royal Party voyaged to South Africa to play its part in arousing emotional unity behind British foreign policy in that strategic region, it did not, apparently, occur to us that we were witnessing a demonstration of Emperor worship and State Shinto, or that the Royal Family was being used by the British Foreign Office to bolster British imperial prestige and

---

9    Ibid., p.111.
10   Ibid., p. 113.
11   Ibid., p. 114.

arouse emotions for the ties of Empire.[12]

During World War II and during the occupation of Japan, a number of documents were produced in the United States on the theme of "historical militarism in Japan." Mears took up each and every one of these documents. For instance, she said, "In his indictment of Japan's historic militarism, Mr. Hornbeck jumps rapidly from Hideyoshi, in 1578, to the Tanaka Memorial (which may have been a forgery) in 1927."

The American biweekly *Fortune* once published a pamphlet called "Pacific Relations," which was believed to be a project designed to provide guidelines for postwar U.S. foreign policy in the region. On this project, Mears said:

> In the first place, it is obviously not history, but propaganda. It reviews some nine to ten hundred years, and can find in that long period only two events worth commenting on—Hideyoshi's invasion of Korea and the persecution of Christian converts. While both of these events are certainly discreditable, it is not easy to see how either of them unfits the Japanese for a respected place in international relations, since there is no Great Power that hasn't invaded its neighbors; and since persecution of some Christians by other Christians was a conspicuous feature of Western civilization during the period of the Japanese persecutions.[13]

She was absolutely right. The sixteenth century was indeed a period when the Catholic church persecuted and massacred Protestants with fire and crucifix.

Mears' analysis remained keen and objective when it was applied to Japan's modern history.

On the Manchurian Incident, which triggered the clash between Japan and the United States in the Far East, Mears said, "From the Japanese point of view, . . . they felt their 'vital interests' in Manchuria to be considerably more important to them than our 'vital interests' in Latin America

---

12 Ibid., p. 116.
13 Ibid., p. 129.

were to us . . .[14]

Reconfirming that Americans were condemning Japan because it had violated its international commitment, Mears questioned whether the international rule that great powers had applied around the time that Japan had learned it as the first lesson from the international community was not much more flexible and resourceful for those in power.

On the Greater East Asia War, Mears observed,

> Preoccupied as we have been with our picture of Japan as a militaristic aggressor determined to "conquer and enslave the world," we have neglected to note that Japan fought both in the China Incident and World War II under the slogan of "liberating Asia" and the Pacific islands from the "enslavement" of the "White bloc" . . . From the point of view of large numbers of Asiatics, the Japanese legal fictions were more plausible than ours.[15]

She continued to apply her objective analysis to Japan's initial victories, saying, "Japan's first victories—in Asia and the British, French, and Dutch colonies—were made possible by the activities of native collaborationists," and "With a few notable exceptions (the Philippine campaign was one of them), Japan's first successes during the war were won with remarkably little fighting."[16] Mears believed that, "it is necessary to point out that the Japanese went as far as we did in making their fictions seem plausible, and considerably further than our European allies did."[17]

On Japan's accomplishments in the liberalization of Asia, she made the following objective observation;

> In relatively calm days after Japan's first successes and before the tide of war swept back again, the local regimes established under Japanese "protection" appear to have achieved a fair amount of stability . . .
>     The evidence is strong that, had the European nations, and the

---

14    Ibid., pp. 266-267.
15    Ibid., p. 288.
16    Ibid., p. 288.
17    Ibid., p. 289.

United States, not carried the war to Asia and the colonies, the native independent regimes would have been glad to work with Japan in developing their Co-Prosperity Sphere.[18]

This may well have been so, considering the frenzy that pervaded all of Asia. Japan was defeated too quickly. Had Japan won the Battle of Midway or, at least, had it avoided the Battle of Midway, it would have been able to endure the war half a year longer. Unlike the glorious days of Napoleon, which lasted ten years, Japan's victorious days were only half a year long. Mears' logic and insight, which came from her clear view of the possible outcome of Japan's continued victory, were truly commendable.

Toward the end of her book, Mears spent a few pages on Japan's war crimes. Admitting that the Japanese military "ruthlessly bombed civilians; they looted and destroyed property," Mears claimed:

Accepting as proved the Japanese guilt in those "crimes against humanity," there remains the major problem of whether our punishment of the Japanese people, which is being carried out, is just; . . . Reviewing the past history of the Western Powers in the Far East, noting our own behavior during the war, following our current policies and those of our wartime allies in the pages of the daily press, makes it perfectly clear that the guilt of Japan does not cancel the shared guilt of the democracies; makes it clear that other potential aggressors cannot possibly know from the record what the Japanese crime really is, or what we are punishing them for, or on what just grounds are we punishing rather than being punished.[19]

There is an old saying in Japan that one should maintain a mental state of *Onshin Ichinyo Jita Byōdō*. Roughly, it refers to an attitude of viewing oneself and others completely impartially and objectively, washing even all the special affections for family and relatives. Only a philosopher can attain this state of mind and it is utterly unthinkable in real politics. Even more so between a victor, who has won a war making tremendous

---

18    Ibid., pp. 290–91.
19    Ibid., p. 298.

human and physical sacrifices, and a loser. It would be a natural response for ordinary people to claim that, if enemies and friends are indeed treated equally, all the sacrifices are hard to justify.

On the basis of all the previous arguments, Mears went further and declared that an attempt to settle an international issue by force would only lead to another international issue, and would continue without end. She concluded her book with a historical philosophy that echoes the lament of Boyi and Shuqi on the foolishness of replacing violence with violence in eleventh century BC China.

Revisiting Mears' arguments thus far, it is not hard to imagine that she was completely ignored not only by the GHQ leadership but also by leaders of the U.S. government who were pressured to prepare the country for an imminent long Cold War with the Soviet Union. Thus, she had absolutely no influence in real politics.

On further reflection, however, this "attitude of viewing oneself and others completely impartially and objectively" must be the ultimate guiding principle for anyone who attempts to write history. Now that all the love and grudges are forgotten as more than half a century of time has lapsed since the end of the occupation of Japan, this Mears-like historical, philosophical approach must become the supreme guiding principle for anyone who writes history.

CHAPTER

# 5

# Shidehara Kijūrō's Agony

*—What Did Shidehara and MacArthur Discuss on January 24?—*

## Abrupt Issuance of the Purge

Shidehara Kijūrō was informed of GHQ's abrupt issuance of the Purge on January 4, 1946, when he was sick in bed from acute pneumonia. The news filled him with rage and deep distress.

In retrospect, the Shidehara cabinet was an excellent government comprised of outstanding people who were bound together in mutual trust and full of zeal to reconstruct their homeland. The heated arguments at each and every cabinet meeting were testimony to the fresh and comradely atmosphere—which was so completely different from the more formal and mundane meetings of subsequent cabinets.

It must have been utterly unthinkable for Shidehara to comply with GHQ's instruction to dismiss his cabinet members. They included Home Minister Horikiri Zenjirō, who had been undertaking electoral reform; Education Minister Maeda Tamon, who had been promoting educational reform; Agriculture Minister Matsumura Kenzō, who had at first declined his nomination, telling Shidehara, "I don't feel confident enough," and thus invited an uncharacteristic outburst from Shidehara who responded, "You are not the only one who doesn't feel confident," by way of encouraging Matsumura; and Chief Cabinet Secretary Tsugita Daizaburō, who

Shidehara Kijūro
(Copyright © KYODO NEWS IMAGES INC.)

had been Shidehara's sworn friend since the days of Shidehara's cooperative diplomacy.

Upon hearing the announcement of the Purge, Shidehara lost all incentive
to continue to serve as prime minister. As major cabinet members visited
Shidehara's sickbed one after another, his rage at MacArthur's ruthless
decision only grew fiercer.

 Prince Higashikuni Naruhito's cabinet, the predecessor of the Shidehara cabinet, had also attempted to reform Japan by its own hand and had
resigned in protest against GHQ's dismissal of a large number of Home
Ministry officials. Shidehara shared the same frame of mind. For such
enlightened gentlemen as Prince Higashikuni and Shidehara, GHQ's
preposterous, rude, and heartless handling of the Japanese government
was utterly unacceptable. The ancient European common sense in international relations that Higashikuni and Shidehara had believed in—i.e., that
a gentleman would treat another gentleman with respect and mutual trust
even when one was on the winning side and the other on the losing side—
was shattered by GHQ.

On the morning of January 14, after a week of no government action
despite GHQ's directive on the Purge, Chief Cabinet Secretary Tsugita

visited Shidehara to confirm his intention before the cabinet meeting. Tsugita found that Shidehara's determination to resign as prime minister remained unshaken. Shidehara said to Tsugita, "My conscience would not allow me to decide who is to be dismissed and who is to remain among my cabinet members, all of whom have been in the same boat until today."

In response, the cabinet meeting on the same day decided to request Shidehara reconsider his resignation. Matsumura took the initiative, joined by Horikiri and Maeda. They argued, "While the Prime Minister's high esteem of friendship is fully understandable, the state of affairs does not allow him to speak rashly of resigning for the sake of friendship." It was those four major cabinet members, the very targets of GHQ's Purge, who suggested Shidehara should not pay heed to friendship with them. They were arguing that Shidehara should remain as prime minister for the sake of Japan, paying no attention to what would happen to them. Theirs were words and deeds of the Japanese in the good old days of Japan.

Shidehara's rage turned out to be the last outburst of a Japanese public figure against an unreasonable decision by the occupation forces. After this, no matter how the Japanese leaders expressed their anger or what kind of admirable course of action they took, all came to naught because Japan had entered the dark age of the occupation.

Meanwhile, no matter what Yoshida Shigeru tried, he could not see MacArthur. It was on the evening of January 10 that he was at last granted a meeting with the head of GHQ. After this meeting, Yoshida debriefed the cabinet meeting as follows:

> Mac said, "That was not my idea. It was a directive from Washington, about which I could do nothing. We have no intention to impose any more unreasonable demands on you, and we'd like the current cabinet to execute this directive . . . I believe in Mr. Shidehara's integrity and sincerity as a statesman and beg you to comply with this directive." When I conveyed this message to the prime minister, however, he was highly agitated, saying, "That unreasonable Mac. How dare he say such a thing!" He would not listen to me any longer.

Hearing Yoshida's report, it was Matsumura's and Tsugita's turn to visit Shidehara's sickbed to persuade him. In response to Shidehara's recommendation of Mitsuchi Chūzō as his successor, Matsumura, after pointing out first that this was a matter that would profoundly affect the country's fate, asked Shidehara if he was confident that Mitsuchi could really be trusted to bear the burden of steering the government at such a critical juncture. By asking, "Can you truly conscientiously recommend Mitsuchi to the Emperor?" Matsumura pressed Shidehara hard with questions on his cowardice, in abandoning Japan in crisis when nobody else could be entrusted with the task.

Pained by these questions, Shidehara shed copious tears, saying, "Your questions burn my heart as if hot water were going down my throat." Subsequently, he remained silent for twenty or thirty minutes before he finally said "It is not time for me to be concerned about my personal matters. I have decided to accept your request and remain as prime minister."

## Shidehara's Visit to MacArthur

Although Shidehara recovered from his illness and returned to his office on January 21, he was not the same Shidehara he had been before.

For instance, he ceased to speak openly of his own convictions that he had cherished since the days of the Taishō Democracy and to act on them. He also stopped quoting Leon Gambetta, a French statesman prominent during and after the Franco-Prussian War in 1870, to express his determination to face the leaders of the Allies with the pride and self-respect of a great nation, Japan's loss in the Greater East Asia War notwithstanding. This apparent self-restraint, or self-constraint, continued until Shidehara's death. Thus, Shidehara decided to remain prime minister of Japan on the recognition of the reality of a loser: that he had to bite the bullet no matter how unreasonable GHQ's demands might be.

From this point on, Shidehara had changed and so had Japan.

At this point, everything was futile, be it Japan's history, tradition, or zeal for reform. The Japanese had to discard everything, be it self-respect as a great nation or pride as an individual. The only thing that was required of the Japanese, instead, was acceptance of their fate as a war loser and resigning themselves to that fate.

On January 24, Shidehara visited MacArthur. The official reason for the visit was to convey his gratitude to GHQ's provision of penicillin. Penicillin, a historical breakthrough in the world of medicine, was still mostly unavailable in Japan in those days. MacArthur presented this precious drug to Shidehara when he was suffering from pneumonia, which in those days was the number one killer of the elderly. Had Shidehara not been provided with penicillin by MacArthur, he might not have survived.

It was this visit that has long been the subject of controversy as the occasion when Article 9 of the Constitution was decided.

In his *Reminiscences* published in 1964, MacArthur said,

> Although I have been accused of having imposed the article on the renunciation of war of the new constitution of Japan by my personal order by those who were not in a position to know what really happened, this is not true, as the following facts should clearly reveal.

Thus, he made it clear at the outset that he was writing this particular section of his memoir to defend himself. Throughout this section, his description remained graphic and dramatic as follows:

> Prime Minister [Shidehara], then, suggested that, when drafting the new constitution, it should include the article on the renunciation of war and declare that Japan would not possess any military organizations whatsoever . . .
>
> I was genuinely flabbergasted. By that time throughout my long career, I have become mostly desensitized to things that surprise or thrill normal people. But that was a breath-stopping experience.

When MacArthur told Shidehara that abolition of all wars had been his long-standing dream, the Japanese prime minister said, according to MacArthur, "Today, the world may make fun of us as two unrealistic dreamers. In one hundred year's time, however, we will be called prophets." Shidehara looked rumpled with tears.

In his *Gaikō 50-nen* (50 Years of Diplomacy), which was a counterpart to MacArthur's *Reminiscences*, Shidehara wrote:

> Oftentimes, Americans come to me and ask me if the new constitution of Japan has not been imposed by GHQ against Japanese

wishes. As far as I am concerned, that is not true. The new constitution has never been coerced on us by anyone.

Having said that, Shidehara continued to argue that it was far better to renounce a war by totally abolishing military means than to possess half-measure war capabilities.

Despite these testimonies of the two top leaders of the time, however, it is said, "There hardly is any scholar today who believes that it was Prime Minister Shidehara who first suggested the inclusion in the constitution of clauses on renunciation of war and non-possession of military capability, as MacArthur so dramatically described in his *Reminiscences*." (Iokibe Makoto. *Senryō-Ki* )

As far as MacArthur's testimony was concerned, it is the reality that the more dramatic his descriptions are, the more doubtful their authenticity becomes. Therefore, it is hard to believe there is any scholar, either in Japan or in the United States, who takes MacArthur's above testimony at face value. It seems safe enough to consider it a MacArthur lie.

Of the two, Shidehara was more skillful in his remarks. His was more of a general remark with time and venue unspecified. His could be interpreted as Shidehara's ex-post facto reflection on the Japanese government's acceptance of the draft new constitution, which had already become an irretrievable policy after the Shidehara-MacArthur meeting on February 21 and the cabinet meeting on February 22. At least there is no reason it should be interpreted to refer to the Shidehara-MacArthur meeting on January 24. "As far as I am concerned" in his description could imply that it was preceded by "While some others might have thought that we had been forced to accept it." While this statement may make sense if made in reference to Japanese passive acceptance of subsequent U.S. propositions, it does not apply to the tête-à-tête dialogue with MacArthur at all.

Since this issue has already been almost settled after meticulous studies by historians, I believe there is no need to introduce the content of those studies here.

Allow me, nevertheless, to introduce my insight as a career diplomat. Experience has made me side with the majority views of scholars.

A professional diplomat never fails to leave a complete record of an important meeting. In the case of a senior diplomat, he may instruct his subordinates to produce a verbatim record. First of all, a diplomat is trained to record what the other party says word for word as accurately as possible. This is because even a subtle difference in nuance could lead to a major misunderstanding. One can be a little relaxed about his own remarks, which he should remember himself, particularly about pleasantries and chitchat. Whenever one makes a specific proposition or a commitment, however, it must be recorded accurately without fail.

This is a practice that any diplomat is trained to carry out to the best of his ability. Therefore, it is utterly unthinkable that Shidehara, a paragon of a diplomat, would have failed to do so. If he had indeed "suggested that, when drafting the new constitution, it should include the article on the renunciation of war and declare that Japan would not possess any military organizations whatsoever" as MacArthur claimed, it was not at all possible that he would not have left any memo about it or that he would have kept silent about it to his subordinates for many days afterwards—indeed, until his death at that.


What was most mysterious of all was the complete absence of a record of the dialogue on the Japanese side, not to mention Shidehara's proposal or MacArthur's response. Kishi Kuramatsu, former secretary to Prime Minister Shidehara, declared that he had heard no explanation on this dialogue from Shidehara nor did Shidehara make any report on it to the cabinet meeting.

This could only mean one of the following two things: either Shidehara spent the entire three hours thanking MacArthur for the penicillin and simply exchanged compliments of the season, or the two talked about something that could not be repeated to others or kept in a record at any cost. If there indeed were some substantial exchanges between the two as MacArthur's *Reminiscences* suggests, this must point to the second possibility. It is also hard to believe that, after one entire month of no contact, Shidehara did not have any substantial exchange with MacArthur during his three-hour visit.

When Kanamori Tokujirō, former Minister of State in charge of constitutional affairs and the Librarian of the National Diet Library, interviewed Shidehara in late autumn 1950 on the earlier days of the occupation, he said, "While it is high time for the Japanese side to prepare an accurate record of its own, there seem to be so many things only you know. I'd like to take this opportunity to ask for your disclosure." In response, however, Shidehara only said, "It is still premature to talk about it" and remained silent on this issue. Because Japan was still under occupation when this interview took place, Shidehara's silence was fully understandable. Shidehara died in March 1951, before the signing of the Treaty of San Francisco in September. It is obvious from this exchange that Shidehara was harboring something that he could not talk about.

The mystery of the January 24 Shidehara-MacArthur meeting becomes all the more outstanding when it is compared with another three-hour long meeting between the two on February 21. Shidehara reported on the content of this latter meeting at the cabinet meeting the following day. Then Health Minister Ashida Hitoshi left the following detailed note about what Shidehara reported:

As usual, MacArthur began to make a speech, saying,

I have given everything I have for the benefit of Japan . . . I hear, however, that discussions at the Far Eastern Commission have been so unpleasant for Japan beyond Your Excellency's imagination. While I do not know how much longer I can remain in this position, I become overwhelmed by anxiety when I think of the day after I am gone . . . The U.S. proposition . . . on Article One of the Constitution . . . is to protect and preserve the Emperor . . . We have struck out all the provisions on the military. At this point, the Japanese government should pay more consideration to how the international community will think of Japan than to how the Japanese people will react. If the Japanese government retains provisions on the military, . . . the international community will surely think that Japan must be considering rearming itself.

For the benefit of Japan . . . I believe Japan should exercise moral leadership by declaring the renunciation of war.

At this point, Shidehara interrupted to say that even if Japan took the leadership, there would be no followers. In response, Mac said Japan had nothing to lose even if there were no followers. He said it is those who do not appreciate this leadership who are at fault.

This exchange between MacArthur and Shidehara is a world apart from MacArthur's memory of the January 24 meeting in which Shidehara allegedly said, "In one hundred year's time, however, we will be called prophets."

## Consistency in Shidehara's Thinking

What, then, was the substance of the January 24 meeting?

Although there has been much debate on the content of this meeting, it is primarily speculation due to the absolute shortage of factual evidence. And speculation is naturally affected by the current of the times.

Against the strong current of the postwar pacifism in Japan, it must have been difficult to openly declare that MacArthur had lied. That in itself would have been nothing but another speculation not fully backed up by evidence. To espouse this stance, one would have had to have been prepared to be called a right-winger or reactionary advocate of constitutional revision—although quite a few courageous people would have been willing to be so labeled.

That being the case, yet another set of groundless inferences that catered to the current of the times started going around. Two examples are, "While Shidehara may not have made a concrete proposal, he must have said something abstract to that effect," and "MacArthur must have grasped Shidehara's true intention and given the appropriate instructions to his subordinates."

Speaking out against these compromise interpretations, Shidehara Michitarō, the eldest son of Kijūrō, wrote at the outset of his commentary on his father's *Gaikō 50-nen* (Fifty Years of Diplomacy) that he wished to "clear my late father of false accusations by reading through his spirit in his book . . . and declare that the notion that Article 9 had been proposed by Shidehara was 100 percent a lie." He then quoted from the memoir of Shibagaki Tadashi, an old acquaintance of Shidehara's, on his meeting with Shidehara as follows:

> Shidehara said, "The constitutional revision this time is also another case of putting up with humiliation today to make a comeback tomorrow, 'enduring the unendurable and suffering what is insuffer-

able' as the Imperial Rescript appealed." Pointing at an unfinished manuscript nearby, Shidehara said, "I am not writing what I truly believe in. It is with the extreme "kanshin's forbearance"—accepting any humiliation—that I am writing this manuscript. This is scheduled to be published when it is finished—but this is one of the lamentable measures required to appease the war victors' deep suspicion and oppression."

According to Shidehara Michitarō, this lamentation must "thoroughly reveal Shidehara's dilemma of believing in one thing and saying something totally contradictory to it."

Allow me to spend the next few pages on my own personal analysis on this issue.

At the outset, let me set straight a few facts.

First is the fact that Shidehara believed it unnecessary to revise the constitution or, at most, that a few minor alterations would suffice.

In his first press conference as prime minister on October 5, 1945, Shidehara began by referring to the establishment of democratic politics in Japan. He lamented the derangement of democracy during the recent period of militarism—the democracy that had been so laboriously accomplished under the Meiji Constitution in the form of the Taishō Democracy. Despite institutionalization through the Charter Oath of the basic philosophy of a political regime that paid regard to the collective will of the Japanese people, Shidehara said, "great principles of constitutional government [were] disturbed in recent years." In this press conference, Shidehara made no reference to constitutional revision at all. When Shidehara set up the Constitutional Problems Investigation Committee, it was meant to "investigate" constitutional problems. As the committee's director, State Minister Matsumoto Jōji, pointed out, avoidance of the term "revision" or "reform" was deliberate.

In the plenary session of the House of Representatives on November 28, Shidehara said, "The provisions of the Meiji Constitution are full of flexibility . . . I do not necessarily find it impossible for them to accommodate the developments of the times." Nevertheless, since there were cases in the past when constitutional provisions had been distorted, Shidehara expressed his wish to apply a few minor alterations to the constitution for the purpose of "eliminating room for uncertainty so as to prevent future abuses." Judging from later remarks by Shidehara and Matsumoto, it seems safe to assume that a revision that would allow the Diet and cabinet members to control the military was what was in Shidehara's mind when he referred to "minor alterations."

Subsequently, the Constitutional Problems Investigation Committee continued its deliberations, submitted a draft constitution to the Emperor in early January 1946, and started article-by-article discussions. Meanwhile, the focus of the U.S. occupation policy shifted to the constitution issue. General directive SWNC228 on constitutional revision arrived from Washington on January 11. The directive instructed that coercion should be absolutely the last resort because it could backfire and obstruct the embedding of the revised constitution in the Japanese mind.

This SWNC228 prompted GHQ to request the Japanese side to submit the draft constitution early. The Japanese government started drafting a revised constitution; the draft was submitted to the Emperor on February 7 after its approval by the cabinet meeting on February 4. The English translation of the draft was submitted to GHQ on February 8.

Incidentally, the draft that had been scooped in the February 1 issue of the *Mainichi Shimbun* was the Miyazawa Toshiyoshi draft. This draft, which GHQ had glanced at and completely disapproved of, was one version earlier than the draft submitted to GHQ on February 8.

The major revisions to the Meiji Constitution proposed by the Japanese side included (a) control of the composition of the military forces and the strength of the standing forces by law and (b) requirement of approval by the Diet in the case of a war declaration or a peace negotiation (except for a case of emergency, in which consultation with the standing committee in charge would suffice on condition that approval would be sought afterwards from the subsequent Diet session). In other words, the Japanese draft proposed to put the conduct of the military under the control of the Diet. Behind the apprehension that Shidehara was said to have expressed on the inclusion of the military-related provisions in the draft was, perhaps, his meeting with MacArthur on January 24. Overall, the Japanese draft was perfectly compatible with Shidehara's line of thinking, and he supported this draft at the time of the cabinet meeting as well as the report to the Emperor.

Going back further, how did Shidehara perceive national security and the functions of the international community?

At the time of the Manchurian Incident, Shidehara was quite negative toward entrusting such a critical international issue to such a "speech contest among minor players" as the League of Nations. The essence of Shidehara's cooperative diplomacy was the traditional notion of cooperation with the world's major powers such as Britain and the United States. Shidehara remained skeptical about the wholesale delegation of Japan's security to the international community.

Shidehara's attitude is more clearly stated in his *Gaikō 50-nen.* What follows are Shidehara's remarks in a conversation with Kenneth Colegrove of Northwestern University who was assigned to GHQ for a while.

Quoting the example of the League of Nations' failure to effectively deal with Italy's invasion of Ethiopia in 1935, Shidehara said,

> When it comes to a matter of one's own life or death, man strives in frenzy to the very end, delivering up one's properties and even life . . . It is, however, against human nature for a man to shed his blood for others afar off who are totally unrelated to him, unless there is some peculiar reason. What the United Nations attempts to do is to force all countries to do this. I am afraid it might be repeating the same mistake that the League of Nations had made . . .

If one recalls that, when MacArthur suggested that Japan should exercise moral leadership by declaring renunciation of war, Shidehara replied that even if Japan had taken such leadership, there would be no followers, it goes to show that, from the time of the Manchurian Incident through the aforementioned meeting with MacArthur on February 21, Shidehara's attitude remained consistent.

In contrast, what MacArthur's *Reminiscences* claims that Shidehara said is truly out of line with Shidehara's thinking.

## An Unspeakable Promise with MacArthur

Next, I like to make inferences on exactly what MacArthur said on January 24, 1946. Actually, given the trend in MacArthur's thinking since the outset of the occupation and given the position he found himself in around January 24, there must be things that were only natural for him to say.

Even before the occupation administration began, MacArthur had been convinced that for the occupation to be successful, it would be imperative to preserve and rely on the Emperor's authority. MacArthur based this thinking on the advice of his protégé, Brigadier General Bonner Fellers. MacArthur kept the Fellers memo of October 2, 1945, a theoretical insight into the Emperor issue, at his elbow and repeatedly consulted it.

MacArthur's thinking around January 24 must be identical with his talk with Shidehara on February 21 or, at least, perfectly consistent with it.

On February 21, MacArthur first debriefed Shidehara on the discussions at the Far Eastern Commission and told the Japanese prime minister that he was worried about whether he could fully protect the Emperor, given the direction the discussions were taking.

It was decided at the Moscow Conference of Foreign Ministers that was concluded on December 27, 1945, that a Far Eastern Commission should be founded to give Allied members other than the United States some say on the occupation of Japan. It was agreed then that important issues, such as revision of the Japanese constitution, would be decided at this Far Eastern Commission.

Upon the decision to launch the Far Eastern Commission on February 26, 1946, a study mission headed by Frank McCoy, who later became chairman of the Commission, spent time in Japan in late January, overlapping the timing of the Shidehara-MacArthur meeting on January 24.

In his meeting with members of the study mission, Charles Kades of GHQ's Government Section announced that revision of the Japanese constitution would be a matter of exclusive jurisdiction of the Far Eastern Commission, as well as its prerogative. On January 29, immediately before McCoy's departure from Japan, MacArthur said to McCoy, "[The constitution issue] has left my hands as the result of the Communiqué adopted in Moscow." But MacArthur added a rather obscure reservation, saying, "Today, in absolute faithfulness to the Communiqué, GHQ has abstained from any interference in the constitutional revision issue, which has been completely left to the discretion of the Japanese government's spontaneous deliberations."

At that time, McCoy failed to note this important reservation made by

MacArthur. And, therefore, when the Japanese draft of the revised constitution was suddenly announced on March 6, after having been confidentially prepared jointly by the Japanese government and GHQ, both McCoy and the then U.S. Secretary of State James Byrnes were dumbfounded.

His explanation to the McCoy Mission notwithstanding, MacArthur instructed GHQ's Government Section to study whether GHQ had the legal authority to revise the Japanese constitution. It is unclear whether this instruction was issued before or after January 24. According to John Dower, the instruction had been issued "a week or so" before February 1 when the result of the study was reported back to MacArthur, which should be just about January 24. It would make perfect sense if the instruction had been issued immediately after MacArthur's meeting with Shidehara.

The reply from the Government Section was that, "unless there is a decision made by the Far Eastern Commission," MacArthur was authorized to be engaged in revision of the Japanese constitution, just as he was in other important issues.

In other words, MacArthur had had the authority to take control of the constitutional issue before the convening of the Far Eastern Commission on February 26. Judging from this reply, it would be more natural to infer that the real reason that MacArthur had ordered the Government Section to look into the issue was not to render an impartial and objective legal judgment but to verify that he was correct in assuming that he had continued authority on constitutional affairs until the launching of the Far Eastern Commission.

This decided the time limit to MacArthur's secret grand scheme to revise the constitution of Japan.

The above are the facts that can be used to infer the content of the dialogue between Shidehara and MacArthur that took place on January 24.

There is indeed only one thing that needs to be inferred. It has been believed that there was something discussed during that meeting that Shidehara could never disclose no matter what. A secret that he could not share even with his cabinet members, his assistants, or his personal friends, to whom he said only, "It is premature to speak of it." The secret that was kept undisclosed because Shidehara died before the end of the occupation. . . . What was this something?

Thinking logically on the basis of the above facts, actually it may not be too difficult to find the answer. It is like a crossword puzzle with only one answer missing, while all the other answers are filled in. It is so obvious that, if it were a crossword puzzle, there would be no need to bother to fill in the empty answer.

Besides, candidates for what had to be kept secret so badly can be narrowed down to a small number of possible topics. One possibility would be that it had something to do with the Emperor, which the Japanese in those days could never mention to others. The only other possibility would be either a gentleman's agreement that Shidehara had promised MacArthur he would never disclose, or a combination of the two.

In the Japanese mind in those days since Meiji, particularly for cabinet members who were supposed to assist the Emperor, it was utterly unthinkable to repeat anything to do with the Emperor to others. If told that disclosure could cripple MacArthur's occupation policy, which could then lead to prosecution of the Emperor as a war criminal and all kinds of humiliations in court, a cabinet member would agree to absolutely any condition. In order to protect the Emperor, it was imperative to establish a constitution that stipulated preservation of the Emperor system. For this to be possible, the new constitution had to be so liberal that even the Far Eastern Commission could not oppose it—including, as MacArthur insisted on February 21, renunciation of war. Moreover, this renunciation of war had to be a spontaneous initiative from the Japanese side, because MacArthur could not defend the new constitution vis-à-vis the Far Eastern Commission or the U.S. government if it were found to have been coerced by the occupation forces. If there were a promise with MacArthur that could never be disclosed to others, it must have been this plot that renunciation of war was a Japanese initiative.

Renunciation of war had remained MacArthur's consistent argument throughout those days and, therefore, it is hard to imagine that he did not bring it up during the discussion with Shidehara on January 24. If he actually did not, then he must have shared none of his own ideas with Shidehara during the three-hour discussion.

Now that we know this much, it really does not matter whether Shidehara cherished a pacifistic conviction at the point of January 24, 1946. Whether Shidehara really stressed the need for renunciation of war with tears in his eyes, as suggested by MacArthur's *Reminiscences*, or made a skeptical comment such as "If Japan took the leadership in renunciation of war, there would be no followers" as he did on February 21, it had no bearing on the outcome. No matter which attitude Shidehara actually did take, MacArthur had to say what he had to say, while Shidehara had to agree with MacArthur's proposal, regardless of how concrete the proposal might have been, and promise that his government would draft a pacifist constitution and make the world believe it was a Japanese initiative instead of coercion by the occupation forces.

All of Shidehara's subsequent words and deeds should be interpreted as "reading a blank scroll as if it were a real one" in order to save his master, the Emperor Shōwa.

## Dumbfounded Washington

After the agreement at the January 24 meeting, MacArthur's confidential operations were carried out at breakneck speed.

On February 3, MacArthur instructed his staff to prepare a draft constitution based on three "MacArthur principles": (1) preservation of the Emperor system, (2) renunciation of war, and (3) abolishment of feudal institutions. MacArthur wanted the draft prepared in one week so that he would have ample time to review the draft before submitting it to the Japanese side on February 13.

On February 13, Major General Courtney Whitney, Chief of GHQ's Government Section, visited Foreign Minister Yoshida Shigeru and Minister of State Matsumoto Jōji. The two had anticipated American responses to the Matsumoto draft, the draft constitution the Japanese side had submitted to GHQ earlier. To their surprise, Whitney announced that the Matsumoto draft was unacceptable and, instead, handed them the U.S. draft prepared by GHQ. While, at a glance, Matsumoto thought the American draft was totally unacceptable, Whitney told Yoshida and Matsumoto that it would be beneficial for Japan to accept this draft when "even the Supreme Commander for the Allied Powers cannot be omnipotent" against the pressure on GHQ to prosecute the Emperor as a war criminal.

Although the Japanese side repeatedly explained the Matsumoto draft until February 19, not even bothering to convene cabinet meetings, in an attempt to obtain U.S. understanding, it received an ultimatum from the

U.S. side to either accept or reject the American draft by February 20.

Then came the Shidehara-MacArthur meeting on February 21, followed by the cabinet meeting on February 22 in which Shidehara did not show any sign of resisting the American draft.

According to the record of this cabinet meeting taken by Health Minister Ashida Hitoshi, while Shidehara appeared to show some understanding for the U.S. draft, Matsumoto expressed his opposition, saying, "As seen in the cases of Germany and several Latin American countries, a constitution that is adopted under coercion by outsiders eventually ends up unobserved and becomes a tool for disturbances by fascists."

In response to Shidehara's quibble that the American draft was no different from the Japanese draft in principle, Education Minister Abe Yoshishige argued, "It is not that I do not accept the American draft, but I must say the American draft's first article on the Emperor and the article on renunciation of war are quite different from our ideas."

It appears that Shidehara was already resigned to accepting the U.S. draft and announcing it as a Japanese initiative in order to save the Emperor from the humiliation of being tried as a war criminal.

MacArthur's operations were carried out in absolute secrecy, completely unknown to Washington. And the Far Eastern Commission was uneventfully launched with its inaugural meeting on February 26.

Meanwhile, Prime Minister Shidehara submitted the draft constitution to the Emperor on February 22 and received the Imperial permission. The final draft was discussed article by article at the cabinet meeting on March 5. While a number of comments were made during the deliberation, the overall tone was that the situation was beyond cabinet members' control. Members found that they had no other option than to yield completely to GHQ's proposal. Every one of them was fully aware of the grave risk that disobedience of GHQ's order could bring to the Emperor.

After a whole day of deliberations at the cabinet meeting on March 6, the "Outline of the Draft of Revised Constitution of Japan" was adopted. This was what was made public with an Imperial Rescript.

In this Imperial Rescript, Emperor Shōwa announced, "Following the earlier acceptance of the Potsdam Declaration . . . we applied fundamental revisions to the constitution, hoping it would provide a foundation for national reconstruction." Thus the requirements for making it formal that the new constitution was at Japanese initiative were completed. At the same time, Prime Minister Shidehara respectfully announced that, with the new constitution, "[We should] establish the foundation of fundamental democracy at home and, internationally, pursue eradication of war ahead of other countries in the world."

Washington was flabbergasted.

On March 20, the Far Eastern Commission unanimously requested postponement of the general election in Japan scheduled for April 10. It was an attempt to halt creation of a fait accompli. In response, MacArthur rejected the request and protested that the U.S. government should have vetoed the decision at the Far Eastern Commission on March 20. On April 10, the day of the general election in Japan, the Far Eastern Commission ordered MacArthur to dispatch his deputy to Washington, D.C. and explain the constitutional issue. Having held his reply to the order until May 4, MacArthur flatly rejected the dispatch of his deputy, saying he himself had been in charge of the constitutional matters and nobody could represent him. On the revised constitution, MacArthur only boasted that it was "the most liberal constitution in the world." Everything went along as MacArthur had schemed.

On May 13, the Far Eastern Commission decided on the principles about the new constitution and formally requested MacArthur to guarantee (a) sufficient deliberation, (b) legal continuity with the Meiji Constitution, and (c) expression of the Japanese people's intent.

The Far Eastern Commission played into MacArthur's hands. This request caused MacArthur no problem. Legal continuity with the Meiji Constitution had already been taken care of formally by the Emperor's Imperial Rescript. MacArthur settled the whole issue by formally submitting the above three requests as messages from the Allies to the Japanese people.

Thus, MacArthur's strategy was beautifully carried out with the Supreme Commander's iron will and soldier-like discipline and efficiency.

Whether one summarizes this process as coercion by the occupation forces or as the success of MacArthur's strategy to save the Emperor for the sake of the successful occupation of Japan should be left to the historical judgments of posterity.

CHAPTER

# 6

# Yoshida Shigeru Comes to the Stage

*—How a Diplomat with No Distinct Ideology or*
*"Ism" Became Prime Minister—*

## Hatoyama Ichirō Purged from Public Service

Then came the era of Yoshida Shigeru.

In the first general election in Japan after World War II, carried out on April 10, 1946 (21st Year of Shōwa), the *Jiyūtō* (Liberal Party) led by Hatoyama Ichirō became the dominant party by winning 141 seats in the House of Representatives, followed by the *Shimpotō* (Progressive Party) with 94 seats, and the *Shakaitō* (Socialist Party) with 93 seats.

This election result was not what the leaders of GHQ's Government Section, including its deputy chief Charles Kades, had expected. What they had assumed would happen was a complete sweep of the conservative elements that had been deeply involved in Japanese politics before and during the war. In their minds, the winner should have been the Socialist Party. This may be hard to understand even for present-day Americans, but this was one of the trends of the Marxist-influenced "New Dealer" syndromes of that generation.

More than half a century after this first general election, John Dower said, "What was truly unfortunate for postwar Japan was that a social democratic force that was powerful enough to take over the government in place of the conservative party failed to rise. For this reason, a two-party system never took off in Japan."

This is a typical and representative view of the American New Dealers. They were so ignorant of history and the tradition of democracy in Japan.

Even someone ignorant about Japan's history would readily realize as soon he visits an electoral district during an election that elections in Japan have a long tradition since the days of the Freedom and People's Rights Movement and Taishō Democracy. Even after Japan experienced defeat in the war, the 1945 election result showed it was old political hands, descendants of the *Seiyūkai* and the *Minseitō* during the Taishō Democracy, that the majority of the Japanese voters chose over novel left-wingers. Not a small number of those elected were successors to the electoral bases cultivated and maintained since the prewar days or even the days of the Freedom and People's Rights Movement. Those chosen by voters in time provided the foundation for the Liberal Democratic Party (LDP), established in November 1955, which subsequently long monopolized the Japanese government until the end of the Cold War days. And this was the basic framework structure of conservatism in Japanese politics.

Nevertheless, the New Dealers continued to refuse to admit that the election result was the expression of the Japanese people's genuine wishes. The first measure GHQ took to sweep away what seemed to them the remnants of the past was the Purge. Because the *Shimpotō* was comprised of mostly incumbent Diet members, all but 14 of its 274 members were purged. Nevertheless, the party won 94 seats in the general election to become the second-largest party after the *Jiyūtō*, outdoing the Socialist Party.

GHQ's Government Section always regarded the *Jiyūtō* led by Hatoyama with enmity.

In an attempt to confront the Japan Communist Party, the darling of the mass media in those days, head on, Hatoyama declared an anti-communist manifesto and appealed to all conservatives in Japan to join forces. His was highly legitimate behavior for a conservative in light of the presence of such a visionary as Winston Churchill, who had warned of the "iron curtain" as early as March of the same year.

But such outright advocacy of conservatism got on the nerves of the Government Section, which was infected by leftist, New Dealer thinking and convinced that people in a defeated country ought to be more downcast and repenting of their sins. Taking advantage of the press conference for the foreign media corps held only four days before the voting, the Government Section compiled Hatoyama's praises of Hitler from his remarks during the war and handed them to American journalist Mark Gayn. Gayn distributed the compilation among participating foreign journalists so that Hatoyama would be tormented with hostile questions.

These and other forms of sabotage by GHQ nevertheless failed to convert the Japanese people's will, which chose the *Jiyūtō* as the dominant party. In response, GHQ's Government Section attempted to engineer a second party–third party coalition between the *Shimpotō*, which had elected Shidehara Kijūro as its president, and the Japan Socialist Party. It is believed that the Government Section not only insisted to Narahashi Wataru, Chief Cabinet Secretary of the Shidehara cabinet, that Shidehara's prime ministership be continued but also even threatened him that Japan could be placed under military administration if the *Shimpotō–* Japan Socialist Party coalition failed to protect the Shidehara government. The Socialist Party, however, deepened its leftist inclination at that time and, as such, chose to overthrow the Shidehara cabinet. As a result, the Shidehara cabinet resigned, and the administration was entrusted to the dominant party *Jiyūtō,* led by Hatoyama.

On the very day that Foreign Minister Yoshida Shigeru intended to obtain GHQ's approval for Hatoyama's becoming prime minister, GHQ purged Hatoyama from public offices. As a result of GHQ's action, it was Yoshida who was given the position of prime minister, raising the curtain on the Yoshida era during Japan's occupation.

The expulsion of Hatoyama was nothing but an interposition by GHQ's Government Section, which was determined to force through its immature progressive ideals, totally ignoring the rule of democracy. This time, however, the Japanese side no longer showed the will to resist—as the Higashikuni cabinet had done by resigning in protest or as evidenced in Shidehara's agony when he received the GHQ directive on the sweeping purges. Rather than censuring GHQ's high-handedness, people around Hatoyama, as well as later historical writings, became more critical of Hatoyama's failure to take a more "moderate" attitude in light of the circumstances of the time. By this time, Japanese politics had fallen into a state of resignation or become habituated to the occupation.

Of Yoshida Shigeru, who succeeded Hatoyama to sit at the helm of Japanese politics from that point on, the late Professor Kōsaka Masataka said that he was a "good loser" who "calmly accepted his fate." Whether "good" was an appropriate adjective or not, the Japanese were left with no alternative other than accepting the reality of a loser.

## Extremely Arrogant and Insolent

Allow me, here, to devote a few pages to a portrait of the person of Yoshida Shigeru.

To write about Yoshida Shigeru is tantamount to once again ruminating on the flow of Japanese politics and society since the Meiji era that I have sketched in the previous four volumes on the diplomatic history of modern Japan.

Yoshida was born to the family of Takenouchi Tsuna, one of the leaders of the *Jiyūtō*'s Tosa faction, as the fifth son. Takenouchi was such a visionary leader toward the end of the shogunate that together with Itō Hirobumi he advocated the abolition of the *han* system and the establishment of prefectures. Takenouchi had been introduced to Itō by Mutsu Munemitsu, a Tosa faction sympathizer. At the time of the conspiracy of Tosa Risshisha in 1878 (10ᵗʰ Year of Meiji), Takenouchi was arrested together with Mutsu and others and sentenced to prison.

Yoshida Kenzō, a friend of Takenouchi who adopted Shigeru in his early childhood, was a unique character. Born to the family of a retainer of the Echizen-*han*, he learned English, sailed to Europe on board a British warship, and became the head clerk of the Japan branch of Jardine Matheson upon his return. Subsequently, Yoshida Kenzō built a huge fortune from highly successful businesses, including soy sauce manufacturing.

This adoptive father passed away when Shigeru was eleven years old. He inherited all of the legacies of the deceased. This allowed Shigeru to spend an extraordinarily wealthy youth among his contemporaries. Even when he was a mere student, he commuted to school on horseback from his own house with his own nameplate on the door. Whenever he went out, he took a rickshaw.

Yoshida Shigeru used up almost the entire inheritance from his adoptive father, excepting a house in Ōiso, Kanagawa, before he died. Hearing of an adoptive son of a millionaire who had multiplied his adoptive father's assets, Yoshida allegedly said, "What an unforgivable man." It must have been his unique sense of humor that made Yoshida say this, knowing it was he who had done an unforgivable thing in squandering his adoptive father's fortune. Yoshida's arrogance and the naked readiness he exhibited throughout his professional career to quit a job when he did not like his superior were attributable, at least in part, to this affluence, along with his own natural disposition.

One thing we can say for the Japanese upper class is that traditionally it has been strict in disciplining itself, advocating a life of simplicity and fortitude, no matter how wealthy or powerful it might have been.

Thus, Yoshida Kenzō made it a rule to get up at four o'clock in the morning, even in the depth of winter, and make family members and house servants clean throughout the vast property, calling out instructions in a loud voice. Shigeru's adoptive mother, Koto, was a granddaughter of Satō Issai (1772–1859), one of the prominent Confucian scholars toward the end of the shognate. Issai was a professor at the *Shōheikō* School (a school based on the principles of Confucianism run by the Edo shogunate). As such, he was a central figure in the shogunate's education with, allegedly, 3,000 disciples, including such dignitaries as Tokugawa Nariaki, Watanabe Kazan, Sakuma Shōzan, and Yokoi Shōnan. Saigō Takamori belonged to the generation that was too young to become Issai's pupil, but he picked up 101 quotations from Issai's *Genshishiroku* and kept them at his elbow.

Particularly noteworthy about Yoshida's boyhood education was the five years he spent at the boarding school *Kōyo Gijuku* in junior high.

*Kōyo Gijuku* was a private school founded by Ogasawara Tōyō, one of Satō Issai's disciples, with the support of wealthy families. Among its supporters was Nakajima Nobuyuki, the then governor of Kanagawa prefecture, who sent his own son, Kumakichi, who later became Minister of Commerce and Industry. Nobuyuki was the brother-in-law of Mutsu Munemitsu, mentioned above as a comrade of Takenouchi Tsuna, who was Yoshida Shigeru's father by blood, in the aforementioned Tosa faction, and he later became Speaker of the House of Representatives.

In other words, Yoshida was educated at a super elite institution in the Meiji era.

The school's curriculum included algebra, geometry, physics, American history, and international law. What made the school particularly unique, however, were the lessons on the Chinese classics. Each year students were given such classics as *Jūhachi Shiryaku* (Epitome of Eighteen Histories), *Bunshō Kihan* (Classic Sentences), *Shiji Tsūgan* (Chinese Historiographical Text), and *Sōgen Tsūgan* (Song and Yuan Historiographical Text) to read .

While Yoshida's writing was not particularly elegant, it was obvious to anyone that it was based on the foundation of his scholarship in Chinese classics. Yoshida was fortunate enough to receive an education that was directly descended from the traditional education of the Edo period, which had been a society under highly sophisticated civilian administration. In those days, such a society was extremely rare in the world.

Makino Nobuaki, who became Yoshida's father-in-law by his marriage after he entered the foreign ministry, was the second son of Ōkubo Toshimichi, one of the statesmen who made an outstanding contribution to the Meiji Restoration. Makino accompanied his father to visit the United States in 1871 (4th Year of Meiji) as a member of the Iwakura Embassy when he was ten years old. Makino continued to stay in Philadelphia to study, which made him a forerunner of the "returnee children" when he returned home. Being a returnee was rare in those days. Upon his return to Japan, Makino joined the foreign ministry where, partially thanks to his blue blood, he continued to be promoted smoothly from Japanese ambassador to Italy, ambassador to the Austria-Hungary Empire, education minister and agriculture and commerce minister in the Saionji Kinmochi cabinet, foreign minister in the first Yamamoto Gonnohyōe cabinet, and, finally, to Imperial Household Minister in 1921 (10th Year of Taishō). Makino was a graceful and polite aristocrat equipped with Western sophistication, and along with Saionji, assisted the Emperor as an Anglophile advocate of international cooperation.

As shown above, Yoshida Shigeru was a product of all the traditions in the upper class and intellectual class of Japanese society throughout the Edo period, the twilight of the shogunate, and the Meiji era. To understand Yoshida's words and deeds, therefore, it would be more effective to put them in the context of this historical background rather than to explore his outlook and philosophy.

# A Stereotypical British-Style Gentleman Who Values Common Sense

Yoshida Shigeru was no philosopher or, for that matter, thinker. He did not pose as an academic. Nor was he endowed with a state strategy based on meticulous theoretical structure like Shigemitsu Mamoru or a personal belief based on highly perceptive analyses like Tōgō Shigenori.

This characterization is endorsed by Yoshida's preferences in reading material. He was fond of reading Nomura Kōdō's *Zenigata Heiji* Edo detective story series in Japanese. In English, he liked reading the adventures of Sherlock Holmes as well as Peter Wodehouse's light humorous novels. Yoshida must have been a stereotypical British-style gentleman who valued common sense more than anything else, including highbrow philosophy or ideology. While Yoshida was fond of history and he was believed to recommend people around him read history books, this is perfectly compatible with the behavioral pattern of a British gentleman.

Here lies the origin of all the confusion about the postwar argument regarding Yoshida Shigeru. According to the popular view, which provides the bottom line to the postwar perception of Yoshida, he was an anti-war liberalist who, during the war, had been imprisoned because he opposed the war. After the end of the war, and particularly toward the latter half of the occupation, according to this view, Yoshida persisted with the policy to prioritize economic reconstruction, resisting U.S. pressure for rearmament. To cite an extreme case, some people labeled the policy of prioritizing the economy over rearmament the Yoshida Doctrine, as if Yoshida had his own distinct state strategy.

Closer scrutiny of Yoshida's personal records as well as his past words and deeds, however, readily reveal that such was a false perception. From this revelation, some would jump to another false criticism that Yoshida was not a liberalist but instead an imperialist.

Yoshida had nothing to do with any "isms" or ideologies. It is unproductive to pigeonhole Yoshida with labels that completely miss the mark because they are based on a distorted historical view of postwar Japan and then, next, to fuss about the fallacy of the labels.

John Dower, author of *Empire and Aftermath: Yoshida Shigeru and the Japanese Experience, 1878–1954*, keenly pointed out this contradiction. Dower noted that Yoshida's diplomacy was permeated with realism and his own diplomatic instinct and that, as such, it cast "a lot of doubts about the absolute dichotomy that has often been adopted regarding this particular period in Japanese history." Dower was referring to such dichotomies as the military vs. the civilian officers, ultra-nationalist vs. internationalist, Tanaka diplomacy vs. Shidehara diplomacy, and pro-Asia faction vs. pro–Anglo-Saxon faction.

Indeed, a historical view that divides a man into two and labels one progressive and the other reactionary based on a simplistic formula, paying no heed to the person himself, would only lead to endless, unproductive debates having nothing to do with the truth of history.

## Argument for the Central Role of Foreign Ministry in Diplomacy

At this point, allow me to briefly review the history of Yoshida's thinking.

It is safe to say that it was after Yoshida was appointed consul-general in Mukden in 1924 (14th Year of Taishō) that he became influential enough to talk about Japan's diplomacy.

It would not be an overstatement to say that, since the beginning of the 20th century, Japan's diplomacy had been almost exclusively about Japan's interest in Manchuria. Thus, remarks by the consul-general in Mukden, capital city of Manchukuo's Fengtian province, naturally carried considerable weight in Japan's foreign policy.

Actually, this was the second time Yoshida had served at the consulate in Mukden. Having passed the foreign service examination in 1906 (39th Year of Meiji), one year after the Russo-Japanese War, Yoshida was stationed in the Japanese legation in Mukden in March 1907 as a junior staff. Here was another connection Yoshida had with the history of Meiji.

In 1907, Yoshida was under Hagiwara Morikazu, Japan's first consul-general in Mukden. In those days, the Imperial Japanese Army stationed in north China would not give up the military government, inviting Qing resentment and British/American suspicion. Facing this situation, Hagiwara reported on the military's conduct by telegraph to the home office in Tokyo. As I wrote in my earlier book, *Komura Jutarō and His Age*, Itō Hirobumi convened the historical Consultative Meeting on the Manchurian Issue on the basis of Hagiwara's telegrams. Seeing as this meeting was convened in Tokyo in May, Yoshida must have been in Mukden right then.

One thing that needs to be clarified at this point in relation to the strife between diplomacy and the military in early Shōwa is the issue of the centralization of diplomacy.

In the telegram that Itō cited at the Consultative Meeting on the Manchurian Issue, Hagiwara, who had just been stationed in Mukden, said: "The authority of military administrators is unjustly expanded, while the presence of the consul-general is hardly recognized, either domestically or internationally, inviting complaints and suspicions among official and private sectors both within and outside the country." As a result of the deliberations, the Consultative Meeting produced a directive that "the military administration in Manchuria should be gradually succeeded by the consulate in Mukden."

Twenty years later, as soon as Yoshida arrived in Mukden as consul-general, he sent letters to the commanding officer of the Kwangtung Army, the president of South Manchuria Railway, and the Governor-General of Korea. Referring to Zhang Zuolin's calls for support that had been previously addressed directly to these institutions, Yoshida in the letter requested that those calls hereafter be forwarded to the consulate or the foreign ministry in order to avoid confusion in Japan's China policy. He also informed the then Foreign Minister Shidehara Kijūrō of this request via classified official telegram. Both of these actions were manifestations of Yoshida's argument that foreign relations should be comprehensively controlled by the foreign ministry.

Tōgō Shigenori, foreign minister in the Tōjō Hideki cabinet, who had expressed his wish to resign in opposition to the war against the United States, initially was persuaded to remain in the cabinet. Nevertheless, he eventually resigned from his post because he opposed the establishment of a new Ministry of Greater East Asia. Tōgō said, "[The new ministry] would deprive the foreign ministry of the most important policy area, disturb the centralization of Japan's diplomacy, and hurt the pride of East Asian peoples, making it impossible to maintain cooperative relations between Japan and these neighboring countries."

Reading this, one gets the impression that what Tōgō was really opposed to was the disturbance of the centralization of Japan's diplomacy by the establishment of the Ministry of Greater East Asia.

Undoubtedly, the centralization of diplomacy is a correct principle. When the foreign ministry and some other government agency, or agencies, start acting in an uncoordinated manner concerning the country's relations with a foreign nation, there will be confusion in the diplomacy. The function of coordinating a country's diplomacy from a comprehensive viewpoint naturally belongs to its foreign ministry.

It is true that, throughout the Shōwa history, arbitrary conduct by the military had often misled Japan's foreign policy. The most outstanding example was the German-Japan Anti-Comintern Pact that the Imperial Japanese Army promoted with Nazi advisor Joachim von Ribbentrop, completely bypassing the Ministries of Foreign Affairs. This incident very much speaks to the legitimacy of the argument for the centralization of diplomacy.

Of course, diplomats' judgments are not always right. When Prime Minister Tanaka Giichi entrusted settlement of a long-standing issue over the railway in Manchuria to Yamamoto Jōtarō, president of the railway in the late 1920s, it was because Yoshida's high-handed attitude toward the governor of Mukden had become the greatest obstacle to the negotiations. Coupled with Yoshida's not-too-cordial relations with Zhang Zuolin, Tanaka judged that the settlement of the issue would be improbable as long as Yoshida remained in charge of negotiations with the Chinese side. While Tanaka's decision allowed Sino-Japanese negotiations to bypass Yoshida, the local representative of diplomatic authority, it seems fair to say in retrospect that Yamamoto's subsequent handling of the situation was far more appropriate than what Yoshida would have done.

On a more mundane level, bureaucrats are without fail bound to engage in turf battles. Once a bureaucrat neglects or fails to engage in this competition, his subordinates will give up on him and his future career itself will be in jeopardy. In the case of Yoshida in particular, it is not hard to imagine that, driven by his overly assertive nature, he was extra sensitive about his territory and averse to someone else meddling behind his back with what he regarded as his own prerogative.

To be sure, it is appropriate for a diplomat to insist on the centralization of diplomacy. Nevertheless, a historical view that regards Yoshida's and Tōgō's engagement in a turf battle, which is routine conduct for any bureaucrat, as heroic resistance to the prerogative of the military is of little value.

Particularly in the case of Yoshida, it is quite conceivable that, had the issue been entrusted to Yoshida, he would have taken a much more high-handed stance toward the provincial government of Fengtian.

## Yoshida's Manchurian Policy: Departure from Shidehara Diplomacy

Yoshida attended to his tasks in Mukden vigorously and sent a large number of suggestions and proposals to the ministry in Tokyo.

Allow me to introduce a lengthy memorandum, dated April 27, 1928, that comprehensively reveals Yoshida's philosophy. Yoshida drafted the document between the time when he returned home from Mukden and when he was appointed vice-minister for foreign affairs.

In the preamble, which opens with the words, "In the era of the Great Emperor Meiji," a reference to an authority that in those days no Japanese could oppose, Yoshida points out that the First Sino-Japanese and the Russo-Japanese Wars erupted when the Japanese economy and politics became deadlocked. Yoshida writes that these wars contributed to economic recovery and political reconciliation. He stressed the importance of aggressive measures for Japan to cope with the slow economy that had not really picked up since the post–World War I recession.

He continued to insist on the complete renewal of Japan's China, Manchuria, and Mongolia policies, saying:

> Even though China is believed to be a world-class source of wealth, Japan has so far idly watched it being tyrannized by warlords . . . When it comes to the management of Manchuria and Mongolia, to which the Great Emperor Meiji was believed to have special attachment, all we have done is to vainly consult Zhang Zuolin's pleasure, . . . [so much so that] we are unable to make a decision because of worrying about Zhang's reaction even when the very foundation of our influence in the region, which we have spent years to establish, is shaken . . .

In retrospect, this is a document that could well be quoted as an ideological argument in defense of subsequent arbitrary conduct by the Japanese military stationed in north China, including the assassination of Zhang Zuolin (1928) and the Manchurian Incident (1931–32). The document's preamble, too, could be interpreted as an approval of a war if it could bring about a breakthrough for a stagnant economy.

Yoshida enumerates the following reasons why Japan's China policy had not been successful:

1. An ideology against war (including the argument for the people's self-determination) emerged after World War I, which people accepted as a matter of course;
2. People became obsessed with such empty slogans as "Japan-China friendship" and "mutual co-existence and co-prosperity"; and
3. Japan's China policy has not been centralized.

Yoshida, therefore, concludes that now is the time for Japan to "pursue its policy with firm resolution." This was, simply put, an open anti-liberal manifesto.

In terms of a policy goal for Japan, Yoshida says, "While it may not be necessary for Japan to physically conquer three eastern provinces of China, it would be imperative to promote political reform in those three provinces under Japan's substantial guidance in order to emulate Britain's accomplishments in Egypt . . ."

This quote reminds me of notes that Mutsu Munemitsu had scribbled during his days at Cambridge University, particularly the following portion touching on Britain's policy toward Egypt:

Since Britain defeated the Egyptian army in 1882, it has de facto ruled Egypt. Britain classified its operation in 1882 a "military action," a term that was not found in international law, instead of as a war. This is because, theoretically, Egypt is a part of the Turkish Empire, with which Britain has maintained peaceful relations . . .

Japan's decision to call the conflict in Manchuria in 1931–32 the Manchurian Incident instead of the Manchurian War was cut from the same cloth as the above British choice of wording. Britain had certainly played an immense role in Egyptian modernization, and it was Britain's de facto rule of Egypt that Yoshida had in mind when he considered Japan's policy toward Manchuria.

In the concluding section of his memorandum, "How to Carry out Policies toward Manchuria," Yoshida enumerates errors that Japan has committed in the past and countermeasures to be taken as follows:

> As a result of the pursuit of vague Sino-Japanese friendship, we have become overly eager, from top to bottom, to please the Chinese side, . . . allowing the Chinese to be arrogant for nothing. As far as I am aware, there has been no case internationally of a plan to advance into another country's territory being launched successfully by relying solely on the goodwill of officials and private citizens of the target country . . . We should never hesitate to carry out a plan just because the locals are not favorably disposed . . . Britain's India policy has never been welcomed by the Indians since the start . . . As long as we plan to advance into China and Manchuria, we should be prepared to face anti-Japanese movements by locals . . .

In short, Yoshida was saying that Japan should not be bothered by such empty slogans as "Wilsonian pacifism" and "Sino-Japanese friendship" and that Japan should stop pampering Zhang Zuoling. Yoshida was proposing that Japan should instead make Manchuria its protectorate, as Britain had done to Egypt, and in so doing be fully prepared for anti-Japanese movements by the Chinese.

Shidehara Kijūrō's cooperative diplomacy and Tanaka Giichi's aggressive diplomacy are often compared. On this point, Yoshida himself said in his memoir, *Kaisō 10-nen* (10 Years in Retrospect), "Pondering whether there was a substantial difference between the two, the truth must be that there was not so much fundamental difference in those days—which seems all the more obvious today."

I sense Yoshida's self-justification in the above quote. In my judgment, he was trying to justify his past conduct. When he wrote "All we have done is to vainly consult Zhang Zuolin's pleasure" in his 1928 memorandum, it is undeniable that his words contained an element of vindication of his failure to win over Zhang Zuolin.

In retrospect, there was a marked difference between the diplomacy of Shidehara and Tanaka. Between the two, Yoshida's stance was closer to

Tanaka than Shidehara. In fact, Yoshida belonged to a more radical right-wing school than Tanaka. Yoshida at one time said of Mori Tsutomu that the two of them were quite in sympathy with each other. Mori was a person who, as parliamentary vice-minister for foreign affairs, led Prime Minister Tanaka, who had the air of a moderate military man matured during the Taishō Democracy, to aggressive diplomacy. And it was via Mori that Yoshida sold himself to Tanaka, who appointed Yoshida vice-minister for foreign affairs. Yoshida later reminisced that those vice-minister days under Prime Minister cum Foreign Minister Tanaka were the most pleasant experiences in his life in officialdom.

Also, Yoshida did not resist at all the general trend of statism and expansionism that formed the main stream of the Japanese ideologies in those days. In 1932 (7th Year of Shōwa), Yoshida wrote a letter to his father-in-law Makino Nobuaki, saying, "While cooperative diplomacy is a decent principle, it would be looked down on as empty do-nothingism if it ignored the national wish to advance externally." This was a clear departure from Shidehara diplomacy.

## Pursuing Rainbows: Partnership with Britain and the United States

At the same time, though, Yoshida was too defiant to be simply carried away by the trend of the times. As a matter of fact, in the midst of the rushing current of anti-Anglo Saxon xenophobia, Yoshida had persisted with the policy line of harmony with Britain and the United States since his days as Japanese ambassador to Britain.

This policy line consistently remained Yoshida's principle of conduct not only while he was ambassador to Britain in 1936–38 but during the period leading up to the defeat of Japan in 1945.

Even after Yoshida returned home from Britain and retired from the foreign ministry, he took two overseas trips and stayed in close contact with U.S. ambassador to Japan Joseph Grew. Although Grew did not think particularly highly of Yoshida as a diplomat or a person influential in Japanese politics, he nevertheless found Yoshida a precious source of information on Japan and called him "a liberalist" and "a good friend of mine and the United States." To maintain friendship, it is important for both parties to

Yoshida in 1931

find each other a good source of information. In later years, during the occupation of Japan, Yoshida and MacArthur found each other precious sources of information. Yoshida cherished his friendship with Grew, and when the latter was detained by Japanese authorities upon the eruption of the Greater East Asia War, Yoshida sent Grew foodstuffs. This benevolent conduct of Yoshida's left a good impression on Grew who toward the end of the war was put in charge of U.S. Japan policy as undersecretary of state.

Upon arriving in London to take up the ambassadorship in 1936, Yoshida stressed the importance of a "clear policy agreement" between the two countries to British Foreign Secretary Anthony Eden. This meeting was followed by the first Yoshida proposal on October 26, 1936, and the second Yoshida proposal on June 2, 1937.

In a nutshell, Yoshida proposed that Britain and Japan should jointly support China's sovereignty and, together, keep its doors open as far as the region south of the Great Wall was concerned. Yoshida also proposed that the two countries should work together to protect their respective vested rights against China's attempts to eliminate foreign interests. In addition, Yoshida included a demand for Japan's preferential position in China. In the first proposal, Yoshida proposed that Japan should monopolize military cooperation with China by concluding a long-term agreement for arms procurement with the Nanjing regime and sending military advisers from Japan. Yoshida cited the need to restrain the Soviet advance to China and discourage warlords from procuring arms on their own.

British probing in Tokyo revealed, however, that Yoshida's proposal had not yet been endorsed by the Japanese government. The future prospects of Japanese politics that Yoshida had referred to—i.e., that the pendulum would swing back in time to allow the moderates to become dominant in Japan—was also found to be nothing but wishful thinking. The British side decided to let Yoshida propose whatever he wanted, but Yoshida's proposals became deadlocked when the Second Sino-Japanese War erupted on July 7.

Yoshida continued his efforts to strike a compromise with Britain and the United States even after the war erupted until his retirement as ambassador to Britain in the fall of 1938. Even after he returned home, Yoshida continued to explore the possibility of cooperation with Britain and the United States through British Ambassador to Japan Robert Craigie and American Ambassador to Japan Joseph Grew. From the following British and American testimonies that John Dower quoted in a chapter of his book, which was fittingly titled "Pursuing Rainbows," it is obvious that those efforts were mostly quixotic:

"I was flabbergasted by Yoshida's remarks." (U.S. Ambassador Joseph Grew on November 1, 1937)

"It is impossible to pay attention each time a foreign ambassador says something in his personal capacity." (British Foreign Secretary Edward Wood, 1st Earl of Halifax on May 7, 1938)

"Yoshida so tenaciously insists that the settlement of all the difficult problems is just around the corner that everyone here suspects that he is prone to wishful thinking by nature." (British Ambassador Craigie on March 17, 1939)

"He [Yoshida] always says a rainbow is just around the corner and tonight was no exception." (U.S. Ambassador Grew on April 16, 1940)

Whether in Manchuria or in London, Yoshida's words and deeds were bound to be accompanied by an air of fighting windmills on the spur of the moment.

## The Substance of the Yoshida Doctrine

An expression that is most fitting to describe the journey of Yoshida's diplomatic strategy—from aggressive expansionism during his Manchurian days and pursuit of partnership with Britain and the United States when he was ambassador to Italy and Britain to, finally, cooperation with Douglas MacArthur during the occupation period—would be *plus royal que roi* (more royalist than the king).

Yoshida was a more outspoken statist and expansionist than Tanaka Giichi in his Manchurian days. In his British days, he was a more quixotic advocate of cooperation with Britain and the United States than Britain itself. Truly, Yoshida was more royalist than the king, indeed. His argument in postwar days against the rearmament of Japan also definitely had an aspect of constantly siding with MacArthur against the swing in the U.S. government's Japan policy between the thorough elimination of militarism from Japan on the one hand and the rearmament of Japan on the other. As I will touch on in a later chapter, Yoshida's reply in the Diet denying Japan even the right to self-defense was indeed more royalist than the king, i.e., more like the leftist tendencies of GHQ than those held by GHQ itself.

Yoshida and MacArthur seem to have had a relationship of genuine mutual trust that went above and beyond a relationship based on mere mutual interests. Thus, a Shōwa political commentator Kase Shun'ichi testifies, "In any event, Mr. Yoshida held MacArthur in high esteem and I think it was reciprocal" (Kase Shun'ichi, *Kakankai Kaihō*, 1969).

Believing that maintaining a political regime with the emperor system intact was imperative to successfully occupying Japan, MacArthur mapped out a grand strategy to promote absolute pacifism in Japan. MacArthur wanted to protect his policy from the Allied countries, which were against the continuation of the emperor system, as well as from the hardliners in Washington. And MacArthur thoroughly defended his grand strategy all the way. Even after the eruption of the Korean War,

MacArthur opposed Secretary of State Dulles' argument for Japan's rearmament and insisted, instead, on using Japan's economic power.

In the meantime, Yoshida's words and deeds perfectly matched MacArthur's like a shadow following an object. Yoshida's remarks in those days are so well known that they do not need to be quoted here. One peculiar case, though, is interesting. In January 1950, Yoshida abruptly spoke out for rearmament during his speech on the administrative policies of his cabinet. While Yoshida was criticized for his sudden change of sides, the substance of his remark was exactly the same as MacArthur's New Year's Day message. While I will come back to the background of this remark later, approval of the right to self-defense without rearmament was tantamount to, at least logically, reliance on protection by U.S. forces—thus foreshadowing the later U.S.-Japan Security Treaty.

It is understandable that, one way or another, Yoshida had to refrain from taking any action against MacArthur's wish at any cost in order to conclude a peace treaty with the United States and restore Japan's independence. It was only natural for Yoshida to find his relations with MacArthur, who actually ruled Japan, more important than those with Washington-based Secretary Dulles. Hypothetically, had MacArthur switched his policy 180 degrees after the eruption of the Korean War to clearly side with Dulles' argument for Japan's rearmament, it was hardly conceivable that Yoshida would have resisted the MacArthur-Dulles argument and persisted with an anti-war, economy-first policy.

To be sure, Yoshida stuck with his own line even after MacArthur was dismissed. But by that time Dulles had ceased putting strong pressure on Japan because the imminent signing of the peace treaty was more or less confirmed. It might be more accurate to conjecture that deep down Yoshida might have started harboring a notion of Japan's rearmament in the future, even though he would not think of stepping over the boundary that he had built with his replies in the Diet.

Meiji-Shōwa journalist/political commentator Abe Shin'nosuke harshly criticized Yoshida's refusal to discuss the pros and cons of rearmament and a constitutional amendment. Instead, Yoshida simply announced that Japan shall not rearm and the constitution shall not be revised. This caused great confusion among the Japanese people.

This goes to show that Yoshida possessed nothing that could be termed a Yoshida Doctrine. To quote Kase again,

Yoshida Shigeru was weak in economics . . . I am not sure, as today's historians and commentators seem to like to believe, that he spoke from an accurate, logical calculation that rearmament should be foregone in order to restore the economy. What I can tell you is that his thinking about Japan's rearmament had begun to change completely about two or three years before his death. His earlier opposition to rearmament had been based on a notion that people had to be fed first before they became strong enough to shoulder arms. Now that the Japanese economy has been successfully restored, . . . Yoshida had clearly become doubtful of the virtue of leaving Japan's security in the hands of a foreign country.

One day, Mr. Yoshida spoke at The America-Japan Society . . . Although he was reading the speech text that I had drafted, he stopped reading it at one point and said, "Ladies and gentlemen, isn't it time for Japan to arm itself with nuclear weapons?" (Kase Shun'ichi, ibid.)

If that was indeed how Yoshida had perceived the issue, then it was no wonder that he could not logically explain why rearmament and constitutional revision had to be opposed.

## Fearless Optimist

Yoshida was a person born under a lucky star.

To begin with, he was fortunate enough to be adopted by the millionaire Yoshida family even though he was born as the fifth son of impoverished former samurai Takenouchi Tsuna, who had been blessed with many children.

When Yoshida was appointed Japanese ambassador to Britain, it had actually been planned that he would become foreign minister in the Hirota Kōki cabinet formed after the February 26 Incident. But Yoshida's appointment as foreign minister was rejected by the Imperial Japanese Army on the grounds that Yoshida was the son-in-law of pro-Britain/U.S. Makino Nobuaki. Hirota in the end had to comply with the Army's demand and instead name Yoshida Japanese ambassador to Britain.

In retrospect, for Yoshida this was the dividing line between a fate like

Hirota's death by hanging and ascent to the highest official position of prime minister. In terms of political conviction, no great difference existed between the two. As a matter of fact, while Hirota only catered to the general trend of statism and expansionism, Yoshida was more of a flag waver, particularly in his Manchurian days.

Nevertheless, Yoshida was labeled an antiwar liberalist just because he had henceforth persisted with his pro-Britain/U.S. stance and ended up being arrested for his role in the peace engineering toward the end of the Greater East Asia War. Consequently, while a number of promising contemporaries of Yoshida were purged from public service, Yoshida alone got ahead.

About Yoshida Shigeru's survival in this period, Abe Shin'nosuke writes,

> Due to the surprise turn of fate, some overestimate Yoshida and even extend him hero worship, while some others underestimate Yoshida and view him as an insignificant snob. Thus, there are fiercely differing views on Yoshida's person, and none of them is accurate. In a nutshell, Yoshida was a mediocre creature just like all of us.

I think this is a fairly impartial assessment of Yoshida Shigeru.

Had Shigemitsu Mamoru and Tōgō Shigenori not been imprisoned to everyone's surprise, either one of them undoubtedly would have shouldered the chief responsibility for steering Japan's diplomacy during the occupation period. Yoshida was not on a par with these two in terms of accurate assessment of situations, penetrating insight, or unwavering policy arguments. Tatsumi Eiichi, who as military attaché served both Ambassadors Shigemitsu and Yoshida, wrote in his memoir, "As far as intellectual capabilities were concerned, I believe Mr. Shigemitsu was superior to Mr. Yoshida" (*Saikō*, December 1982 issue). Tatsumi defended Yoshida by characterizing him as a strong-willed person who acted in accord with his convictions.

It is not my intention here to badmouth Yoshida. Admittedly, he might not have been on the same level as a diplomat as Shigemitsu or Tōgō. Nevertheless, he was a first-rate diplomat who served the country as vice-minister for foreign affairs and ambassador to Britain. Moreover, in terms of personality, Yoshida was much more accommodative, humorous, and broadminded than such cool, bureaucrat-types as Shigemitsu and Tōgō.

What I would like to take up here, rather, is the generally accepted notion about Yoshida in postwar history. It is totally misguided to perceive Yoshida as a great statesman who showed the Japanese mettle by resisting Dulles' demand for rearmament because he was convinced of a comprehensive state strategy that put top priority on the economy.

I do not intend to deny that Yoshida was, in a somewhat different sense, a great statesman. After all, it was indeed a great accomplishment of Yoshida to protect the emperor system and conclude the peace treaty with the United States by constructing firm relations of mutual trust with MacArthur and by cautiously following MacArthur's policy line, while secretly looking forward to rearmament some time in the future.

As Shidehara had something he could never reveal to others, it is not hard to imagine that Yoshida, too, must have had a lot of things he could not put into words under the humiliating circumstances of the occupation, given his stubborn and arrogant disposition.

In the end, Yoshida should be understood as one of the patriots who, like Shidehara and Ashida Hitoshi, devoted himself to defending the emperor system and realizing an early conclusion of the peace treaty for the benefit of Japan. Seen from the flip side, this was tantamount to what Abe Shin'nosuke meant when he referred to Yoshida as "an average Japanese who is no different from an ordinary citizen."

Yoshida contributed to the process of negotiations with the United States before the eruption of the war, including drafting a compromise proposal, and he started peace engineering immediately after the start of the war. His idea about the negotiations at that time was to have Konoe Fumimaro stay in Switzerland and make it a venue for contact with various countries, including Japan's adversaries.

Although it appeared that Konoe, too, found this idea appealing at one point, the idea never materialized. Objectively speaking, the possibility of an early peace was less than one percent, if any, after the Japanese attack on Pearl Harbor had inspired the American will to fight.

Admittedly, there might have evolved a situation in which the peace talks might not be totally meaningless for countries, depending on how the war developed, such as the Soviet Union having a hard time defeating

Germany. Also, had it not been for Japan's defeat in the Battle of Midway, leading to a delay in the U.S. counteroffensive for a year or two, a trend such as India's independence movement might have been perceived as irreversible. Then, Japan might have been able to obtain the support of American public opinion, which was against colonialism.

If the above situations had really come about, there might have been a chance for Japan to negotiate peace in Geneva while continuing to fight the United States, delivering more casualties on the U.S. side—just like Vietnam did during the Vietnam War.

In any event, if the plan to post Konoe in Switzerland had been carried out, Japan would have been able to see its situation much better. Japan may have been able to avoid committing its fate solely to success in battles—i.e., the Battle of the Philippine Sea, the Battle of Okinawa, and the homeland defense war—and to isolating itself from the rest of the world, abandoning all diplomatic efforts. At least Yoshida's discernment as a diplomat to propose peace negotiations in Geneva without caving in to the trend of the times should be properly appreciated.

In 1945, the year of Japan's defeat, Yoshida was imprisoned for his role in the antiwar movement. The codename for the movement among police authorities was the Yohansen Movement. This was not a Swedish name. The movement's full name was the Yoshida Hansen (antiwar) movement. This shows clearly that the police regarded Yoshida as the ringleader.

In February 1945, Konoe Fumimaro visited Yoshida at his residence to stress the need to promptly stop the war. After this visit, Konoe drafted the so-called *Konoe Jōsō-bun* (Konoe's address to the throne), which was submitted to the Emperor on February 14.

The address first predicted that the defeat of Japan would be inevitable. Based on that, it pointed to the danger of a communist revolution, which would be far more dangerous than the defeat itself. Konoe analyzed that things were moving exactly as Ozaki Hatsumi, the Soviet spy whom Konoe had unknowingly trusted, had calculated, and now Japan had entered a war with Britain and the United States, two of the world's major capitalist countries, preparing a perfect opportunity for a communist revolution. The address revealed that, at last, Konoe had come to full realization of this possibility.

Yoshida's actions in this period were detected by the military police, resulting in Yoshida's detention for 40 days from April to June. And this turned out to be one of Yoshida's great pieces of good luck. Almost all of those who participated in this antiwar movement together with Yoshida later became subject to purging, including Hatoyama Ichirō. Detention by the military police provided Yoshida with vindication.

The end of the Greater East Asia War gave Yoshida a tremendous sense of liberation.

In his letter of August 27 addressed to Kurusu Saburo, former Japanese ambassador to the United States, Yoshida wrote, "Up to this point, I must say Japan has been the best and most gracious loser in the history of the world."

Admittedly, it is true that Japan ended up missing a chance to promptly surrender after the release of the Potsdam Declaration, but that must have been inevitable given the domestic situation in Japan at that time. Nevertheless, Japan wasted hardly any time after the atomic bombs on Hiroshima and Nagasaki and the Soviet Union's participation in the war. Japan surrendered on the decision of its own government, without losing governmental control both within and outside Japan. This successfully prevented the mainland from becoming a battlefield and contained coup d'état attempts by the military. Historically speaking, it was indeed a highly unusual way to lose a war.

It gives me shivers to imagine what would have happened if the Japanese government had not been courageous enough to suppress the Imperial Japanese Army's demand the war continue for a few more months. All the rest of the cities in Japan must have been completely destroyed, and 100 million Japanese people surely would have had to face the winter literally homeless. It is said that the U.S. government even had a plan to burn down agrarian villages in the harvest season; if carried out, Japan in the winter to early spring of 1946 would have been a living hell where a few million starved to death. There was ample possibility for Japan to be divided and occupied, with northern Japan including Hokkaido coming under Soviet rule until the 1991 dissolution of the Soviet Union. If the entire Japanese population had been chased off from northern Japan as the Germans of Königsberg in eastern Germany had been, the territory might have been under Russian rule even indefinitely.

It is easy to make accusations about the delay in the decision to surrender. Yet had it not been for the wisdom and courage of the Emperor, Suzuki Kantarō, Tōgō Shigenori, and Yonai Mitsumasa, Japan as we know it today would not have been.

Yoshida never abandoned his optimism about militarism being just a temporary phenomenon. The country, like the swing of a pendulum, was destined to return to normalcy in time, he felt.

In a letter Yoshida sent to Grew ten days after the attack on Pearl Harbor, he wrote, "In recent years, we have witnessed a number of unfortunate incidents. It was beyond anyone's anticipation that the everlasting friendships between our two countries would result in such a tragic outcome," as if to declare that eruption of the Great East Asia War had been totally unexpected to him. In his letter to Kurusu immediately after the surrender, Yoshida concluded, "After a storm comes a calm, as the proverb goes. Our current defeat may not necessarily be that bad if we can reconstruct our economy by promoting science and technology and attracting American capital."

This bold optimism, which can only be termed fearless, was the very essence of Yoshida Shigeru.

CHAPTER

# 7

# The First Yoshida Shigeru Cabinet

## —From Addressing the Food Problem and Agrarian Reform to Promulgation of the New Constitution—

## The Price of the Prime Ministership

Upon hearing the announcement of his purge from public services, Hatoyama Ichirō on May 4, 1946, formally requested Yoshida Shigeru to succeed to the prime ministership. As a matter of fact, Hatoyama had always suggested that Yoshida should take over if something happened to him. But each time, Yoshida had dodged the suggestion, saying, "That's not for me." This time, too, Yoshida declined Hatoyama's formal request.

Yoshida continued to turn down the appointment even after May 4, citing his lack of experience in domestic politics and his own disposition as reasons why he was unfit for the position. In the course of repeatedly declining the offer, however, Yoshida appears to have been preparing mentally to accept the post in the event that he could no longer fend off the offer. When Yoshida finally made up his mind to accept the nomination, he shared his aspirations with Takemi Tarō, who was related to Yoshida by marriage. Takemi was a highly reputed physician in those days, particularly among dignitaries who often used Takemi's clinic as a perfect venue for secret meetings. Yoshida told Takemi, "In history there have been cases of losing a war but winning in diplomacy."

During a man-to-man talk with Hatoyama presumed to have taken place on May 14, Yoshida named three conditions for accepting the appointment. Of those three conditions, by far the most important was the demand for carte blanche regarding cabinet appointments. Hatoyama did not mention these three conditions even to Kōno Ichirō, secretary-general of the *Jiyūtō*, because Hatoyama was sure Kōno would never agree with them. Thus, by repeatedly declining the nomination, Yoshida was able to raise the price of his becoming prime minister.

Yoshida's three conditions later proved to be truly significant.

As introduced earlier, the gravest and, possibly, the only shortcoming of the Meiji Constitution was the lack of a provision regarding the prime minister's power to appoint and dismiss cabinet ministers. While the new constitution, which was about to be promulgated in 1947, was amended in this regard, ordinarily the prime minister would still have to pay due consideration to various political groups, which would tie his hands somewhat in forming a cabinet of his choice. What Yoshida did was to snatch a carte blanche on personnel from *Jiyūtō*, his power base, in 1946 when, legally speaking, Japan was still under the Meiji Constitution.

Subsequently, on the basis of the landslide victory by the ruling *Minshu Jiyūtō* (a product of the 1948 merger between those who seceded from the *Minshutō* and the *Nippon Jiyūtō*) in the 1949 general election and the absolute authority of Douglas McArthur, Yoshida was able to secure near-autocratic power in personnel affairs in terms of the appointment and dismissal of cabinet members. No one else between the Meiji era and today has enjoyed such power. This became one of the factors that contributed to the myth of Yoshida's one-man rule and the hero-worship-like adoration of what people believed to be Yoshida's political capability.

## Food Crisis and Imperial Properties

Among the whole set of devastations that plagued the Japanese economy immediately after World War II, the greatest and gravest was the food shortage.

In July 1945, on the eve of Japan's defeat, the rice ration was reduced from the previous 2.3 *go* (approximately 345 grams) per person per day to 2.1 *go* (approximately 300 grams). This reduction might be insignificant today; in fact, nowadays a Japanese person might consume only 300 grams of rice a day because of the abundance of side dishes people now eat with their rice. But in 1945, the Japanese had to rely almost solely on rice for nutrition. The caloric intake per day from 300 grams of rice should have been less than 1,000 kcal, far short of the starvation line of 1,640 kcal, not to mention the 2,500 kcal that nutritionists say a healthy Japanese needs daily.

Three main factors caused the food shortage: (1) the more than 30 percent reduction in the rice harvest in 1945 from the previous year due to bad weather and damage to rice paddies caused by air raids; (2) the termination of rice supplies from former overseas territories, including Taiwan, Korea, and Manchuria; and (3) reluctance on the part of producers to make their obligatory supply of rice available at a low price. The fall in the government's authority encouraged the producers' reluctance; in the end, producers supplied less than half the amount they had during the war.

It was anticipated that, in the spring/summer of 1946, before the crop-moving season of the 1946 harvest, Japan would be facing the greatest food crisis in history. The Japanese people stood in fear of what seemed to be imminent starvation.

It appeared that Emperor Shōwa played a great role in this food problem.

According to the memoir of Matsumura Kenzō, who was minister of agriculture and forestry at that time, he was summoned to the Imperial Palace in December 1945. The Emperor said to Matsumura:

> It is utterly unbearable for us to allow many of our people to die of hunger after having forced them to suffer the misery of war. . . . We are told that there are quite a number of items of international value among the imperial properties, and we have had an inventory made. It is our wish to obtain food from the United States in return for this inventory so that our people may be freed from hunger even for a day.

Prime Minister Shidehara Kijūrō immediately requested a meeting with MacArthur, in which Shidehara conveyed the imperial wish. Deeply moved by the Emperor's proposal, MacArthur replied,

> While the imperial offer is fully appreciated, the United States

would lose its face, and I mine, if we agreed to provide the Japanese people with food in return for confiscated imperial properties. Thus, I wish to return this inventory to His Imperial Majesty. . . . As long as I remain in my current post, no one in Japan shall starve to death. I will take whatever measures necessary to bring over food from the United States. Please advise His Imperial Majesty that he should rest assured about this matter.

In retrospect, this promise by MacArthur went a long way. The world's food situation deteriorated further after MacArthur made his commitment. That year, Europe suffered a massive shortage of wheat, Burma and Thailand experienced a poor rice harvest, and China and India faced famines. Under normal situations, a war loser like Japan could not complain if it were forced to suffer from famine as a punishment.

The above promise between top leaders notwithstanding, the food crisis remained imminent because it was by no means certain the promise would really be carried out. Even the 2.1-*go* rations began to see delays in the spring of 1946; after March, rationing constantly lagged behind schedule. In Tokyo, the delivery was one full week behind schedule toward the end of April. The "Give Me Rice" movement grew in force after International Labor Day (May Day) on May 1. On May 19, the "Mayday for Food" rally convened in the open space in front of the Imperial Palace: 250,000 citizens forced their way onto the palace grounds from Sakashitamon Gate.

The movement became so annoying to GHQ that, on May 20, MacArthur had to make an announcement, warning, "The act of violence that the undisciplined elements are about to launch will no longer be allowed to continue."

## Conditions to Form a Cabinet Are Now Complete

It was on May 16 in the midst of this rice upheaval that Yoshida received the Imperial command to form his cabinet.

As soon as Yoshida accepted the nomination, he invited Takemi to the prime minister's office and said, "My cabinet will be a food crisis cabinet in which the agriculture minister will be the key player. Go ask for Mr. Ishiguro Tadaatsu's advice."

Having served the Konoe Fumimaro cabinet as its agriculture minis-

The first Yoshida Cabinet
(Copyright © KYODO NEWS IMAGES INC.)

ter, Ishiguro was the guru of agriculture policy in Japan. To the visiting Takemi, Ishiguro recommended University of Tokyo professor Tōhata Seiichi as agriculture minister.

Hearing of Ishiguro's recommendation, Tōhata rushed to consult with Wada Hiroo, director-general of the Agricultural Policy Bureau of the Ministry of Agriculture and Forestry.

Wada was a socialist who had once been arrested on suspicion of violating the Security Preservation Law in 1941 when he said, "If the war continues for two years, there will be no food in Japan." When Tōhata asked if Wada would be willing to accept the vice-ministership under Tōhata, Wada replied affirmatively, saying, "Let's do it even if it costs us our lives."

Wada's reassurance notwithstanding, Tōhata was, after all, too scholastic to feel comfortable with a political post. In the end, he bowed out of the nomination. When Yoshida suggested the nomination of Wada as agriculture minister instead, Tōhata offered to assist Minister Wada as vice-minister.

Meanwhile, Emperor Shōwa continued to call Yoshida at 8:00 o'clock every evening to urge the early formation of his cabinet, saying, "We urge you to form your cabinet as soon as possible to cope with the imminent food problem." Yoshida always replied that he was doing his best.

Today, Yoshida's unhurried formation of the cabinet has become something akin to legend. Some claim that they heard Yoshida brag, saying, "The cabinet formation can wait until MacArthur's announcement on food provisions. Let red flags fly all over Japan for a month or so, and the United States will surely bring food." When MacArthur confirmed the provision of food to the Japanese people on May 21, Yoshida is believed to have said, "Now the conditions to form my cabinet are complete." It has also been quoted that, hearing this, Takemi said, "For the first time, I have witnessed diplomacy at work."

A review of Yoshida's journal, however, reveals that he was not deliberately postponing the formation of his cabinet.

Yoshida had to spend half of the time it took to form his cabinet persuading Tōhata. Even after Wada was appointed agriculture minister, Yoshida had to face opposition to this appointment from the majority of *Jiyūtō* members who demanded that Kōno Ichirō be appointed to the post. At one point, when Hatoyama conveyed his opposition to Wada's appointment over the phone, Yoshida had to flatly reject Hatoyama's demand, reminding the latter of the three conditions for Yoshida's acceptance of the prime ministership.

While it can be easily imagined that Yoshida may have chuckled to himself over the delay in the completion of his cabinet as he looked forward to the impact of the "Give Us Rice" rallies on GHQ, he was certainly not in a position to deliberately delay the process.

Of course, it would be perfect if Yoshida could form his cabinet after he was assured that MacArthur's promise to Shidehara was really going to be kept. Thus, after MacArthur invited Yoshida to GHQ on May 21 to repeat his promise—i.e., "As long as I remain Supreme Commander for the Allied Powers, no Japanese citizen shall starve to death"—Yoshida said to Wada and Takemi, "Now, at last I can form my cabinet," when he returned to his office.

From MacArthur's viewpoint, the most crucial thing was to successfully carry out occupation policies. His reassurance to Yoshida on May 21 was only a natural extension of his own announcement on May 20 in response to the Mayday for Food rally on May 19. It is easily conjectured that the delay in the formation of the Yoshida cabinet was not such a major determinant for MacArthur.

MacArthur made the United States release some flour reserves before the end of May as well as send 200,000 tons of food in June/July and

200,000 tons each in August and September. These supplies enabled Japan to overcome the worst period. According to the *Tokyo-To Shokuryō Eidan-Shi* (History of the Tokyo Food Public Corporation), more than 90 percent of all the food supplies that Tokyo citizens received in July and August and more than 70 percent in September were imported from the United States.

The Japanese people who experienced this episode of the war victor Americans rescuing the loser Japanese from starvation must have felt that Japan really had been no match for the United States. It would not be an overstatement to say that at the bottom of the pro-American sentiment and the sense of trust toward the United States that are observed today among the Japanese is the memory of this gift from the Americans.

## Dreams and Efforts of Agricultural Administrators

It was in conjunction with land reform that Wada, Yoshida's pick specifically to address the food problem, fully demonstrated his worth as the most appropriate person on this matter.

The root cause of Japan's agricultural land problems was the tenancy farming system. Tenant-landlord relations had always been a grave social problem in Japan since the end of the shogunate period. In a myriad of ways, the country had long tried to tackle this problem through trial and error.

Although a variety of agricultural reform plans were made in the cabinet or in Diet committees during the Taishō Democracy period, reform of the tenancy farming system itself almost never made it into a bill due to strong resistance from landlords. Consequently, reform bills emphasized the promotion of owner farmers and the protection of landed farmers from bankruptcy. Large fiscal expenditures would be needed to finance reforms, which is what, in the end, blocked the passage of those bills.

The first agricultural reform law that was enacted was the Farmland Adjustment Law of 1938 legislated around the same time as the National Mobilization Law. Even though the importance of creating and maintaining landed farmers as a "nucleus of agriculture in the empire" was stressed during the Greater East Asia War, the necessary coercive acquisition of farmland that the agricultural authority had initially planned was never implemented. Such farmland acquisition had to await the postwar agricultural reforms.

Nevertheless, during the war, all of the rice harvests of absentee land-lords except for the household reserves of resident landlords were put under direct control of the government. Also, the gap between produc-ers' rice price and landlords' rice price widened, leading to a significant decline in the power of landlords and an increase in independence of tenant farmers.

It is a global phenomenon for citizens' rights and the burden of civic duties to become more equalized during an all-out war. In this sense, a war often has the effect of laying the foundations for postwar democratization.

Matsumura Kenzō was parliamentary vice-minister for agriculture and forestry in the Hiranuma Kiichirō cabinet during the war. By that time, there already was a law to promote the creation of landed farmers as well as a draft act on the arbitration of tenancy disputes. After the war, Matsu-mura was appointed agriculture minister in the Shidehara cabinet. In that capacity, he reminisced as follows: "We were convinced that we could carry out land reform just by adding the legal force [to the draft act during the war]. Behind the successful implementation of the land reform in Japan was, thus, the preparations that had been made much earlier."

After Matsumura resigned as vice-minister for agriculture and forestry, Wada, Tōhata, and several others continued the study of land reform. When Matsumura became agriculture minister after the war, he immediately appointed Wada to be director-general of the Agricultural Policy Bureau.

Matsumura was an advocate of making all peasants landed farmers and insisted on limiting a landlord's property to 1 *cho* and 5 *tan* (approxi-mately 14,850 square meters). Even though Wada was a socialist, he knew from experience that a radical reform would only trigger resistance. So he suggested an upper limit of 3 *chō* (approximately 29,700 square meters) and made the imposition of property tax on farmland the centerpiece of reform. Although the consensus was reached within the agriculture minis-try on the upper limit of 3 *cho*, Minister of State Matsumoto Jōji spoke up against this proposal at a cabinet meeting, calling it a violation of private property rights. Thus the cabinet decided on the upper limit of 5 *cho*.

In those days, GHQ had not yet pressured Japan to carry out land reform. Giving Japan's spontaneous agrarian reform without pressure from GHQ high marks, the late Professor Ōishi Kaichirō of the University of Tokyo said,

The fact that such an agricultural reform bill was worked out when the GHQ's positive attitude toward agrarian reform was not yet known to the Japanese government points to the significance of the accumulation of the vast experience of the agriculture ministry officials in farmland policies before and during the war.

Although it was feared that powerful landed representatives would not allow the bill to pass in the Imperial Diet before the first postwar general election, GHQ's release on the promotion of agricultural reform supplied a nice tailwind for the bill. The bill was enacted on December 18.

Actually, GHQ had not been too enthusiastic about this field at the beginning.

In GHQ, Robert Appleton Fearey from the Department of State and Wolf Isaac Ladejinsky from the Department of Agriculture were put in charge of agriculture policies. When Fearey proposed the creation of landed farmers through the purchase of farmland from landlords in June 1945 before he was stationed in Tokyo, the idea was turned down. Fearey, who had served under Ambassador Joseph Grew as a personal secretary prior to and during the outbreak of the war, once again proposed the same scheme when he was stationed in GHQ toward the end of September. This time, the idea caught MacArthur's attention and found its way into the GHQ memorandum of December 9.

Surprisingly, it was the Allied Council for Japan that strongly stressed the inadequacy of Fearey's proposal. At the council meeting convened in 1946, the Soviet Union submitted a revolutionary proposal for coercive confiscation of land from large landowners and free redistribution of the confiscated land to peasants. Such a proposal was only natural for a communist country. In those days, the intention among the Allies to penalize the war loser Japan was more prominent than the wish to reform Japan. Coupled with the perception that the impoverishment of rural villages had been behind Japan's militarization, Britain, which had suffered from Japan's "social dumping" (Japan's export offensive taking advantage of its low labor cost), submitted its own proposal on Japan's agricultural reform as a counterproposal to the Soviet suggestion. Britain's ideas were adopted into the GHQ proposal issued in June. This proposal provided a base for the second revised proposal to the Japanese government, which was passed by the Imperial Diet without modification on October 10. The main focus of the revised proposal was on lowering the upper limit of land ownership from 5 *cho* that the cabinet meeting had decided earlier to 1 *cho*, which was close to Matsumura's original proposal.

Although the agrarian reform in Japan during the occupation period thus took the form of a reform imposed by GHQ, it should be regarded as the fruition of long-standing dreams and efforts by agricultural officials since the Taishō Democracy.


## Diet Deliberation on a New Constitution

The greatest task given to the first Yoshida cabinet was to accomplish the amendment of the Meiji Constitution. A draft of the revised constitution was introduced in the House of Representatives on June 25 and passed by the House on August 24. After undergoing a few modifications in the House of Peers, the draft was once again passed by the lower house to be promulgated on November 3.

According to Thomas Bisson, through the above deliberation some 30 modifications were applied to the draft. He said, "All the modifications were, de facto, revisions that GHQ had demanded."

Bisson had been dispatched to China as a missionary before becoming a China scholar at Columbia University. Having participated in a movement to support the "Chinese People's Resistance against Japanese Aggression," he was a typical pro-China individual and a radical leftwing activist who, according to John Dower, believed that only those Japanese who had been suppressed or imprisoned during the war could create a new Japan. Assigned to GHQ's Government Section from March 1946 until May 1947, when constitutional reform was the central issue there, Bisson's memoir is filled with the record of successes and setbacks of the radical New Dealers' attempts at the leftist reform of Japan.

As Bisson describes above, the Diet deliberation on the new constitution was almost totally under GHQ's thumb except for the following few cases. When the wish of GHQ was known, nobody dared to oppose it. While freedom of speech was severely restricted and no remark against GHQ policy was tolerated outside the Imperial Diet, people were supposedly free to speak their minds inside the Diet. And yet, hardly any remark was heard against GHQ's policy. Everyone in Japan was aware that, even though the Japanese investigation had found that Hatoyama should be spared from the purge he was purged, nonetheless only because his words and deeds incurred the wrath of the occupation forces. Because everyone in Japan had cooperated with the country's war effort in one way or another during World War II, anyone suspected of saying or doing something against GHQ's policy was liable to a sudden purge based on his past "wrongdoings." Diet deliberations on the new constitution were conducted at a time when Japanese politicians were all caught up in such fear.

At the outset of the deliberations, Yoshida announced that, while the Imperial Diet was "theoretically" entitled to modify the draft constitution, "in light of the current international situation," discretion was called for when proposing revisions because the draft had been prepared "in full consideration of various possible developments within and outside Japan." Everyone who heard Yoshida could read between the lines.

Thus, such a perfunctory argument that the new constitution was "supported by the majority of Diet members whom Japanese voters had elected of their own free will" was far removed from the reality of Japan under occupation.

Nevertheless, the Diet deliberations raised several critical issues.

The first issue was the procedures to be taken to amend the constitution. Because the Meiji Constitution had been laid down by Imperial edict, its amendment was possible only when, by Article 73, the Emperor ordered the Imperial Diet to deliberate the revision. Under the Meiji Constitution, therefore, nobody other than the Emperor was entitled to propose a constitutional amendment.

During discussions at the Privy Council before the Diet deliberation, Minobe Tatsukichi remained adamantly insistent on revising the amendment procedures. His stance was that the current procedure was a violation of the Potsdam Declaration's article 12—i.e., ". . . in accordance with the freely expressed will of the Japanese people."

This issue of inconsistency with the Potsdam Declaration was taken care of by an Imperial rescript issued after the draft constitution was submitted to the House of Representatives. The Imperial rescript read, "We . . . wish to have the constitution of Japan revised in accordance with the freely expressed will of the Japanese people and, by Article 73 of the Imperial Constitution, submit a draft of the revised Imperial Constitution to the Imperial Diet for members' deliberation." There would have been no other way out.

There was, however, one thing that the Japanese could not concede no matter what GHQ said and that was the issue of *kokutai* (国体) or national polity centered around the Emperor. When Japan accepted the Potsdam Declaration, it adamantly demanded preservation of *kokutai* as the condition for acceptance.

And it was also over this issue that Bisson, who had been engaged in the constitutional amendment at GHQ's Government Section, expressed his disappointment on the "unfortunate compromise," after discussing intensively on this point with hardly any reference to other points, including Article 9.

In a nutshell, Bisson's discontent concerned a single point. The Japanese side unbendingly insisted on the word "*kokumin*" where the original U.S. draft used "people," which should have been translated as "*jinmin*." The Japanese side also insisted on the use of "nation" in the English version instead of "people." The debate was over a portion of the Constitution of Japan's preamble that reads ". . . do proclaim that sovereign power resides with the people" and Article 1 which says, "The Emperor shall be the symbol of the State and of the unity of the people, deriving his position from the will of the people with whom resides sovereign power."

As aptly pointed out by the interpretation of the new constitution contributed jointly by Ashida Hitoshi and Abe Yoshishige to the *Asahi Shimbun* newspaper on October 18, 1946, the view of Bisson and his associates was based on the perception that "From ancient times, a state has been perceived in the West as a dualistic entity composed of those who govern and those who are governed."

The American War of Independence, for instance, was a war of resistance by the American people against the British king. The French Revolution, too, was a people's victory over the monarchy. By extension, Bisson believed that the purpose of the new constitution of Japan should be to retrieve sovereignty from the Emperor and give it to the Japanese people. But the above-quoted *Asahi Shimbun* commentary co-authored by Ashida and Abe declared that "sovereignty resides in the community of people and the Emperor," and "sovereignty belongs to the people as a whole, which includes the Emperor" and concluded that "Because the new constitution does not alter the foundation of Japan's existence as a state, it would not affect the national polity centered around the Emperor."

This was a consistent stance of the Japanese government.

On June 26, 1946, the *Jiyūtō*'s Kita Reikichi said in the representative interpellation at the Diet, "Since ancient times, Japan has long been co-governed jointly by the Emperor and his subjects. If one has to use the term sovereignty, it resides in the entity that encompasses both the Emperor and his subjects." In response, Prime Minister Yoshida Shigeru replied,

> I believe the Imperial family is our national polity itself that has emerged spontaneously in Japan. There exists no distinction between the Imperial family and the people, forming a so-called sovereign-subjects unity or a sovereign-subjects family . . . The national polity centered around the Emperor shall not be affected at all by the new constitution (applause).

Bisson deplored this remark, saying, "Yoshida schemed to integrate the Emperor into the people so that there would be no conflict or disunion of will between the two." He then expressed his concern, questioning, "If the interpretation that the Emperor shares a part of sovereignty is justified, would it not mean that it is constitutionally justifiable to strengthen the Emperor's power and authority when political situations become more favorable in the future?"

The Japanese government thus succeeded in making the preservation of the national polity centered around the Emperor, which had been its consistent position since the acceptance of the Potsdam Declaration, somehow compatible with the new constitution, at least on the surface if not in substance.

In this way, Japan became the only state in the 20th century that maintained its monarchy even after losing a war.

To what, one wonders, was this unique accomplishment attributable. In his representative interpellation, Kita Reikichi said:

> Unlike European countries, [Japan] does not have the history of direct contests for political power between the Emperor and the people. Contests for power in Japan, instead, have taken the form of strife among feudal elements, court nobles, and samurai clans, who were positioned in the middle between the Emperor and the people, as well as between samurai clans and court nobles.

Certainly, at least as far as the modern era was concerned, the emperor system of Japan was different from the three monarchies in Russia, Germany, and Austria, all of which perished by World War I. Even Emperor Meiji, who was called "Emperor Meiji the Great," did not use his power in a way that made his behavior subject to calls for responsibility like Kaiser and the Czar. Nor did Emperor Shōwa.

Japan's history and tradition that regarded the Emperor not as a substance with power but as an object of worship, coupled with Emperor Shōwa's distinct personality that evoked people's love and respect, must have contributed to such an outcome—that is, the survival of the emperor system even after defeat in a war. Such a thing was rare in the history of the world.

## Forever Renounce War . . .

The issue of Article 9's renunciation of war had already been settled with the draft constitution that the U.S. side delivered to the Japanese government on February 13 and the Shidehara-MacArthur talk on February 21.

After this, there was a tacit understanding among members at cabinet meetings as well as the Imperial Diet that this article already was an unmovable fait accompli. It was only the Communist Party, which as an outsider to the power center had no fear of being purged, that dared to challenge such fundamental issues as the right of self-defense. What was left for the Japanese side to do was to sort out peripheral issues.

At the Imperial Diet discussion on the renunciation of war, Hara Fujirō of the *Shimpotō* party questioned what measures (treaties with other countries, etc.) the government was contemplating in case Japan was invaded. Even as he posed his question, Hara acknowledged the inevitability of the war renunciation clause, saying, "In light of various international situations, it is more than easy to imagine that, in the end, Japan was cornered into accepting insertion of this clause."

In response, after clarifying at the outset that "the current draft does not directly deny Japan's right to self-defense," Yoshida said:

So far, many modern wars have been fought in the name of self-defense . . . Japan has been seriously suspected of being a belligerent country that could threaten world peace any time by rearming itself and waging a war of vengeance. This has been the gravest misunderstanding of our country today . . . Therefore, Japan's spontaneous renunciation of the right of belligerency would provide the foundation for world peace under whatever name . . .

When, subsequently, the Communist Party's Nosaka Sanzō requested that Yoshida reply to Nosaka's question that "When there are justified wars and unjust wars, would it not be more accurate to say that Japan would renounce a war of invasion," Yoshida responded by saying that it would do more harm to recognize a country's right to justifiable defense.

It seems undeniable that these and other remarks by Yoshida brought confusion to subsequent discussions on self-defense or, more specifically, on the establishment of the National Safety Forces in 1952 and, eventually, the Self-Defense Forces in 1954.

And Yoshida cannot escape the charge of saying something so thoughtless that he himself had to ask, "Did I really say that?" later.

At this point, however, Yoshida must have spoken for MacArthur, who wanted to impress the zero percent probability of Japan's rearmament on the Far Eastern Commission, being *plus royal que roi* (more royalist than the king) or, in this case, more MacArthur-like than MacArthur himself.

The situation in those days was such that the basic principle adopted on July 2 by the Far Eastern Commission included abolition of the Emperor system as its primary choice. And GHQ's Government Section had even implied replacement of indirect rule with military administration. Whether conversion to a military administration after one year into the occupation was possible at all or not, it must have been best for the Japanese government to play it safe by sending a message that it would be absolutely inconceivable for Japan to rearm. It must have also been deemed that playing it safe would contribute to early termination of the occupation.

It is not hard to imagine that these remarks by Yoshida, which were fully aligned with MacArthur's strategy, pleased MacArthur.

One of the shortcomings of a military man's strategy is the lack of long-term perspectives. For a war, winning or losing is everything.

But politics and wars are quite different in certain aspects.

The legal contradiction over the interpretation of the right of self-defense was regarded as only of secondary significance in light of the importance of the mission to protect the emperor system and indirect rule by eliminating the Far Eastern Commission's interference. It is this kind of attitude that eventually elicited confusion regarding Japan's security policies for more than half a century after the occupation.

It should be noted, however, that politicians in Japan did not leave this issue of the right of self-defense entirely unattended to even though they were fully aware of the position that Japan was placed in those days.

A Committee on the Bill for Revision of the Imperial Constitution, for instance, was launched on July 1, 1946, with Ashida Hitoshi as its chairman and a subcommittee was established under it, again with Ashida as its chairman. The issue of the new constitution was intensively discussed in the subcommittee. This intensive deliberation resulted in the draft constitution compiled on August 20, including the so-called Ashida revisions on Article 9.

These Ashida revisions are still visible today in the Constitution of Japan. The phrase "Aspiring sincerely to an international peace based on justice and order" at the outset of Article 9 was added as the result of the Ashida revisions.

The Article says that the Japanese people would not aspire to just any kind of peace. Peace is no good if it is not "based on justice and order." And this kind of peace would require either an international organization like a world government that can maintain international justice and order or maintenance of international order through the balance of power among countries capable of self-defense and protecting freedom. The logical conclusion of this clause was that it would not be enough to simply repeat the mantra of peace. That was what the Ashida revisions added to the Japanese constitution.

Then came a much more important revision. "In order to accomplish the aim of the preceding paragraph, land, sea, and air forces, as well as other war potential, will never be maintained" was added to Article 9 by the Ashida revisions.

The addition of this clause made it possible to interpret that Japan would not "maintain land, sea, and air forces as well as other war potential" specifically to "accomplish the aim of the preceding paragraph." The war referred to in the previous paragraph was a "war as a sovereign right of the nation" and a war as "means of settling international disputes," and, therefore, a war of self-defense was clearly not included. This way, the Ashida revisions provided room for interpreting it that Japan could maintain means for a war of self-defense.

During the deliberations at the subcommittee, Ashida never explained clearly that this revision was applied so that Japan would be able to exercise its right of self-defense in the future. Omission of this explanation was only natural. Had Ashida overtly explained, it would have nullified Yoshida's laborious efforts to fend off the Far Eastern Commission's critical eyes. And yet, the unspoken purpose of this revision by Ashida, a scholar diplomat whose brain was always clearly organized, should be obvious.

When Ashida asked for Charles Kades' approval on his revisions, Kades agreed with them immediately. To Ashida who asked if Kades should not consult with MacArthur or Courtney Whitney first, Kades replied, "It's OK. No problem."

When, subsequently, Kades' subordinates started making a fuss about the Ashida revisions, saying "they would allow Japan to rearm," Kades argued back that it would be too much to deprive Japan of its right of self-defense, which resulted in his subordinates' bringing the matter up directly with Whitney. To the Government Section's staff who complained that Japan could now rearm, Whitney brushed off their complaints, saying, "So what? Don't you think it is a good idea?"

As a matter of fact, the three principles of the Japanese constitution that MacArthur presented to GHQ staff members on February 3 included a clause proclaiming that Japan would renounce "even a war to maintain its own security." When Kades deleted this particular clause, MacArthur acknowledged his action. And that was why Kades approved the Ashida revisions then and there without consultation with his superiors.

This means that approval of Japan's right of self-defense had already become a consensus among top leaders of GHQ without Kades' subordinates' knowledge and that Yoshida, unknowingly, forged ahead along MacArthur's line of thinking. Whether Yoshida had known of this or not, though, it can be said that Yoshida must have felt that he had no other option than to go along with this line in public in order to cope with the Far Eastern Commission.

Ashida, on the other hand, had absolutely no knowledge of this consensus among GHQ's leadership. But, then again, it was not a case of an aimless attempt hitting the mark. In the end, both Kades and Ashida just followed where logic directed.

The Far Eastern Commission also became aware of the implication of the Ashida revisions. On September 21, the Chinese delegate to the Commission pointed out the possibility of the Ashida revisions to Article 9 paving way for the future rearmament of Japan. Accordingly, the Commission demanded insertion of a clause that cabinet members would be limited only to civilians, with which GHQ concurred.

It was actually strange to ban appointment of a military man to the cabinet when there was no longer any military and, therefore, no military men in Japan. Although the Imperial Diet took issue with this, it had to accept the insertion of this clause particularly in the face of strong pressure from GHQ. This insertion is still intact in Article 66 as "The prime minister and other ministers of state must be *bunmin* (civilians)."

A civilian in English is an antonym to a soldier, warrior, and samurai. But in Japanese *bunjin* or *bunshi*, the traditional antonyms to *"gunjin* (military man)" mean "a man of letters" and "a literary man." This is somewhat different from what the word *civilian* refers to. If cabinet members were limited to men of letters or literary men, it would be next to impossible to form a cabinet. Also, since politicians were not bureaucrats, however, they could not be referred to as civil servants, either. Hence, *bunmin*, a word that had not existed in the Japanese vocabulary, was invented and is still in use in the Constitution of Japan.

In retrospect, it was theoretically possible to officially recognize Japan's right of self-defense when the Far Eastern Commission did not demand withdrawal of the Ashida revisions and, instead, requested insertion of a clause on the limitation of cabinet members to civilians. Nevertheless, there were objective conditions in those days that made the Yoshida cabinet, as well as MacArthur himself, hesitate to openly declare Japan's right of self-defense.

On October 17, 1946, just before the promulgation of the Constitution of Japan on November 3, the Far Eastern Commission decided on a regulation on reassessing the new constitution. In line with that decision, MacArthur gave the following notice in his letter of January 3, 1947, to Yoshida:

> The Allies of World War II decided that the Constitution of Japan should be officially reexamined one or two years after promulgation. If the Allies find it desirable, they may request implementation of such procedures as a national referendum in order to directly ascertain the Japanese people's views on the new constitution.

While the true intention of this notification can be interpreted in various ways, one thing that was clear was that, whether Japan adopted a new constitution or not, it was the Allies that ruled Japan and they had not yet restored sovereignty. Shidehara Kijūrō never disclosed the content of his talk with MacArthur on January 24, 1946, and that was because the occupation had not been terminated before he died. Until the end of the occupation, Japan was in no position to talk freely about its right of self-defense.

After prohibiting the February 1 General Strike, MacArthur wrote a letter to Yoshida on February 7, 1947, instructing that the Diet be dissolved and a general election be held under the new constitution. The results of the House of Councilors election on April 20 and the general election on April 25 put the period to the first Yoshida cabinet.

# CHAPTER
# 8

# The Tokyo Trials (1)

*—The Worst Hypocrisy in History—*

## Was It a Fair Trial? (Willoughby)

What was the International Military Tribunal for the Far East, or the Tokyo Trials all about?

Even though this event has been discussed repeatedly, I would still like to briefly review all the facts of the Tribunal for the benefit of my readers and give some thought to the content of the trials.

First I have to point out that before World War II there had been no precedent for this kind of war tribunal. While it was decided at the end of World War I that Kaiser of Germany had to be tried in accordance with the Treaty of Versailles, the trial did not take place because the Netherlands, where Kaiser sought asylum, refused to hand him over to the Allied Powers. In the course of events, views were expressed questioning the legal grounds for the proposed trial. While Britain retained its positive stance toward the need for a trial, the United States and Japan became skeptical. Thus, this attempt did not quite succeed at setting a precedent for a war tribunal.

During World War II, the Allied countries had expressed their intention to punish war criminals once the war was won. They were stimulated by the international criticism of the Jewish Holocaust and the forced labor of residents of the occupied territories.

Once Germany surrendered, the United States, Britain, France, and the Soviet Union concluded an agreement on the treatment of war criminals on August 8, 1945. During the consultations on the agreement, the four powers determined that, "The war initiated by Germany was a war of aggression and an international criminal act. Therefore, acts by the United States to assist peoples who had been unlawfully and unjustly attacked by Germany were justifiable."

One of the intentions behind this agreement was the justification of the political and economic pressures that the United States had imposed on Germany before its participation in the war against Germany. These pressures included the provision of arms to Britain and giving permission to the U.S. Navy to fire on German submarines—both violations of neutrality.

In light of this background, it might have been futile from the start for Japan to insist that the Greater East Asia War was a war of self-defense against the economic blockade by the United States or to contemplate the consequences had it not attacked Pearl Harbor. If it had already been established that all of Japan's wars after the Manchurian Incident were unjust, and that, thus, the American economic blockade was a justifiable sanction against Japan, and that both the United States and the Soviet Union, which participated in the war at its last stage, had fought to punish Japan because it had started an unjust war, it would have been useless no matter what Japan had argued. Simply put, losers are always in the wrong. As a matter of fact, it seems undeniable that this view not only formed an undercurrent of the International Military Tribunal for the Far East but also that it continued to affect the historical view on Japan for a long time to come, even in Japan.

Article 10 of the Potsdam Declaration issued on July 26, 1945, declares, ". . . stern justice shall be meted out to all war criminals, including those who have visited cruelties upon our prisoners." The Japanese government accepted this Declaration. The Declaration did not say that war crimes included starting an unjust war. It only singled out "those who have visited cruelties upon our prisoners"—which had been clearly prohibited by international laws of wartime. This became a source of controversy during the Tokyo Trials. Nevertheless, it was decided that Japan would be tried

The Tokyo Trial

by a war tribunal even though it had not conducted any acts that could arouse the intense hatred comparable to that incited by the actions of Nazi Germany. Today, there remains an attitude to put the Nanjing Incident on a par with the Holocaust. This is one of the causes of resentment and grudges among the Japanese people toward the Tokyo Trials.

The war tribunal to try Germany, the so-called Nuremburg trials, started on November 20, 1945. All the major sentences were passed by October 1946.

The Tokyo Trials more or less followed the pattern set by the Nuremburg trials with a few minor procedural modifications such as the compositions of judges and prosecutors. The Tokyo Trials lasted for two and a half years from May 1946 through November 1948.

The Tokyo Trials began with a debate on the legitimacy of the court to pass judgment on war crimes. Upon rejection of the motion by the chief justice, chief prosecutor Joseph Keenan gave an opening statement on June 4. The presentation of evidence by prosecutors began the same day and continued until early 1947.

On January 27, 1947, a *pro forma* appeal for discontinuance of the trial was submitted by counsels on the grounds that the prosecutors had failed to establish the guilt of the accused. The appeal was naturally turned down.

Defense by counsels commenced on February 24, 1947, and lasted until January 12, 1948. Each of the accused, including Tōjō Hideki, had submitted an affidavit. Defense was followed by refutation by prosecutors, surrebuttal by counsels, closing arguments by prosecutors, and the summation—after which the court was adjourned for six months. The judgment was read in November; the seven defendants who were sentenced to death were executed on December 23, 1948.

At a glance, it appeared as if due procedures of a war tribunal had all been implemented and thorough discussions had been exchanged before sentencing. In actuality, however, it can be said that, by conducting all the necessary procedures within a limited time, the discussions at the tribunal ended up being empty in terms of substance. As a matter of fact, the legitimacy issue raised at the outset of the tribunal remained shelved throughout the trial. And, substance-wise, the final verdict was almost like a carbon copy of the prosecutors' opening statement.

The only deviation from prosecutors' accusations that the sentence showed were such nonsensical arguments as a conspiracy among defendants to conquer the entire world and the accusation that Japan had invaded Thailand. In the first case, sufficient evidence was lacking, although the defendants were proven to harbor a conspiracy to conquer the Far East. The second case was found to be groundless.

Although it took two and a half years to try the war crimes of the accused, it would have taken an equal amount of time to try a single murderer in peace time and much longer to hand down the death sentence. It is, therefore, unthinkable that the responsibility of each and every one of dozens of the Japanese in leading positions during 15 years of world turmoil could be examined in such a short period of time and that seven of them could be executed so quickly.

The only way to make such a thing possible must have been to prepare a scenario at the outset and manage to reach the conclusion as laid out by the scenario. This would make it necessary to meticulously follow due procedure, lining up all the favorable testimonies and rejecting all the inconvenient ones. This must have been the only way to reach the same conclusion. And it would not be an overstatement to say that this was exactly what took place during the Tokyo Trials.

The Tokyo Trials have been repeatedly talked about in Japan and continue to be discussed even today.

It is already obvious to anyone that the tribunal was a unilateral measure toward a war loser taken by the war winner. Should it, then, be lost in history? Japanese still talk about the Tokyo Trials because the historical view that permeated the Tribunal still continues to affect the way that they view history.

And one of the reasons this peculiar historical view still remains with the Japanese is GHQ's severe control of freedom of speech for the near-seven years of the occupation: GHQ did not tolerate the questioning of this view. Another reason is the role of the strongly communist-affiliated Japan Teachers' Union and Japan Federation of Newspaper Workers' Unions, which take an anti-government, self-loathing view of Japan, in protecting this perception in GHQ's stead.

Thus, it all boils down to whether the Allies had the authority to conduct a war tribunal to begin with. If they had not been authorized to do so, then, the argument goes, all of the tribunal's verdicts as well as the permeating historical view would have been invalid.

In this chapter, the legitimacy of the Tokyo Trials will be discussed. Chapter 9 will revisit the issue of the controversial historical view. This is really the very theme that permeates this entire volume.

## Winner Judges Loser

First we must contemplate whether the Allies had the legitimacy to try the war criminals. For this purpose, I think it best to revisit the words of Kiyose Ichirō and Takayanagi Kenzō, two of the chief counsels at the Tokyo Trials.

Readers, however, should be informed that the reading of part of Kiyose's and the whole of Takayanagi's opening statements had been banned at the Tribunal until final arguments. The chief justice dismissed Kiyose's argument without giving the reason, saying, "The time will come in the future to disclose the reason." Takayanagi's argument was rejected for the reason that it was essentially the same as Kiyose's and that Kiyose's argument had already been dismissed. The chief justice turned away their arguments, so to speak, at the door.

Had this issue been dealt with squarely, the Allies would have had no theoretical grounds for winning the debate, which would have made the Tribunal itself invalid. Therefore, the Allies had no choice but to push through their own way, saying that the opening of the Tribunal had already been decided.

The Japanese side argued that Japan had accepted the surrender per conditions stipulated in the Potsdam Declaration before the Allied forces landed on Japan. The claim was that this differentiated Japan from Germany, which had continued to fight until its entire territory was occupied.

Certainly, Japan and Germany were different.

At the Nuremberg trials, it was clearly stated that the regulations of the court were "based on the supreme legislative power of the Allies to which Germany surrendered unconditionally."

Before Germany surrendered, its government had already ceased to exist due to the physical occupation by the Allies. Because the occupation forces monopolized power, they could do anything they pleased. This situation was endorsed by the surrender document signed by Karl Dönitz, who was named Hitler's successor as Head of State, with the title of *Reichspräsident* (President) and Supreme Commander of the Armed Forces, after Hitler's death. While the concept of *nulla poena sine lege* ("no penalty without a law," meaning that one cannot be punished for doing something that is not prohibited by law) is a grand principle of civilized countries ruled by law, state sovereignty is by no means bound by it. Although the United States makes much of the formality of a court trial, it could have done anything if it had declared itself an uncivilized country. It could have even decided to simply hang Hitler without taking the trouble of trying him in a court of justice and justified that as an act of sovereignty. As a matter of fact, Robert Jackson, chief United States prosecutor at the Nuremberg trials, once said, "If we so wish, we can execute defendants without a trial." Justice Radhabinod Pal, representing India, at the Tokyo Trials deplored this statement, saying, "It is unbelievable that someone can speak like that in the 20th century."

In contrast, Japan was not yet occupied by the Allies when it surrendered. Japan could have gone on fighting and inflicted more sacrifices on the Allied forces. And yet, Japan chose to stop fighting and surrender, following the conditions offered by the Allies.

The Potsdam Declaration that Japan accepted did include an article on an unconditional surrender by the Japanese military, but it did not refer to the unconditional surrender by the Japanese government. Recognizing the presence of a functional government in Japan, the Declaration stipulated that the orders of the occupation forces authority would be executed by the Japanese government. The Japanese side could have insisted that, following the principles of international law at the time of Japan's surrender, the relations between the Allies and Japan within Japan should follow Japanese laws.

It would have been a perfectly valid legal argument. Nevertheless, public opinion in the United States and other Allied countries at that time were in no mood to differentiate Japan from Germany. All the public cared about was to punish the likes of Hitler, Mussolini, and Tōjō.

Even today, Japan is affected by its one-time alliance with Germany. As I have mentioned in various places, the Nazi's Holocaust was an ethnic cleansing policy unrelated to a war. Nevertheless, it has been treated as if it were on par with the Nanjing Incident. The Nanjing Incident was a problem of noncombatants being victimized in the course of a war. In that sense, the Nanjing Incident belongs in the same group with the atomic bombings on Hiroshima and Nagasaki, the massive air raids on Tokyo and Dresden, and the brutal conduct of the Soviet military in Berlin and Manchuria.

Matsuoka Yōsuke's reckless, arbitrary conduct in concluding the Tripartite Pact adversely affected Japan even after the end of the war.

The hearings at the Tokyo Trials proceeded even though the issue of the legitimacy of the court remained shelved. The court clarified its position on this issue in the final verdict.

First, it argued that the Tokyo Trials derived legitimacy from the Charter of the International Military Tribunal, which was laid down by the Supreme Commander of the Allied Powers. Therefore, the court argued, the Japanese side had a duty and a responsibility to comply with the Charter. In effect, the court brushed off the issue of the Charter's legitimacy right from the get-go.

The final verdict argued that the Tokyo Trials completely agreed with the rulings at the Nuremberg trials. But readers should be reminded that the major emphasis of rulings at the Nuremberg trials was placed on Germany's violation of the international law at that time. As counsels for the Japanese defendants at the Tokyo Trials pointed out, however, there was an insurmountable gap between the violation of international law and the opening of a trial to pronounce death sentences on those who were responsible for the crimes. While an explanation that this gap was ignored by an act of sovereignty by the occupation forces might be acceptable in the case of Germany, it would not be conceivable at all in the case of Japan.

Seeing as the Nuremberg trials' rulings came out after Japan had accepted the Potsdam Declaration, there was no international custom at that time to try war criminals. According to Takayanagi, Japanese leaders would have considered the option of not accepting the Potsdam Declaration if they had known that its acceptance would mean such an outcome as the Tokyo Trials.

In the portion of his opening statement that he was banned from reading at the Tokyo Trials, Kiyose argued that the Potsdam Declaration did not necessarily allow the occupation forces to behave as they pleased, quoting the declaration's phase, "Following are our terms 'We will not deviate from them." Kiyose stressed that the occupation forces must follow the principles of international law and refrain from blaming individuals for a country's conduct.

Of course, it was utterly useless to argue these points. In one word, you ought to win a war if you want to have your own way.

On these interactions, Kobori Keiichirō, Shōwa scholar of literature and conservative commentator, offered a highly vivid metaphor based on the peace negotiation scene in William Shakespeare's *Henry IV* between Prince John, son of Henry IV, and his archrival the Archbishop of York.

The Archbishop's side showed a determination to put up thorough resistance if its peace conditions were not accepted and stressed there would be others to follow the Archbishop when he fell. In response, Prince John said, "We accept all the conditions on our honor as the king's family . . . Your Excellency, you have my word that we will correct all the inconveniences. Please dissolve your forces and we will do the same." These words induced the successful conclusion of the peace negotiation.

As soon as it was known that the Archbishop's forces were dissolved, Prince John arrested the Archbishop for treason.

Suppressing protests from the Archbishop's side against the unfairness, Prince John ordered, "Take these traitors to the guillotine, their proper bed and place of death." Once a loser is disarmed, it has no physical power to force the winner to keep its promises, giving the winner a free hand.

## Punishment by an Ex Post Facto Law

Because the Tokyo Trials were from the outset a kind of high-handed conduct by the Allies, they displayed countless procedural shortcomings.

To begin with, the appointment of judges itself was heteroclite. Having appointed the American lawyer Joseph Keenan as chief prosecutor in accordance with MacArthur's wishes, GHQ appointed the Australian lawyer William Webb, with whom MacArthur had gotten acquainted during the Pacific War, as president of the Tokyo Trials in order to avoid both the chief prosecutor and the president of court being Americans.

Before the appointment, Webb had written a report that said there had been a massacre of noncombatants by the Imperial Japanese Army at the time of its attack on Rabaul. It is unthinkable in a country ruled by law for a person who has been personally involved in a case to be a judge of a court that tries the very case. Even in Australia, Webb's homeland, criticism was heard on what appeared to be something akin to appointing a detective who had investigated a crime as a judge of the court trying that case.

Counsel Kiyose Ichirō proposed a motion to challenge President William Webb at the outset of the trial, but the judges rejected it because "all the judges of the Tokyo Trials were appointed by General MacArthur and none can be absent from the trial." What really happened was that Joseph Keenan crashed the gate as the judges were consulting on this motion and denounced the consultation, saying, "Such a waste of time is against MacArthur's policy. He is hoping for a prompt trial." In a nutshell, Keenan insisted that there was no time to waste on such a matter.

American lawyer Ben Bruce Blakeney, who served as a defense counsel at the Tokyo Trials, made a more fundamental argument as follows:

> The plaintiff of this trial is the countries that have fought with and defeated Japan. Moreover, all the judges of this tribunal are representatives of the plaintiff countries and so are prosecutors. Therefore, the trial cannot escape suspicion of being unfair today as well as in the eyes of future historians. Only a trial by neutral countries is legal, and only such a trial by neutral parties can make fair and commonsensical judgments.

Also at play here were differences in the styles of a trial between Anglo-Saxon courts and continental courts. This difference provided a background to Judge Bernardo Roling from the Netherlands and Judge Henri Bernard from France, who each attached a minority view to the verdict.

In the continental legal system, the prosecutor acts to represent fair public interest as a state institution. Under the Anglo-Saxon legal system, in contrast, prosecutor and counsel confront one another, presenting only favorable evidence and withholding unfavorable evidence, sparring vigorously with one another in order to convince the neutral and impartial judge to decide in their favor.

In other words, the Anglo-Saxon legal system assures an impartial check-and-balance of power between plaintiff and defendant, but it works only when the presiding judge is neutral and impartial.

When judges are all from war winners, i.e. representatives of the plaintiff, however, there is obviously no hope for an impartial judgment. Nor can there be an impartial balance of power between a war winner and a war loser.

Particularly disadvantageous for the defendant side was the difficulty in gathering evidence. With nothing to start with, counsels had to run around in the midst of hunger and destitution to collect relevant material. In contrast, all the GHQ side had to do was to order the Japanese government to submit, for instance, "reference material on so and so conference convened on so and so date."

Also noteworthy was the fact that decisions on the adoption or rejection of evidence was left to a majority vote among judges. This system of sorting and rejecting evidence has been well developed in the Anglo-Saxon courts to prevent juries, who are laymen in the law, from making the wrong decisions based on evidence lacking evidential capacity. In short, it is a system to protect juries from erroneous information. What happened at the Tokyo Trials was an abuse of this system by which judges representing plaintiff countries decided by majority vote to adopt or reject evidence. It was obvious that this was disadvantageous for the Japanese defendants.

In 1995 (7th Year of Heisei), the Tokyo Saiban Shiryō Kankō-kai under the leadership of Kobori Kiichirō published an eight-volume, few-thousand-pages-long *Tokyo Saiban Kyakka Miteishutu Bengogawa Shiryō* (Compilation of Defense Counsels' Evidence that Was Rejected and Unadopted by the International Military Tribunal for the Far East). This compilation was a historic accomplishment.

According to Kiyose Ichirō, who is quoted in the preamble of this document,

A massive amount of material submitted by counsels was rejected. Particularly, statements by the Japanese government were right from the start not even considered because they were judged to be self-serving . . . Even the statements issued jointly with the Chiang Kai-shek and Wang Jingwei regimes of the time, which were really historical documents, were all rejected. I would say perhaps eight out of ten pieces of evidence that the counsel side submitted were rejected.

On this remark by Kiyose, Kobori reflected that "the total rejection by the Tokyo Trials of all the official statements of the Japanese government at that time" was "an interesting testimony to the fact that this court had no ear for 'Japan's say' from the beginning."

The most fundamental question concerning a war tribunal is the issue around the principle that laws must not be retroactive. It is a matter of *nulla poena sine lege* (no penalty without a law) or that of an ex post facto law. It is argued that a war tribunal violates a grand principle of the civilized world that one should not be punished for legal conduct that becomes a crime only under a law enacted after the conduct has taken place.

Over this issue, a legal expert could develop a meticulous argument or, more properly, talk like a pettifogger. It can even be argued defiantly that there is no rule that a law cannot be applied retroactively. As a matter of fact, the Nazi law of 1935 allowed judges to try defendants based on "healthy national sentiment." This means a German at that time could be punished if he committed an act that the public opinion found intolerable even when there was no law that was applicable. The rise of such ex post facto law is and, indeed, has been possible in a totalitarian society like Nazi Germany and in the height of flared up national sentiment in a war winner.

By quoting an antiwar treaty, one could also argue that a war tribunal is not a case of ex post facto law. However, when a country signs an antiwar treaty, it customarily attaches various reservations. Among the rejected materials submitted by defense counsels were the proceedings of the U.S. Congress' session in December 1928 on the so-called Kellogg-Briand Antiwar Pact. It was recorded in the proceedings that U.S. Secretary of

State Frank Kellogg stated that this pact would not prohibit the right of self-defense and that it would be up to the government concerned to determine whether a combat was an act of self-defense. He continued to say,

> The government of the United States would by no means agree to entrust the issue of self-defense to any court at all. . . . The right of self-defense is not confined to the mainland U.S. . . . The United States itself must be the judge of this issue. . . . If what the United States is facing is not a justifiable act of self-defense by the opponent, we can appeal to the public opinion of the world. That is all it takes.

If that was indeed what the United States had believed in, then Japan, too, had had the right to determine itself whether Japan's war had indeed been a war of self-defense.

Even if Japan's war was judged to be beyond the boundary of self-defense, the punishment it should expect would have been, at most, criticisms from international public opinion. One should recall the case of the Soviet Union being expelled from the League of Nations after attacking the Baltic countries and Finland and, later, condemned by the United Nations as the result of suppression of the Hungarian Revolution of 1956 and interference with the Prague Spring in 1968.

And, even in these cases, it was the state, not an individual, that was condemned. If an individual was to be punished, Stalin would have had to have been executed. Nowhere in the Kellogg-Briand Antiwar Pact was there even a hint of the possibility for leaders of a war-losing country to be condemned and executed after the war.

Setting these detailed legal arguments aside, it is plain to anyone that, from a broader perspective, a war tribunal is a trial based on an ex post facto law.

According to legal scholar Taoka Ryōichi, Robert Taft, one of the most respected senators in U.S. history, stressed in his October 1946 speech after the Nuremberg trials that it would be useless for the war winner to try and punish war losers with an ex post facto law in order to prevent future wars of aggression. Taft explained the reason was that those who started a war of aggression were always confident that they would win. He continued to say:

Far from being a realization of justice, the Nuremberg trials were an expression of vengeance of the part of the Allies. The execution of German prisoners of war was a huge blot on the history of the United States, and I earnestly hope the same error will not be made in Japan.

Taft's wish notwithstanding, the same error was repeated in Tokyo in the form of the International Military Tribunal for the Far East.

As Pal, an Indian judge at the International Military Tribunal, wrote, "A trial of war criminals according to definitions of crimes given by the war winner would be tantamount to denial of the development of civilization in the past few centuries that divide the ancient times when the defeated was completely annihilated and our own time."

War tribunals have been conducted even in the post–Cold War world against Cambodia's Pol Pot and Slobodan Milosevic of Yugoslavia. International tribunals in the name of humanity will continue to be carried out in the future.

Only time can tell whether this is a good thing or not. As far as the Nuremberg trials and the International Military Tribunal for the Far East are concerned, however, it cannot be said that they followed historical precedence.

Even if an international norm should be established in the 21st century that allows punishment of atrocious inhumane conduct with an ex post facto law, the question still remains whether Japan's conduct during the Pacific War, which was tried at the International Military Tribunal for the Far East, was indeed comparable to the Nazi's Holocaust, Stalin's Great Purge, the mass tortures and murders during the Great Proletarian Cultural Revolution, the annihilation of the Cambodian middle class by Pol Pot, and the ethnic cleansing attempt by Milosevic.

Even President Webb of the Tokyo Trials, who harbored an inherently strong anti-Japanese sentiment, admitted the existence of this question. In the personal view that he submitted as a supplementary remark to the court decisions, which he supported, Webb pointed out that "crimes committed by German defendants were much more atrocious, versatile, and extensive than those of the Tokyo Trials defendants. . . ."

On five German defendants, including Rudolf Hess and Karl Dönitz, who were spared from the death sentence by the Nuremberg trials, Webb continued to write as follows.

I believe the Nuremberg trials decision took into consideration the fact that a war of aggression in general had not been regarded as conduct punishable by a court when Germany started the war in Europe. Up until today, many authorities of international law are of the view that the Kellogg-Briand Antiwar Pact made no change to this.

In dealing with the Japanese defendants, unless it is determined that the same consideration as had been paid to the German defendants should not be paid to them, no Japanese defendant of the Tokyo Trials should be sentenced to death for having conspired to wage a war of aggression, designed and planned this war, and initiated and implemented this war.

In other words, Webb contended that all the Japanese defendants did was wage a war and that they by no means committed inhumane acts that deserved to be punished by death. William Webb himself—president of the International Military Tribunal for the Far East—admitted that no Japanese defendant should be sentenced to death if the same criteria that the Nuremberg trials had applied to German defendants were adopted.

## The Greatest Defect of the Tokyo Trials

While I have so far discussed the legal framework of the Tokyo Trials, now I shall proceed to discuss their substance. As readers will find out, the trials were truly pathetic.

The substance of the Tokyo Trials all comes down to the wording in the first count of crimes against peace in the indictment and the court's conclusion on this charge.

The first count can be summarized as follows: From 1928 through 1945, all the defendants participated in a joint plan or conspiracy. The purpose of the plan/conspiracy was for Japan to control the East Asia/Pacific/Indian Ocean areas, for which Japan waged a number of unlawful wars.

The next three paragraphs summarize the explanation on the history in those years (i.e., between 1928 and 1945) given by the court's ruling along with the argument of the indictment.

There had been strife within the Japanese government since the time of the Tanaka Giichi cabinet (1927) between co-conspirators who wished to expand Japan's influence in the Asian continent by force and those who wished to accomplish the same goal by more prudent means. In the end, the co-conspirators became dominant in the Japanese government and they prepared, organized, and controlled the Japanese people's minds and material resources toward the war of aggression that was planned to accomplish their goal.

After the co-conspirators succeeded in suppressing all the opposing voices in Japan, Japan began to launch aggression to accomplish Japan's control of the Far East.

The Imperial Japanese Army occupied Manchuria in 1931, invaded north China in 1934, started a large-scale war of aggression against China in 1937, prepared a war of aggression against the Soviet Union, and launched a war of aggression against Britain and the United States in 1941.

All of these acts were conducted by "co-conspirators" according to the court judgment, which said, in a nutshell, that there had been such a thing as "co-conspirators" in Japan and it was these co-conspirators who had schemed and carried out all the evil deeds.

To begin with, "co-conspirator" is a highly ambiguous notion as a legal concept. Thus, it would be unthinkable to apply this concept in an international court of justice that included countries outside the sphere of Anglo-American law.

According to Takayanagi Kenzō, one of the two chief counsels at the Tokyo Trials who was known for his extensive knowledge of law history, "co-conspirator" was a notion peculiar to British law. Because it was not found in the system of laws in other countries, according to Takayanagi, it was not general enough to be applied to international law.

"Co-conspirator" was a useful notion with which those in power could punish an undesirable individual or group of individuals; it was a perfect tool with which Britain's rulers in the first half of the 19th century could penalize undesirable labor unions for example. Even today, legal experts in Britain and the United States regard this notion as something like a relic from the past, saying, "Under this principle, anyone's freedom can be prey to a judge's prejudicated likes and dislikes or societal prejudices any time after [the defendant] collaborates with someone else."

In actuality, in the case of Japan, as American prosecutors at the Tokyo Trials themselves admitted, "There existed a sharp conflict of views and vehement strife within the Japanese defendants," a situation that was far from the unity among "co-conspirators." The Japanese defendants, therefore, unfortunately caught a side blow from the German defendants at the Nuremberg trials. The Third Reich was basically solidly unified among comrades completely indoctrinated by Hitler's philosophy as expressed in his *Mein Kamph* and they carried out premeditated plans steadily in conformity. This was by no means the case in Japan.

In order to stress the existence of "co-conspirators," prosecutors quoted the so-called Tanaka Memorial. Obviously, this document was a forgery. But even if it had been authentic, a consistent conspiracy would have been impossible because the *Minseitō* returned to power after the Tanaka cabinet, reviving Shidehara's cooperative diplomacy.

This "co-conspirator" theory was perhaps the largest flaw among many of the Tokyo Trials. All the Japanese agreed that while everyone involved had been swept away by the times, each had had different views concerning what Japan should do and that nothing was further from the truth than thinking that there had been a well-thought-out plan which had been systematically carried out. They all sneered, gave a wry smile, and smiled with pity at the accusation of co-conspiracy. And this was precisely why none of the Japanese defendants was satisfied with the logic of the Tokyo Trials.

Actually, the prosecutors, too, were aware of this incongruence. Thus, they had to say, "Even though there may not have been a concrete scheme or conspiracy, the defendants shared a similar, albeit vague, idea about the use of force to advance Japan's national interest." If this excuse could be accepted, Takayanagi argued, then a conspiracy should be recognized among any politicians and military generals in Britain, France, the United States, and even the Soviet Union who had shouldered the burden of developing their respective countries.

This "co-conspirator" accusation was a strong-arm argument designed to make individuals take responsibility for a state's conduct. According to Takayanagi, it was an utterly revolutionary theory to accuse not only the state but also individuals who acted on behalf of the state when the state waged a war that was against international laws. As such, this argument was strictly rejected by international laws. Takayanagi declared that there could be absolutely no politician in any country that had even thought of this kind of principle when negotiating an international treaty.

Judge Bert Rolling, one of the judges at the Tokyo Trials, from the Netherlands, was a frequent tennis partner to Major General Charles Willoughby, GHQ's Chief of Intelligence and MacArthur's right-hand man. Rolling recalled what Willoughby said when the departing Rolling visited him to bid farewell:

> Willoughby solemnly said to me, "This trial was the worst hypocrisy in history." He also told me that, because of this trial, he would prohibit his son from entering the military. When I asked him why, he said that the United States would undoubtedly fight a war if it were put in the same situation as Japan found itself in . . .
>
> . . . And this has just been proven in recent years. When the Arab countries threatened an embargo of their oil supply, the United States intimidated these countries with military force. U.S. Secretary of Defense James Schlesinger stated in his January 1974 speech that maintenance of the oil supply was a military duty and the United States might mobilize its military forces to secure the oil supply.
>
> According to Willoughby, before the attack on Pearl Harbor, Japan had only two options. One was to sit idly by and watch its oil reserve run out and thus diminish itself into a country that begged for others' mercy. The other option was to wage a war. And Japan chose the second option. If its very survival was threatened, Willoughby swore to me, any country would choose to fight a war.

When faced with the obligation to inspect the rulings of the Tokyo Trials, MacArthur made the following announcement:

> While I have fulfilled a great number of heartbreaking and miserable duties in my long official life, nothing has ever been more unpleasant than inspecting these rulings.
>
> . . . I must confess that I am not equipped with the outstanding wisdom that is required to assess the fundamental and humanly universal issue that this trial entailed. The human race has struggled to find a solution to this issue since before recorded history, and it will perhaps never be completely solved . . .
>
> Within the limit of the current duty imposed on me as well as the limited authority bestowed on me, I wish to say the following. In

light of principles and procedures instructed by the Allied countries concerned, I do not find any flaw in the proceedings of the trial at all that calls for my interference in the court decisions.

. . . In the current process of the evolution of an imperfect civilized society, I believe there is nothing whose sincerity is more trustworthy than this military tribunal. Henceforth, I command the commander-in-chief of the 8th Army to carry out the sentence.

Although MacArthur bent over backward to justify the court's decisions in consideration of his official position, it seems unnecessary to explain his genuine sentiment that can be read between the lines.

## About Time to Settle Accounts on the Tokyo Trials

We can well imagine the resentment of those who were executed as the result of such a sloppy trial. While all the defendants must have been prepared to accept whatever fate might befall them by way of taking responsibility as leaders of a war-losing state, they did not deserve what they got: two and a half years of humiliating treatment as war criminals; death by hanging in their prison garb without any honor; and their surviving families being deprived of retrieving their ashes. It was only by the daring act of the counsels, including Samonji Shōhei, who had inferred the location of the disposal of the defendants' ashes, that the ashes were collected on Christmas night behind American soldiers' backs. The ashes were then buried in the Kōa Kan'non temple in Atami, Shizuoka Prefecture. The temple had been erected in 1940 to enshrine both Japanese and Chinese war casualties in the spirit of the "equality in reposing dead enemies' and friends' souls" by General Matsui Iwane, who was among the seven defendants executed. Some of the ashes were also enshrined in the Jun'koku Nanashi Byō (Tomb of Seven Martyrs) on top of Mt. Sangane in a suburb of Nagoya City.

Subsequently, at the time of the effectuation of the peace treaty in 1952, a campaign was started to demand release of the imprisoned war criminals. As a result and in accordance with the peace treaty, all of the imprisoned were released with the consent of all the countries concerned. The process was completed in 1958.

At the same time, another movement was started to allow surviving families of the executed and those who died in imprisonment to receive the bereaved family pension and the governmental pension. The bill passed the Diet by unanimous decision, winning the support of both the right and left wings of the socialist party at that time. While the governmental pension was normally suspended for criminals who were sentenced to imprisonment for three years or longer, the Diet found it proper to treat those who were executed and those who died while in imprisonment not as criminals under Japanese law but as war victims.

This episode reveals that there was unified national sympathy toward the defendents at the Tokyo Trials among the Japanese people in those days. Taking into account the lists of beneficiaries of the Act on Relief of War Victims and Survivors and the Act on Governmental Pension, the Repatriation Support Bureau of the Ministry of Health and Welfare selected war criminals to be enshrined at Yasukuni Shrine. Those selected were enshrined there starting in 1959. By 1978, a total of fourteen Class-A war criminals had been enshrined at Yasukuni Shrine, providing the spirits of victims of the Tokyo Trials a final resting place.

It is about time to settle accounts on the Tokyo Trials. As a matter of fact, things were supposed to have been settled a long time ago. Under the Treaty of San Francisco, Japan was obliged to accept the International Military Tribunal for the Far East and the Japanese government was bound to carry out the sentences of the Military Tribunal.

The sentences have long since been executed. The only remaining duty that was imposed on Japan by the Treaty of San Francisco, if any, was to refrain from demanding compensation for obvious mistakes of fact and unjust assessments of culpability. Otherwise, it can be declared that Japan has fulfilled all of the obligations imposed by the peace treaty.

Beyond that, it is obvious that no court of justice can make a decision that binds the future eternally.

In ancient Greece, Socrates obeyed the court's death sentence, even though he claimed the decision was at variance with the facts and unjust. Socrates reasoned that the sentence was handed down on the basis in due course. Nevertheless, subsequent history has received no restriction on the assessment of Socrates' conduct from the court decision even though he was found guilty by the court. And Socrates' tomb has continued to be respected by people long after his death.

The only thing MacArthur said about the decisions of the Tokyo Trials was that they had followed the due procedure.

Japan also complied with the clauses of the peace treaty. It seems quite commonsensical that the Treaty of San Francisco cannot forever bind future judgments of future generations.

For the honor of Japan and for the honor of those who were executed, we must settle accounts regarding the Tokyo Trials one way or another. Even today, an occasion arises every once in a while for the Japanese government to express its view on the Tokyo Trials, including the controversy over the enshrinement of war criminals at Yasukuni Shrine.

In a nutshell, after making it known to the world that Japan had indeed accepted and fulfilled all the obligations imposed by the Treaty of San Francisco, the Japanese people need to form a consensus that the Tokyo Trials are unacceptable as a fair trial and that its victims deserve national sympathy. Actually, such a consensus did exist at one time, but it needs to be reconfirmed today due to crooked leftwing, anti-establishment movements in Japan since the 1980s. In other words, what we need to do is to return to a pre-1980s state. What is required of the Japanese government is only to take an attitude that is helpful for the formation of such a consensus.

CHAPTER

9

# The Tokyo Trials (2)

*—Insight of the Two Who Squarely Argued Against*
*the Tokyo Trials' Historical View—*

## What Does It Mean to Judge History?

The International Military Tribunal for the Far East (Tokyo Trials) left a deep scar in the psychology of the Japanese people.

The Tokyo Trials were different from the Nuremberg trials on this account. In the case of Germany, there had been a clear-cut agreement among the Germans themselves as well as the Allies that the Nazis were categorically evil. At the Tokyo Trials, Japan and its entire history, not the particular elements, were degraded. This view of Japan's history as projected by the Tokyo Trials was forced on the Japanese people by GHQ during the occupation of Japan under the policies of strict censorship, which prevented counter-arguments, and it continued to be protected and preserved by left-wing education and publications in postwar Japan for more than half a century.

Against this, some Japanese elements naturally harbored strong resentment. Controversy about it lingers even today.

And this is not the only negative legacy of the Tokyo Trials. Although a court of justice by nature cannot judge a history or a war, the Tokyo Trials nevertheless attempted to try it. Subsequent debates on history were reduced to forums discussing the rights and wrongs of history. Why did we start such a war? This is a cliché that is always repeated when the Japanese discuss early Shōwa history. Even today, TV programs simple-mindedly label those who opposed the war good guys and those who supported the war bad guys; those who resisted the military were, according to TV, good guys and those who supported the military were bad guys. The debate over the war has been degraded to a cheap morality play about good and bad.

This tendency to divide historical conduct into good and bad has also been reinforced by the tide of leftwing thinking in postwar Japan. The Marxist historical view tends to apply conceptual schema to history instead of looking at the facts.

The Marxist historical view labels everything past feudalistic and makes it an object of hatred. In post-revolution China, for instance, every work unit regularly convened a grievance meeting to repeatedly revisit how pre-revolution Chinese had been exploited and abused—completely shelving the failure of the Great Leap Forward and the miseries caused by the Cultural Revolution. In Tibet today, Tibetans are taught repeatedly how miserable serfs had been before the country's occupation by China.

I should hastily add, however, that this practice is by no means confined to the communist countries. Such a practice has been a well-worn device in propaganda by conquerors. In fact, Japan, too, once stressed to citizens of Manchukuo how Manchurian people had suffered from the rampancy of warlords before the independence of Manchukuo.

Since the 1980s when the so-called textbook issue arose in Japan, monuments commemorating the brutal conduct of the Japanese military during World War II have been erected one after another in various places in China. This shows that the chain-reaction habit of passing judgment on history—that is, whether it was good or bad—still lingers on.

The German historian Leopold von Ranke famously wrote: "To history has been assigned the office of judging the pasts of instructing the present for the benefit of future ages. To such high offices this work does not aspire: It wants only to show what actually happened."

And this is the conviction that I have consistently followed in writing the current series on the diplomatic history of modern Japan. If I should ever discuss the right and wrong of Shōwa history, my entire efforts to impartially pursue the truth of history would come to naught.

History is an accumulation of efforts made by states and men to survive given conditions. And history is the great flow of those efforts. It is in this great flow of time that wars occur and peace is achieved. From the beginning, history is not something that we should discuss as being good or bad.

The Japanese people's perspective on their history has been torn apart by (a) the militaristic view of the 15 years from the time of the Manchurian Incident until the defeat in the war, (b) the occupation forces' view that lasted seven years, (c) the subsequent leftwing, anti-establishment historical view that lasted until the 1970s, and (d) the masochistic historical view that emerged in the 1980s.

In order to build a Japan for the 21st century, we must leave behind all the distorted historical views of the past and start anew from scratch. To accomplish this, I believe we must start with looking squarely at what has happened and accepting historical facts as facts.

Assessing history from the viewpoint of "good or bad" tends to lead to simplistic hindsight. Japan won the First Sino-Japanese and Russo-Japanese Wars and succeeded in building the Empire of Japan. Subsequently, Japan failed in wars after the Manchurian Incident, leading to the fall of the empire. Given these facts, a view that concludes the former history to be good and the subsequent history to be bad is almost inevitable.

As exemplified by historical writer Shiba Ryōtaro, whom the Japanese people like to quote often, it has been a popular historical view in Japan to praise everything Japan did in the Meiji period and admire Japanese leaders in those days, while denouncing everything Shōwa Japan did as evil and calling the people of that time corrupt degenerates.

I wish to hastily add that I will be the first to praise the contributions made by the so-called Shiba historical view manifested in Shiba's works after *Saka no Ueno Kumo* (Clouds above the Hill). This work on Japan in the First Sino-Japanese and Russo-Japanese Wars cried out to the world that Meiji Japan had indeed been magnificent. This work appeared in the midst of the postwar historical view spread among the Japanese since the occupation, which regarded Japan between the Meiji Restoration through the defeat in World War II to be in a dark age, whose dawn arrived only with the U.S. occupation forces. The situation in Japan at the time was such that it was safer for anyone, lest he be labeled a rightwing reactionary, to also say that Shōwa Japan in contrast was bad. Shiba was no exception. And this trend continued to hover over Japan for a long time.

To be sure, objectively speaking, the generation that accomplished the Meiji Restoration was full of magnificent individuals. People like Yoshida Shōin and Sakuma Shōzan, who were killed before the Restoration; Saigō Takamori and Katsu Kaishū, who accomplished the Restoration; and Fukuzawa Yukichi and Mutsu Munemitsu, who shouldered the modernization of Japan in Meiji were all gems of Edo-period education. From the viewpoint of world history, Japan in the Edo period was an unprecedentedly civilized society. These were intellectual giants to whom contemporary Japanese are no match in, for instance, mastery of the classics.

Yet such Meiji leaders as Katsura Tarō, Komura Jutarō, and Kodama Gentarō, who actually won the Russo-Japanese War, do not seem to be too much different from Shōwa leaders in terms of their personality.

After all, we are all the same Japanese. Every one of them put his heart into the defense and well-being of Japan, albeit in different international environments.

## Did the Nanjing Incident Really Take Place?

Behind the dichotomy of the good Meiji and bad Shōwa historical view has been the influence of the International Military Tribunal for the Far East. This is because the prosecution included all of Japan's conduct after the Tanaka Giichi cabinet of 1927 (2nd Year of Shōwa) as the object of the trial.

Even today in Japan, all the wars after the Manchurian Incident are put together and called the 15-Year War with China. The Hundred Years' War (1337–1453) between Britain and France was actually a series of conflicts interrupted by periods of peace. This goes to show that the name of a war may not accurately depict the reality of the war. In that sense, the name of a war really does not matter. Thus, it is all right to call those wars with China a 15-Year War. Nevertheless, it was problematic to try all of those fourteen years (between 1927 and 1941) as a unit in a court of justice.

After the Manchurian Incident, agreements were reached between Japan and the Kuomintang regime that succeeded in restoring a degree of peace. Moreover, border disputes with the Soviet Union, including the Nomonhan Incident, had already been settled before the Tokyo Trials.

Therefore, there was no reason for Japan's responsibility to be questioned anew.

If it were only the United States judging Japan, it would have been sufficient and proper to bring a charge against Japan's conduct starting with the attack on Pearl Harbor. In fact, it is believed that MacArthur himself once murmured to people around him that he was of the opinion that the Tokyo Trials should be a simple court martial to deal only with the attack on Pearl Harbor.

Needless to say, defense counsels harshly criticized the inclusion of those fourteen years instead of the years after the attack on Pearl Harbor. This issue not only damaged the impartiality of the trial but also tenaciously contributed to the popular historical view that everything Shōwa Japan did was bad.

The aftereffects of the Tokyo Trials have mostly been overcome thanks to the efforts of countless intellectuals. The distorted historical view of the Japanese has been increasingly eliminated, though there still remain a few spots at the bottom of the educational system where it survives.

The Tokyo Trials also gave birth to another type of aftereffect in the form of a different good-or-bad historical view. This perspective believes that there was nothing wrong with what Japan did.

The most forthright manifestation of this perspective is the argument that the so-called Nanjing Incident did not take place. At one point, this argument was supported even by some highly educated Japanese. This kind of argument could well damage the international perception of the intellectual integrity of the Japanese.

Of course, this line of argument owes its origin to the injustice of the Tokyo Trials.

While a large number of witnesses testified about the Nanjing Incident during the Tokyo Trials, Judge Pal from India raised serious questions about the credibility of each and every testimony. For instance, a witness testified to an incident where all the family members of two women who had been raped on board a boat committed suicide by jumping into the river; the witness said he had heard about the incident from a boatman. It was hearsay, to begin

Radhabinod Pal

with. The women's fathers and husbands showed "they valued honor more than their lives" by committing suicide. Judge Pal questioned whether it was possible for those Japanese soldiers to rape the two women given that the fathers, husbands, and the boatman were present at the time of the alleged incident. Judge Pal also questioned whether the witness detected any artificiality in the boatman's account.

When another witness testified that he had seen Japanese soldiers slaughtering Chinese people one after another in three different locations, Judge Pal said, "This witness strikes me as somewhat out of the ordinary. It appears that some Japanese liked him so much that they took him around to show him a variety of wrongdoings by the Japanese military and yet let him go unharmed."

Actually, the actual scene of a sexual assault is not easily observed. According to an Arabic law, it is said that a naked man and woman found embracing cannot be found guilty of sexual misconduct if a string can slice through the two from head to toe. It would have been difficult for a conventional court of justice to find that a rape had been committed if the only testimony available was a witness's account that he saw a Japanese soldier walking away and a naked woman crying. Nevertheless, the Tokyo Trials adopted this witness's testimony.

A normal court of justice would have found these testimonies to be insufficient evidence. And, had each of the prosecutor's pieces of evidence been refuted one by one like Pal had done, it might have been possible to conclude that the Nanjing Incident had never taken place. Had a competent lawyer currently active in U.S. courts been hired, it would not be too difficult for him to win an acquittal for all the defendants from an impartial judge, given the inconsistency of the evidence presented by prosecutors at the Tokyo Trials.

But history is no court case.

It is not unusual for a defendant accused of murder to be found not guilty by a court. Humanitarian organizations may find it a victory for them. But relatives of the victim wish to know who, then, killed their loved one. The court is not obliged to find an answer to this question. All that matters for a court is that it conducts a fair procedure and that the evidence examined under such procedure was found to be insufficient. However, that will not be sufficient for history.

On the Nanjing Incident, Ishii Itarō, the then Director-General of the East Asian Affairs Bureau of the Ministry of Foreign Affairs, entered the following reflections in his journal: "Telegram arrived from consulate in Shanghai with details on unruly conduct by our military. It says their acts of plunder and rape were too horrible to look at. Were these acts really done by our Imperial Japanese Army?"

Horiba Kazuo of the Imperial Japanese Army General Staff Office left the following observation:

> . . . a few cases of undisciplined conduct were observed. The misconduct by the occupying troops in Nanjing would damage the prestige of the Imperial Japanese Army in the coming decade.

General Matsui Iwane, Commander-in-Chief of the Japanese Central China Area Army, was compelled to deplore, "My god, what have you done?"

What triggered these reactions? Since none of these three actually saw what happened with their own eyes, their testimonies might be regarded as hearsay and as insufficient evidence in a court room. But, history can consider the testimonies as signs of something larger than the usual irregularities that were inevitable in ordinary occupations.

After severely criticizing all the testimonies on the Nanjing Incident, Judge Pal, nevertheless, wrote that it was beyond any doubt that the Japanese military's conduct in Nanjing was nothing short of an atrocity.

It was simply absurd to claim that more than 200,000 Chinese nationals were victimized in the Nanjing Incident. And the court decision that endorsed this estimate was unjust. At the same time, though, it had to be recognized that there indeed had been atrocities in excess of what might be called normal. This should be a starting point for a reasonable historical view.

Unless we in Japan overcome all the actions and reactions derived from the unjust Tokyo Trials, we will never be able to nurture a healthy historical view.

Because the Japanese people had believed that the Japanese military, which boasted the tradition of austere discipline to the world during the Boxer Rebellion (1898–1900) and the Russo-Japanese War, would never resort to brutal conduct, the disclosure of the Nanjing Incident during the

Tokyo Trials sent a shock wave among the public. However, by squarely facing the vulnerability of the Japanese to be carried away by extraordinary circumstances—a tendency that seems to be universally shared by the entire human race—and by acknowledging the Nanjing Incident, the Japanese people should be able to view other peoples much more fairly and objectively.

It should be added that in any other battlefield, the Japanese military persevered with its traditional discipline. Particularly after the Nanjing Incident, the military became all the more resolute never to repeat the same mistake. This was proven in the subsequent occupation of Hankou, where no aberrant conduct whatsoever was observed. Even during the Tokyo Trials, so much evidence on the stringent discipline shown by the Imperial Japanese Army was presented that the judges had to declare it enough. The military's conduct in Hankou should be interpreted as an outcome of its self-criticism on its conduct in Nanjing. Ironically, this proves that aberrant conduct did indeed occur in Nanjing. It is a historical fact, nevertheless, that General Okamura Yasuji, commander-in-chief of the China Expeditionary Army, saw to it that the spirit of benevolence was strictly enforced throughout the troops under the slogan of "Don't burn, don't rape, don't kill"—and this allowed the Japanese military in China to maintain cordial relations with local residents for seven years until Japan's defeat in 1945. Thus, evacuations of Japanese military personnel and Japanese residents after the end of the war were carried out more or less peacefully. It was reported that in some cases the local people regretted the departure of the Japanese for the chaos that was likely to come afterwards in the vacuum created. Therefore, the Japanese should not let their pride be affected by the masochistic historical view based on propaganda that the Japanese military continued to repeat brutal and outrageous conduct all over China. And Japan's neighbors would also welcome Japan's moderate behavior on the basis of its pride in its own tradition as a nation.

The conviction that the Japanese cannot maintain their pride unless the occurrence of the Nanjing Incident itself is categorically denied has ironically led to the loss of international credibility for the Japanese historical view. This vicious cycle must be severed.

# We Should Blame the Military for Everything

Another aftereffect of the Tokyo Trials relates to anti-militarism in post-war Japan.

While each defendant at the Tokyo Trials had a different position, one thing they all agreed on was the absolute necessity of sparing Emperor Shōwa from any war responsibility. Counsel Kiyose Ichirō had planned to defend, first and foremost, the emperor, and then to defend the state. Kiyose intended to carry out the defense of each defendant under these two principles.

Naturally, though, among the defendants, the civil officials and the military officers showed different attitudes. Throughout the entire first half of the Shōwa era, there were countless cases of the military unilaterally deciding important national policies, oftentimes in the name of the prerogative of supreme command. In these cases, the civil officials had been completely left out from the beginning.

Besides, some believed it best to cast all the blame on the military. In his December 10, 1945, diary, Kido Kōichi, Lord Keeper of the Privy Seal at the end of the war, entered the following suggestions of Tsuru Shigeto, a prominent economist who was knowledgeable of the American way:

> According to the American way of thinking, unlike Japan, even when the Lord Keeper tries to take all the blame by admitting his guilt, the emperor will not be spared from blame. In the American way, when the Lord Keeper is found not guilty, the emperor, too, should not be guilty. When the Lord Keeper is guilty, so should the emperor be. This is something that you should keep in mind when dealing with the Americans.

This is indeed where the Japanese way of thinking was completely different from that of Americans. While Japan has had a tradition of letting other defendants go free in honor of the gallantry shown by the one defendant who decides to shoulder all the blame single-handedly, Americans would take the admission of the one as a confirmation of the crime and accuse all of those involved in the crime. In order to protect the emperor, therefore, Kido decided that he should cast all the blame on the military.

At the outset of his affidavit, Kido stated that his entire life had been devoted to fighting against militarists. He wrote, "As far as my duty allows me, I have resisted the military's high-handed maneuvers and tried to redirect them to appropriate outlets. In this document, I intend to write about those futile struggles of mine during those days of extreme fanaticism." And throughout the entire trial, Kido continued to offer testimony that was unfavorable to the military on almost all the incidents during the war.

At this point, counsels' attitudes diverged between those who were defending military officers and those who represented civil officials. Some began to criticize Kido's conduct.

Because Kido's criticism of the military was an intentional and artificial testimony designed specifically to defend the emperor, it was inevitable that his intellectual honesty became questionable. For instance, Kido had occasionally accommodated the military's hardliner argument before and during the war together with his close friend Prime Minister Konoe Fumimaro. There was a portion in the diary of Harada Kumao, Saionji Kinmochi's private secretary (*Harada Nikki*, a detailed record of Saionji's words and deeds), which criticized Kido's accommodative attitude toward the military. Because of this diary, Kido became a target of pointed questioning by the prosecution.

It was Tōgō Shigenori, the cool-headed, impartial, perceptive, and uncompromising foreign minister when Japan surrendered, who confronted the military more squarely than anyone else among the defendants.

In his affidavit, Tōgō wrote, "Immersed in a war atmosphere for ten years since the Manchurian Incident, Japan's diplomacy became so increasingly pressured by the military that it became extremely difficult for a foreign minister to make himself heard in matters related to national policies." On the attack on Pearl Harbor, Tōgō testified that, "the Imperial Japanese Navy expressed its wish to attack Pearl Harbor at the Imperial General Headquarters Liaison Conference." When the prosecution pointed out that other defendants had denied the allegation, Tōgō testified that he had been pressured inside the prison by other defendants not to refer to this fact, leading him to fierce confrontation with other defendants.

Tōgō's criticism of the military had no limit. In fact, Tōgō directed criticism not only at the military but also at the likes of Hirota Kōki, who had gone along with the general trend of the times. The following *tanka* poems written by Tōgō show his state of mind:

When I realize that these men had once led the country
I cannot help but being appalled by the pettiness of their human scale

Convinced that it is best to compromise [with the military]
These people were tossed by waves when they tried to fend off the
wind

And,

These people are without philosophy or ideal
They just followed where the frenzy took them

These poems well reveal Togo's stubbornness and the proud independence of his mind.

Hatred of the military has long constituted one of the underlying tones of
the social psychology of postwar Japan.

It is undeniable that some young officers were rampant, taking advantage of the autonomy of the military command; that senior military leaders did not restrict those young officers and, instead, accommodated
them; and that excessive hazing such as slapping someone in the face was
directed at conscripted civilians to an extent unthinkable in the militaries
of other advanced countries.

When it comes to whether it was really the military alone that was
responsible for leading Japan to disaster and whether restraint of the military alone could have saved Japan from the disaster, the answer is not so
easy to come by.

While it is obvious that the Manchurian Incident was an arbitrary action
by the military, it was something the Japanese residents in Manchuria had
strongly longed for and was supported by public opinion in Japan once
the incident had erupted. As far as the Second Sino-Japanese War is concerned, as I wrote in *Shigemitsu/Tōgō to Sono Jidai* (Shigemitsu and Tōgō
and Their Time), nobody could have prevented it from erupting as long
as the Chinese side had intended to provoke Japan into a war. Actually,
the fact of the matter was that the Imperial Japanese Army General Staff
Office tried to prevent the eruption of a full-scale battle only to find its
efforts were futile in the face of provocations from the Chinese side and

the rising tide of patriotism in public opinion and the mass media in Japan. And as for the Greater East Asia War, it was an arbitrary and runaway deed of Foreign Minister Matsuoka Yōsuke at the time, not the military's conduct, that led to the signing of the Tripartite Pact and rejection of the U.S.-Japan draft agreement. By the time the Hull Note was delivered, it was no longer possible for anyone, be it civil officials or the military, to oppose the war. While the military was certainly responsible for several factors that contributed to the start of the war, it would be way too loose to blame the military for every step toward the war.

Let me pose a hypothetical question here. What would have been the conclusion of a war tribunal had it been conducted not by the occupation forces but by Japanese, as Shigemitsu Mamoru had insisted? First of all, if the Japanese had opened a war tribunal, it would be confined to discussions on suspected violation of international laws, never to judge history. Suppose that the *Daitōa Sensō Chōsakai* (Study Committee on the Greater East Asia War), which was proposed by Shidehara Kijūrō only to be shot down by GHQ, had explored the causes of the war and Japan's defeat in it as originally planned. What would have been its conclusion?

When the Allied countries opposed the launching of the Study Committee on the Greater East Asia War, some on the Japanese side proposed to appease GHQ by excluding former military personnel from its membership. It is said that, hearing this proposal, Shidehara became indignant and said, "What kind of a study can be done about a war when you eliminate the military personnel from the membership? It would become, at best, something akin to a popular journalist account," (*Senpū 20-nen* (20 Years of Storm) by Mori Shōzō.) His was a very orthodox proposition to let the military analyze its own errors so that it could start anew on the basis of its self-reflection.

Shidehara was of the opinion that, "The Ministry of Foreign Affairs and the military both must pursue their respective duties but cooperate closely with one another to carry out national policies." Had the Committee really taken off, its conclusion probably would have been to integrate the military command into the prerogatives of the prime minister. And the Committee would have proposed that Japan pursue cooperative diplomacy based on its insight into the big picture of the world—a function required of the foreign ministry—without being driven by public opinion that called for a hardliner foreign policy no matter what.

Had this been the conclusion of the review on Japan's war and defeat, the military would have been deprived of the autonomy of its command but allowed to retain its own role, while, at the same time, the entire Japanese nation would have been made aware of what had gone wrong and what needed to be corrected. Most of all, it could have prevented rampancy of the unrealistic historical and political view that has plagued Japan for more than half a century after the war—that is, the view that regarded the military as the sole source of all evil and understood everything in terms of strife between the military and all peace-loving forces.

## Judge Pal and Tōjō Hideki

Finally, we have to make a judgment on the historical view that governed the court decisions of the Tokyo Trials. Because this is the very theme throughout the entire five-volume diplomatic history of modern Japan that I have endeavored to complete, it is simply too big an issue to be settled in a few lines here. Instead, let me introduce two individuals, Judge Pal from India and Tōjō Hideki, who challenged the historical view contained in the Tokyo Trial's decisions head on.

At the Tokyo Trials, Judge Radhabinod Pal submitted a minority opinion, whose Japanese translation was 1,200 pages long, and insisted on the acquittal of all the defendants. His minority opinion was not allowed to be read at the time of the verdict. According to Judge Bert Roling from the Netherlands, this incident alone proved the unfairness of the Tokyo Trials.

Pal was born in 1886, three years ahead of Jawaharlal Nehru, to a generation of Indians who were ecstatically inspired by Japan's victory in the Russo-Japanese War. Although no reference is available on Pal's view on Japan, it is not hard to imagine that, born to the generation of Indians whose sole wish was independence of their homeland along with such patriots as Chandra Bose, he must have had a moment of expectation and goodwill toward Japan, whose army had advanced all the way to Burma, expelling British colonial rule on the way. Thus, Pal's argument can be regarded as the last expression of hope and expectations that Asia's nationalism had held for Japan after the Russo-Japanese War.

Pal showed understanding on the reasons that the Japanese side called the war an act of self-defense—such as Japan's distinct positions in China on the Manchurian Incident and the Second Sino-Japanese War; the right to protect Japanese residents in China from the anti-Japanese movements; and the threat from the prospective advance of the communist forces on the Chinese continent. Pal continued to argue that, now that the Tokyo Trials had turned down all the evidence on these reasons that the Japanese side submitted, it would be difficult for the court to make decisions.

Japan had had its own reasons for its actions and arguments concerning its conduct. Whether all of Japan's conduct before and during the war was justified by these arguments or not, Judge Pal argued that court decisions made without hearing the Japanese arguments were simply invalid.

Against the court decision, which found Japan's negotiation with the United States to be a means to buy time to prepare for a war, Judge Pal argued that it was indeed the United States that tried to buy time since the longer the negotiation lasted the more disadvantageous it would be for resource-poor Japan. He also pointed out that the Hull Note had contained the maximum amount of demands, including some that had never been submitted before, and said, ". . . the Principality of Monaco, the Grand Duchy of Liechtenstein, would have taken up arms against the United States on receipt of such a note."

In the conclusion to his voluminous remarks, Pal wrote as follows, quoting Jefferson Davis: "When time shall have softened passion and prejudice, when Reason shall have stripped the mask from misrepresentation, then Justice, holding evenly her scales, will require much of past censure and praise to change places."

At this point, the author intends to devote a few lines to describing the person of Tōjō Hideki. In writing this modern history of Japan, I have not yet attempted to describe Tōjō. In a way, the International Military Tribunal for the Far East was a grand human drama of 28 defendants. While there was an abundance of moving anecdotes about each of those 28 defendants, I must concentrate on Tōjō alone. After all, it was Tōjō who started the war and led Japan's war effort as its supreme commander. If one has to select one defendant to represent Japan's position during the Tokyo Trials, it will have to be Tōjō.

Furthermore, even before the court decision was issued, it was objectively obvious to anyone's eyes that, if someone had to be executed, Tōjō would be the prime candidate. Thus, since Tōjō knew from the beginning that there was no need for him to vindicate himself, during the Tokyo Trials he spoke candidly and in even tones about what he believed in. In this sense, it can be said that Tōjō's testimony represented the thinking of the Japanese during the war most accurately.

After Japan's surrender, Tōjō confided his determination to commit suicide to his wife. He even consulted with his doctor and marked with black ink the critical spot on his chest that he should aim at to shoot his heart.

On September 10, 1945, one day before he was scheduled to be arrested, in response to a question from an Associated Press reporter asking for his view on General MacArthur, Tōjō said, "Escaping the Philippines leaving his men behind was something a military commander should never have done." Appalled, the translator quickly told the reporter that Tōjō thought of MacArthur as a great general. This episode clearly indicated that he had no intention whatsoever to curry favor with GHQ at that point. Tōjō must have behaved that way based on the anticipation of certain death.

The next day, on September 11, when the occupation forces arrived at Tōjō's house to arrest him, he shot the marked spot on his chest with a handgun. It was a handgun prized by his son-in-law, the late Major Koga Hidemasa, with which Koga had killed himself on August 15. Miraculously, though, the bullet missed the vital spot and Tōjō was resuscitated at a hospital.

Tōjō's failed attempt at suicide incurred ridicule from the entire nation. Those who had known of War Minister Anami Korechika's splendid disembowelment despised Tōjō for using a handgun instead of committing hara-kiri like a good warrior. Rumor had it that his was a small handgun designed for American females. Nobody knew that the gun used to belong to his son-in-law because newspapers did not mention it. Some even rumored that Tōjō must have deliberately missed the vital spot so that he could be resuscitated. According to traditional Japanese values, it has been vitally important to die beautifully or not to die dishonorably.

Tōjō's father, Tōjō Hidenori, was an outstanding military man on whom Klemens Meckel, general in the Prussian army and foreign advisor to the government of Meiji Japan, had pinned high hopes. Hidenori climbed the ladder of the military ranks and finally became Lieutenant General in the Imperial Japanese Army before he retired. Tōjō Hideki was Hidenori's eldest son. While in the Imperial Japanese Army Cadet School, Tōjō devoted his time and energy to studying, driven by his unyielding nature, after which, it is said, he put everything he had into whatever he was tackling throughout his life. Judging from both the praise and censure his attitude attracted, he must have been what we call today a nerdy student.

Throughout his entire life, Tōjō was totally devoid of an anecdote that is normally associated with a hero. Furthermore, nothing of a national strategy, national policy, or recommendation written by Tōjō has been found. To put it coolly, he was an uninteresting bore. To put it more nicely, Tōjō was free from the pretentions of an Oriental hero or a patriot. His choice of a handgun over the traditional disembowelment should be understood in this context.

If there was anything about Tōjō that was distinct from others, it must have been his propensity to emphasize discipline and keep a watchful eye on everything, never delegating details to others. In the factional strife within the Imperial Japanese Army, he belonged to, true to his propensity, the Control Faction and tried to suppress arbitrary conduct by his subordinates. It was his nature that earned him the nickname of "military police politics." As prime minister, Tōjō concurrently served in several key ministerial posts in order to control the detailed corners of his administration, revealing what a pragmatic military bureaucrat he was. His image was the total opposite to that of a manly, bighearted, and yet tender-hearted hero that the Japanese had loved.

For these qualities, Tōjō never inspired nationwide popularity even though he was prime minister during an all-out war. And the cold reaction that the Japanese people showed when Tōjō failed to kill himself was a reflection of this negative sentiment.

When Tōjō attempted to kill himself, he left a suicide note.

Addressing himself to "Peoples of the western countries," Tōjō first criticized Britain and the United States, saying,

> Today, you are victorious, while we are the loser . . . Nevertheless, yours is a victory of force, not that of justice or morality . . . Even though one should not hesitate to resort to all available resources to win a war, the instant annihilation of hundreds of thousands of innocent people, young and old, male and female, with atomic bombs is an act of excessive brutality and inhumanity . . .

Turning his attention to his fellow Japanese, Tōjō continued to say,

> We were provoked to start the Greater East Asia War by the Allied countries. We had to stand up against the enemy for the survival of the country and the self-defense of our people . . . My fellow Japanese citizens . . . may you believe in the future of the empire, overcome the great difficulty the empire faces currently with diligence and utmost efforts, and, thereby, hope for the return of the sun.

Particularly, to "my dear young Japanese citizens," Tōjō urged them to firmly hold on to the spirit of the Japanese man even though many in Japan might be misled by fallacious arguments. "What, then, is the spirit? It can only be loyalty and patriotism."

The thinking on which this suicide note was based was exactly the same as the idea that permeated the 220-page affidavit that he submitted to the Tokyo Trials. When he finished writing the affidavit, Tōjō was heard to say, "I have done all that I can do and I have no regrets."

## Why Did Japan Have to Choose the War Option?

The characteristics of Tōjō's affidavit are most concisely summarized in the *Asahi Shimbun* editorial published at the time of the affidavit's public release:

> . . . It is nothing more than a documentary-like chronology of the events that took place during the four years when he was in the position of responsibility, compiled in his own distinct style. There is nothing that has been previously unknown. Nevertheless, in contrast to many of the other defendants whose testimonies consisted of nothing but personal vindications, Tōjō's affidavit is unique in its positive attempt to explain why Japan had to choose the option of war and, concurrently, to justify Japan's choice.
> (*The Asahi Shimbun*, December 28, 1947)

In short, Tōjō straightforwardly put down all the tasks he had faithfully accomplished as they had been perceived and described at that time without any consideration for the occupation forces or self-vindication.

Didn't Tōjō have anything to regret? In fact, he had. In the concluding section of his affidavit, Tōjō said, "Whether the Greater East Asia War was justified by international laws and whether I am responsible for the defeat are two obviously separate and different issues." Stressing that the war was an act of self-defense and, as such, it did not violate international laws, he nevertheless concluded his affidavit as follows: "I am to be blamed for the defeat of Japan in the Greater East Asia War as Japan's prime minister at the time. Not only do I accept this responsibility in this sense, I sincerely wish to shoulder this burden from the bottom of my heart."

In short, while Tōjō felt no responsibility to the Allied countries whatsoever, he willingly wished to take responsibility for the defeat for the sake of the state and the people of Japan.

There is a poem that is believed to be Tōjō's farewell *tanka* even though it has only been transmitted by word of mouth:

> Even if my body is smashed and torn into a thousand pieces
> I can never atone for the sin of
> Devastating the flourishing era of Emperor Shōwa

Incidentally, former foreign minister Tōgō Shigenori wrote:

> I am here showing my compunction
> But you should know
> That my compunction is for the emperor's land and its people

Although Tōgō was in penitence, he said it was not addressed to the war winners. The only object of his penitence was either the state or God.

> Let us now entrust our fate to divine judgment
> Since their [Allied countries'] judgment is
> Highly unreliable

War criminals detained in Sugamo Prison met their death calmly despite the unfairness of the Tokyo Trials because they felt a responsibility to the nation for having lost the war.

Even though Tōjō's affidavit provides a convincingly thorough account of the situations that forced Japan to choose the war option, it is too long to be introduced in its entirety. Let me instead introduce a portion of its concluding "summary":

> I have so far described the reasons and causes that led to the outbreak of the Pacific War. As a person who knows the situations leading to the war completely, I am thoroughly convinced that this war was caused by provocations on the part of the Allied countries to lure the United States into the war in Europe. As far as Japan was concerned, it was an unavoidable war of self-defense.

Because pre–World War II Japan policies had been so full of errors and failures, those who have only viewed Japan-centered history might find this interpretation by Tōjō to read as if he had attempted to thrust responsibility onto others. Taking a macroscopic view of World War II from the viewpoint of British/American world strategies, however, Tōjō's assessment must strike one as objective and reasonable.

In fact, Henry Kissinger's monumental *Diplomacy* does not refute Tōjō's assessment. Moreover, it appears to tally exactly with Tōjō's argument. On the Hull note, Kissinger writes, "Roosevelt must have known that there was no possibility that Japan would accept [it][20]" and continues to argue that,

> America's entry into the war marked the culmination of a great and daring leader's extraordinary diplomatic enterprise.[21] . . . Had Japan focused its attack on Southeast Asia and Hitler not declared war against the United States, Roosevelt's task of steering his people toward his views would have been much more complicated . . . there can be little doubt that, in the end, he would have somehow managed to enlist America in the struggle he considered so decisive to both the future of freedom and to American security.[22]

---

20    Henry Kissinger. *Diplomacy*. Simon& Schuster. 1994. p.392.
21    Ibid.
22    Ibid. p. 393

In other words, Kissinger is of the view that, had Japan not attacked Pearl Harbor, Roosevelt would have somehow found a way to bring the United States into the war with Japan.

In response to the allegation on "co-conspiracy," Tōjō said,

> Against the allegation that we had had a consistent invasion plan throughout the Manchurian Incident, Second Sino-Japanese War, and the Pacific War, I have used the simplest method to prove that the allegation is truly absurd. It is simply unconceivable for any reasonable man to think that, in our administrative system, a small number of individuals could continue to co-conspire for a consistent goal for a long time over several cabinets. It is indeed hard for me to understand why the prosecutors chose to accuse us of such a fantasy.

It is the gravest defect of the Tokyo Trials that they prosecuted defendants for such a "fantasy" crime and issued decisions that accepted this fantasy. This is today indisputable.

Inside the courtroom, the more agitated and crude the prosecutors and judges became, the cooler and calmer Tōjō was. Reading the trial record, the stark contrast between the two sometimes is comical to readers.

When, for instance, Tōjō argued that Japan had fought a war in China to protect Japan's interests and Japanese residents there, Prosecutor Keenan highhandedly said, "Did Japan need a million-strong army to protect its interests and residents there?" Tōjō replied, saying, "That's a leap in logic. All I did was to explain the cause of the war. The subsequent escalation of the battle was the nature of a war."

When the prosecutors questioned whether Proposals A and B, two proposals concerning the negotiations with the United States, were de facto ultimatums from the Japanese side, Tōjō, after conceding it, said, "But diplomacy is something that is carried out against opponents. Diplomacy alters according to opponents' moves. Any nation has that much latitude in diplomacy."

When the prosecutors, then, made a totally uncalled-for remark, i.e., "A couple days ago, you characterized yourself as a single soldier. Today, are you changing your position and pretending to be an expert in diplomacy," Tōjō said, "While the other day I spoke about where I came from, I am a politician serving the country as prime minister."

The prosecutors attempted to corner Tōjō with the fact that the Combined Fleet of the Imperial Japanese Navy had already sailed out before the Hull Note was issued:

> Prosecutor: Do you deny that this fleet was one of the most powerful mobile units?
> Tōjō: Powerful in comparison with what? The U.S. Navy?
> Prosecutor: I am asking if you deny that it was one of the most powerful forces in history?
> Tōjō: What do you mean "in history?" I believe it is only recently that an aircraft carrier was developed . . .

As for Manchukuo Emperor Puyi, Tōjō testified that his trust in Puyi had been betrayed and deplored how unwise he had been to have trusted him. To a follow-up question from the prosecutor—"Does this mean that you had supported Puyi as emperor of Manchukuo for close to ten years as prime minister, when you realized that you had been unwise?"—Tōjō replied, simply, "I was not prime minister for ten years."

## To Speak for Japan and Defend the Emperor

As exemplified above, Tōjō maintained a natural posture throughout the entire interactions during the trial, answering all the questions without pretension. There was, however, one occasion on which Tōjō was forced to make a very harsh decision. And it was about the emperor's war responsibility.

MacArthur had been firmly convinced from the beginning that he had to defend the emperor in order to successfully carry out his occupation policies. And he had gotten agreement from American prosecutor Joseph Keenan on this matter in advance. Nevertheless, some judges from the Allied countries, including the court's president William Webb, continued to believe in examining the emperor's responsibility for the war.

It would be no exaggeration to say that it was only after the final verdict was issued that this mood to prosecute the emperor was finally dispersed. Viewed from the flip side, Japan was in a situation for three years after the defeat until the end of 1948 during which its leaders had no choice but to obey MacArthur's orders, be it about the constitution or about other laws, knowing that the emperor was, so to speak, taken as a hostage. From MacArthur's viewpoint, too, it could be said that he had somehow gotten through the three years during which a single mistake could have implicated the emperor in the war responsibility.

When Keenan and Counsel Kanzaki Masayoshi jointly approached Tōjō with a proposition that Tōjō should say that the Japanese government leaders had started the war against the emperor's wish, he at first rejected the plot, saying, "It would be unacceptable. We started the war because we obtained His Imperial Majesty's sanction. Do you think I can die in peace if I give a fallacious testimony that I, a humble subject, started the war against His Imperial Majesty's order?"

In the end, however, Tōjō agreed to testify that the emperor had reluctantly approved the start of the war.

But on the second day of Tōjō's testimony, he made a slip of the tongue. When asked if Lord Keeper Kido had ever acted against the emperor's wish, Tōjō decisively declared, "It is utterly impossible for a Japanese subject to act against His Imperial Majesty's wish."

Because, by implication, Tōjō testified that nobody could oppose it if the emperor wished for peace, his remark went to mean that it was the emperor's wish to start the war. As soon as court was adjourned that day, Prosecutor Sergei Golunsky from the Soviet Union advised Keenan that they now had enough evidence to prosecute the emperor.

Realizing his mistake, Tōjō made an attempt at modifying his testimony on the fifth day as follows:

> Prosecutor: Was it Emperor Hirohito's wish to start the war?
> Tōjō: Maybe we acted against His Imperial Majesty's wish. In any event, the truth is that His Imperial Majesty reluctantly approved the advice submitted by me and other individuals in the Imperial Japanese Army General Staff Office . . . His Imperial Majesty's statement to that effect was clearly added to the Imperial Edict of December 8, 1941. It was a statement added at His Imperial Majesty's request. It was added as an expression of His Imperial Majesty's reluctance.

This settled the issue. Toward the end of the day's testimony, Prosecutor Keenan requested Tōjō's response, saying, "I wish to know the defendant's view on whether he does not think starting the war as prime minister was morally or legally wrong." Tōjō triumphantly replied, "I have done nothing wrong. I am convinced that I have done the right thing."

Keenan further tried to follow up by saying, "Does it mean that when you are acquitted you are prepared to repeat the same thing with your colleagues?" But this question was rejected by the president of the court, who sustained the counsels' objection.

Throughout the entire trial, Tōjō remained calm and poised.

The only time he became enraged was when, after the death sentence was passed, his execution was postponed due to an appeal to the U.S. Supreme Court. Throwing the papers he held in his hand, Tōjō pounded on the witness stand and shouted, "If you are to execute me, execute me quickly. Goddammit!"

He had long been prepared to die to take responsibility for the defeat. When he failed to kill himself earlier, he decided to live only to present Japan's views and concurrently protect the emperor. And this had enabled him to endure a chain of humiliations, including daily physical examination and labor services under supervision of low-ranking soldiers. Postponement of the execution was, from Tōjō's viewpoint, a prolongation of the humiliation at which he was enraged. His frame of mind at that time is easy to understand for us today.

A little past midnight on December 23, 1948, Tōjō Hideki was executed along with Doihara Kenji, Mutō Akira, Matsui Iwane, Itagaki Seishirō, Hirota Kōki, and Kimura Heitarō.

His death poem reads:

> Now I am departing
> But I shall return to this land
> Since I have not done enough to serve my country

CHAPTER

# 10

# Absolute Power of GHQ

*—The Deep Scars to the Japanese Mentality—*

## Occupation Administration That Resembled Colonial Rule

The occupation forces under GHQ had absolute power. It was the first encounter with such power for the Japanese, a colored race that had never before been colonized or semi-colonized.

In chapter 6 (titled "Neocolonial Revolution") of his book *Embracing Defeat*, John Dower referred to Douglas MacArthur, commander-in-chief of the occupation forces, as a "viceroy" after the "Viceroy and Governor-General of India," which was the title of the chief British government official in India. In this way, Dower likened the occupation of Japan to colonial rule.

To be sure, the lifestyle of the occupation forces—that is, the victor in the war—was indeed that of colonial rulers when the white man's supremacy was unchallenged. Any mansion of note that had survived the air raids was confiscated for use as an officers' residence. There, Japanese citizens served as house servants, while the residence's new masters enjoyed golf and tennis in daytime and cocktail parties in the evening.

To starving Japanese children on the street, who were kept remotely removed from the privileged areas, officers and soldiers of the occupation forces gave chewing gum and chocolates. In this way, they satisfied their need to show mercy as well as their sense of superiority. It was a manifestation of the same psychology that had prompted the Imperial Japanese Army to give away sweets to Chinese children when it occupied China.

And it should be pointed out that all of these activities were financed by the taxpayers of Japan. In the draft budget of the Japanese government compiled in July 1946, one-third of expenditures was devoted to monies for postwar processes—that is, shouldering the expenditures of the occupation forces. Thus, even the orchid corsages worn by the wives of officers of the occupation forces at a party, for example, were financed by the Japanese taxpayers.

While the San Francisco Treaty did not require Japan to pay reparations to the United States, the shouldering of the costs of the occupation forces during the occupation of Japan should be considered as de facto reparations. As a matter of fact, the minister of finance at the time, Ishibashi Tanzan, regarded this expenditure as a form of war reparation. Remembering that the major cause of the runaway inflation in post–World War I Germany was the reparation imposed on Germany by the Entente countries, Ishibashi requested that GHQ reduce expenditures for postwar processes. This incurred the wrath of some in GHQ because, to them, it was presumptuous for the loser to make such a request.

Also, the construction of residential facilities for the occupation forces further depleted Japan's already scarce supply of materials for reconstruction. In his letter to MacArthur in December 1946, Prime Minister Yoshida Shigeru complained that, among materials that were planned to be produced in the third quarter of 1946 (October–December), as much as 57 percent of steel pipe, 89 percent of cast-iron pipe, 85 percent of galvanized sheet, and 53 percent of cement were demanded by the occupation forces. It was an act of exploitation, something akin to stripping a destitute person of clothes.

It seems to be beyond doubt that members of the occupation forces indulged in the pleasures of a winner, enjoying life filled with a victor's sense of superiority. In these circumstances, one would not be surprised to find some who feathered their own nests through nasty business, taking advantage of the power of the occupation forces. And, in fact, there indeed were some who did. Charles Kades, "New Dealer" deputy chief of GHQ's Government Section who exercised an overwhelming influence in the political reform of Japan, made the wife of Viscount Torio Takamitsu his mistress. The immoral pleasure that the two shared was a well-known fact.

While it should be possible to spotlight many other examples of self-indulgence by the occupation forces, the behavior of the American officers and soldiers was, objectively speaking, no more tyrannical or dissolute than other occupation forces in history. After all, the behavior of an occupating force directly reflects the level of civilization of the occuping country.

In his memoir, Ishibashi wrote that GHQ had listened attentively to his request that expenditures for postwar processes be reduced and did not touch on the antipathy that his actions had caused among some GHQ members. As a matter of fact, GHQ agreed to cancel construction of nonessential roads. Lieutenant General Robert Eichelberger, commander of the Eighth United States Army who had highly praised the bravery of the Japanese military during the war, even stopped spending money for flowers for his residence. Meanwhile, after the beginning of the Cold War, economic assistance for Japan was initiated.

Thus, this almost colonialistic occupation administration by the United States did not leave as deep a scar in the Japanese psychology as the scars inflicted on other Asian peoples by their colonizers. This was partly due to GHQ's news censorship, which blocked these facts from reaching the ears of the public. As a matter of fact, as the war losers, the Japanese people were in the frame of mind to tolerate some degree of abuse by the occupation forces. Overall, it can be said that, with only a few exceptions, the occupation forces impressed the Japanese people with the Americans' bighearted generosity and Christian virtues.

Rather, it was the meticulous and high-handed (to the extent of crudeness) mechanisms for occupation that GHQ constructed in order to maintain its absolute power that left a deeper impact on subsequent Japanese mentality. How these mechanisms narrowed the subsequent vision of the Japanese people and fixated their thinking should not be overlooked.

The purpose of exploring what the occupation period really was is certainly not to dig up grudges against the occupation forces. Nevertheless, in order to understand contemporary Japanese society and its background, it is essential that we look squarely at the factors of the occupation era that have affected the Japanese way of thinking even today.

# A Wide-Ranging Purge List

It was the power of the United States—its overwhelming military power particularly after the Japanese military had been disarmed and dissolved, as well as its superior economic power unrivaled by a destitute Japan—that provided the source of the absolute power of the occupation forces. The Purge and the control of freedom of speech were two highly effective means for GHQ to exercise absolute power.

As for the Purge, I have already touched on MacArthur's directive of January 4, 1946, which forced Prime Minister Shidehara Kijūrō to grudgingly accept the harsh reality of defeat in war—even though he shouted, "That unreasonable Mac!" in indignation. Subsequent GHQ directives on January 4, 1947, and six months later purged a total of 201,815 individuals from public service.

The Purge list was not confined to individuals in politics, political associations, and publishers. It extended far more widely to include private businesses.

Executives of more than 300 companies in various industries became the target of the Purge. While there were a few national policy corporations and companies founded in the occupied territories, the majority were ordinary private corporations. Among the Mitsubishi group of companies, for instance, thirteen of them became targets of the Purge, encompassing all major industries from Mitsubishi Corporation (trading company), Mitsubishi Bank, and Mitsubishi Holding Company to group corporations in heavy industry, the chemical industry, shipping, petroleum, mining, steel, trust companies, trading companies, and warehouse companies. Executives were purged in other Mitsubishi-related companies such as the Tokyo Marine & Fire Insurance Co. Ltd. Thirteen companies in the Mitsui Group also became targets of the Purge.

When the creamy top of fresh milk that has just been milked from a cow is scooped off, the rest is spoiled in a matter of minutes. Those top-notch people in the industry who were purged were actually the cream of Japanese society that Japan's families, schools, and society had laboriously nurtured since the Meiji Restoration. What GHQ attempted was to scoop off that cream and throw it away.

The list was prepared by the Japanese government, starting in the autumn of 1946, following criteria instructed by GHQ. In the course of this listing process, Yoshida sent the following letter to MacArthur:

> After the U.S. Congress delegation visited Europe last year, it issued a memorandum saying, "If those who had been involved in the movement that ruled Germany for twelve years should all be eliminated, the only expected consequences would be anarchy and chaos." This commentary very well represents the situation in Japan that I am now witnessing, although I would personally add communism to "anarchy and chaos" in the case of Japan.

Together with this letter, Yoshida enclosed a copy of the list that he had submitted to GHQ's Government Section.

While yielding to the order of the Government Section, Yoshida did not fail to warn the United States that what GHQ had instructed would not only lead to chaos in Japan but also invite communism to plague Japanese society, which would not be beneficial to the United States.

As a matter of fact, about a month prior to this letter, Yoshida got back at the Government Section's highhanded interference.

At a meeting with the Japanese side around that time, Deputy Chief Kades said,

> Since there have been cases in which officials of the Japanese government did not follow GHQ's instructions, General MacArthur announced to Prime Minister Yoshida on September 19 that we had no other choice than to shift the occupation policy "from a flexible one to an uncompromising one," giving the Japanese side directives instead of consultations.

Obviously, this was bluffing on the part of Kades. Upon hearing this, Yoshida first obtained confirmation from American officials who had attended the September 19 meeting with MacArthur. Subsequently, Yoshida wrote to MacArthur on September 27 to officially request clarification, saying courteously and humbly that what Kades had said was different from his own memory.

In response, MacArthur immediately replied on the same day that the Government Section confirmed that Kades' remarks were based on utter misunderstanding and misinterpretation.

Japan was under occupation at that time and, as such, the Japanese side could not refute even a remark by a mere colonel directly. The refutation had to go through the Prime Minister's direct appeal to the Commander-in-Chief of GHQ.

It was immediately after this exchange that GHQ issued the directive to implement the second installment of the Purge. Thus, one can clearly see between the lines of Yoshida's letter above his message that, "The Government Section has been unreasonable again. We will of course follow the directive, but do you really think it is wise?"

Even if MacArthur were in principle of the same view as Yoshida on this issue, he nevertheless had to demonstrate the absolute authority of GHQ. Perhaps, he could not let his men lose face by making another compromise here, either. Yoshida's letter might have backfired to make the Government Section issue a high-handed instruction as retaliation or penalty, in anticipation of Yoshida's appeal to MacArthur.

Yoshida continued to request through letters that the Purge be relaxed, but his requests were mostly rejected.

For instance, in his letter of November 21, Yoshida argued against the Government Section's instruction to ban relatives within the third degree of kinship and the spouses of the purged from engaging in public service for ten years, saying, "I believe, under the modern concept of fairness, even the relative of a murderer should be fully guaranteed his/her freedom." The ancient Chinese custom of nine familial exterminations notwithstanding, Yoshida stuck to his position.

Nevertheless, GHQ rejected Yoshida's plea in the form of MacArthur's reply letter on December 3, which said, "It is obvious that the influence of the purged will linger on if that person's power position should be succeeded by his father, uncle, or nephew." The purpose of the Government Section's instruction was to prevent the Purge from becoming a laughing stock by letting a proxy take over the purged person's position.

It is said that almost the only success in mitigating the Purge that the Japanese side accomplished was that of limiting those targeted to company executives above executive managing director rank for major corporations. It would still have been a major blow for any company to be deprived of its executive managing director, senior executive director, vice president, president, and chairman. While this might have saved young and competent directors who were expected to be president someday, it might also have had an adverse impact in giving incompetent old-timers who had been treated as directors before they were transferred to subsidiary companies a chance to make a comeback.

The most outstanding study, or, rather, almost the only study, on the Purge is Masuda Hiroshi's *Kōshoku Tsuihō* ("Purge," University of Tokyo Press, 1996). There also is a compilation of reference materials under the title of *Kōshoku Tsuihō*, volume 6 of *GHQ Nippon Senryō-Shi* (History of GHQ's Occupation of Japan, Nippon Tosho Center, 1996), to which Masuda also contributed commentaries.

Masuda's writings are precise, accurate, academic, and free of biases. Therefore, I beg for readers' tolerance of the frequent quotes from Masuda's works in the following pages.

Masuda's book, *Kōshoku Tsuihō*, is constructed around the case studies of three Japanese politicians who were purged in this period: Hatoyama Ichirō, Ishibashi Tanzan, and Hirano Rikizō.

As Masuda himself pointed out in his book, in the Purge, which was carried out more or less impartially, these three were the exceptional cases in which GHQ's absolute authority was used politically.

I submit, however, that it was the essence of an absolute authority.

Simply put, in order for an absolute authority to demonstrate its absoluteness, it has to prove that it can get its own way even for exceptional occasions.

When a Briton shot to death a defiant Indian during the British colonial rule, the British-administered court found the defendant not guilty because he fired at what he had mistaken as a dog or a monkey. The British and even the Indians were fully aware that this was a pure fabrication—and that it was an exceptional case. If this kind of fabricated trial had been conducted daily, even the colonial authority would not be able to rule and govern the locals. By demonstrating that, occasionally, this kind of exceptional handling was possible, however, the colonized would be made to know that even the slightest defiance would not be tolerated.

As discussed earlier in Chapter 6, the purge of Hatoyama Ichirō was caused by his defiant attitude, such as the issuing of an anti-communist statement, to the New Dealers, the mainstream in GHQ's Government Section in those days, which hoped for the establishment of a leftwing regime in Japan. To quote Masuda, "It was a political warning and extortion on the part of GHQ that it would not hesitate to purge a Japanese person who shows any sign of rebellion against the policy of the occupation forces."

Hatoyama's past words and deeds were a mere ancillary pretext. Originally, the Purge was targeted at those who had collaborated with Japan's war effort. In the case of Hatoyama, however, it was his defiance of the occupation forces that was the chief cause of his purge. And this warning was proven to be immensely effective. After Hatoyama's purge, a mere reference to "GHQ's wish" would make anyone submissively obey the "wish" in all the subsequent political activities, including the deliberations on the constitution during the first Yoshida cabinet. Because every single person in Japan had collaborated with the country's war effort one way or another, anyone could be subject to purge on whatever pretext GHQ chose. In a Japan facing destitution and starvation, being purged meant the ruin of oneself as well as one's family. The only exception to this horror was members of the communist party, who would never have to worry about being questioned on their conduct during the war. Their free and candid words and deeds became one of the causes of their popularity among the Japanese people in the earlier stage of the occupation

## Even Ishibashi Tanzan Had to Be Purged

As Masuda wrote in the afterword of his book, why Ishibashi Tanzan, "a rare liberal journalist in Japan," had to be purged was the direct motivation for Masuda to start studying the Purge. It was, indeed, a peculiar case.

Ishibashi's insight and robust liberalism that had permeated the editorials he had written before and during the war, which I have liberally quoted earlier in this five-volume series, are truly marvelous. It would be no overstatement to say that there was no one else among the Japanese people who was less responsible for leading Japan to war and the defeat than him. Seen from the opposite angle, it was a warning from GHQ that, if Ishibashi could be purged, nobody in Japan, excepting the communist party members who had been imprisoned during the war, was safe from the purge if he/she should displease GHQ. It can be said that this warning or threat was decisively effective.

Although Yoshida was not close to Ishibashi, Yoshida nevertheless had heard that Ishibashi was "a man of considerable wisdom" and that was why, when finding Ishibashi's name in the list of recommended cabinet members prepared by the *Jiyūtō* party, he appointed Ishibashi finance minister without hesitation.

The main cause of Ishibashi's purge was his upright and uncompromising attitude. In those days, even the finance minister had to visit GHQ to meet Major General William Marquat, Director of Economic and Scientific Section, once or twice a week to obtain his approval on financial policies and receive various instructions.

In retrospect, the difference in Ishibashi's policy and that of GHQ was only technical. When everything was needed but was also in short supply, and when whatever economic policies were implemented would be blown away by inflation sooner or later, any policy would have been futile anyway. There would be no gain, therefore, from an argument on which policy was better than another.

Even though Marquat was a mere military man, quite a layman in economics, he made full use of his official authority to interject his modifications wherever he could and delay decision-making. There naturally emerged friction between him and Finance Minister Ishibashi, who was proud of his own insights into economic affairs. In addition, Ishibashi's request to reduce the expenditures for postwar processes, i.e. expenditures for GHQ, fixed his image as a rebellious person in the minds of GHQ officials.

Meanwhile, there emerged a movement inside the *Jiyūtō* to replace Yoshida with Ishibashi. This annoyed some in GHQ, including Kades, who started to engineer the ousting of Ishibashi.

Because Ishibashi's accomplishments as a liberalist were so prominent, the screening committee on the Japanese side repeatedly concluded that Ishibashi did not deserve to be purged. This brought the committee into a confrontation with GHQ.

At this standoff, Colonel Courtney Whitney, Chief of the Government Section, himself visited Yoshida to hand him GHQ's order to purge Ishibashi. Masuda attributed this action to failure to "apply provisions of treason against the occupation administration" to Ishibashi and evaluated

Ishibashi Tanzan's purge as having "left a bad footprint on the Purge, which had otherwise been assessed to be implemented quite fairly, smearing the history of the occupation of Japan."

Ishibashi did not hesitate to openly state that he would never approve GHQ's judgment that the weekly *Tōyō Keizai* (Oriental Economist), at which Ishibashi had served as editor-in-chief, had advocated militarism. There was a rumor that, because Ishibashi rebelled against GHQ, he would be arrested. Of this rumor, it was said that Ishibashi would not mind being arrested because that would give him an opportunity to vindicate the magazine and himself in the court room.

History books in postwar Japan praised Yoshida's diplomacy as that of "a good loser," while they criticized Ishibashi's "political immaturity." On the contrary, in contrast to other Japanese leaders, who were not categorized as "politically immature" but who misled the country, accommodating public opinion and compromising with the power of the Imperial Japanese Army throughout the prewar and wartime days, Ishibashi alone fearlessly defended his solitary position. Given this fact, it can be said that it was Ishibashi Tanzan who deserved to be praised as a person who genuinely maintained his intellectual integrity.

While space does not allow me to introduce the case of Hirano Rikizō's purge in detail, let me quote Masuda again. He said,

> [Hirano's case was] an exceptional case with a heavy political connotation from beginning to end. . . . In short, this case helped spread among the Japanese people's minds a negative image of the Purge as if the entire operation were a tool of GHQ's capricious political strife."

Thus, as Lord Acton's famous dictum tells us, "Power tends to corrupt, and absolute power corrupts absolutely."

Admittedly, Kades must have been a man of considerable competence. Nevertheless, this abuse of the Purge was an inevitable outcome of the use of GHQ's absolute power by a mere army colonel in an attempt to change at will a country like Japan with a 1,000-year history with his immature New Deal philosophy.

Given that some Americans, including John Dower, regret that Kades' measures were not fully pursued, however, I must conclude that we still have a long way to go to before a fair evaluation of the history of the occupation of Japan can be held between Japan and the United States.

## Historical Accomplishments of Etō Jun

Etō Jun, a Shōwa-Heisei literary critic, killed himself in 1999, leaving a suicide note full of despair and self-denial—"What remains now is a bare skeleton of Etō Jun." However, his book, *Tozasareta Gengo-Kūkan* ("Closed Linguistic Space," Tokyo: Bungei Shunjū, 1989), which he published ten years earlier, must be a historical accomplishment that will remain in days to come.

At the outset of the book, Etō confesses that, while reading literary works day after day to contribute literary comment to a newspaper throughout the 1970s, he felt "irritation, as if the linguistic space in which we live and breathe is queerly closed and strangely constrained." Seeking the source of this irritation, he claimed that he had finally found the control of freedom of speech during the occupation period as the origin.

If I dare to interpret what Etō tried to say, I would conjecture that he must have found that, without exception, there was something authors would not say or were made to believe that they could not say in all the Japanese literary works, which he had to read in the hundreds and thousands, as if the Japanese mentality were confined in a narrow, enclosed frame.

In the concluding chapter of the book, Etō characterized GHQ's control of freedom of speech as "a scheme that was supported by a tenacious intention to destroy the Japanese identity and trust in their own history by whatever means it took." When this scheme took hold in the Japanese media and educational system,

> the Japanese identity and the trust in their own history continued eternally to collapse internally. That identity and trust have since become subject to a continuous threat from international censorship. This is exactly what happened at the time of the so-called textbook issue in the summer of 1982.

Admittedly, Etō's works may contain a few oversimplifications and/or opinionated remarks such as are often found among men of literature. Nevertheless, there is more than some truth in Etō's remarks. In fact, his insight was right on the heart of the truth in Japan's modern history. And it can be said that this work was the greatest, and the last, gift that nationalist Etō Jun left to the Japanese people.

Before Etō, there had been few studies on the censorship by GHQ. The precious few studies that existed were mostly based on the experiences of those who were censored plus a few publicized materials. It was Etō who first introduced the entire picture of GHQ censorship to the Japanese people through his encounter with the colossal Prange Collection in the University of Maryland library in 1979–1980.

One of the reasons for the dearth of information on GHQ's censorship was that it had been a strictly confidential operation to outsiders. To begin with, censorship was a violation of the Potsdam Declaration's Article 10, which stipulates that, "Freedom of speech, of religion, and of thought, as well as respect for fundamental human rights, shall be established." Censorship was also a violation of the Constitution of the United States, which bound those American personnel engaged in censorship, as well as the new constitution of Japan that GHQ had imposed on Japan. While, of course, the absolute power at GHQ's disposal allowed it to ignore those international commitments and Japan's constitution, censorship, nevertheless, remained a secret operation due to its inherent nature.

Thus, the dates that censorship began and ended are not made public. Implementation of censorship was announced to each newspaper and publisher in the form of GHQ notification. The notification clearly stated that reference to censorship would be the first subject to be subject to censorship, and that leaving traces of censorship was banned.

This last stipulation had a much more profound implication than expected.

Censors under Japanese authority before and during the war left XX or ○○ on portions of material that was deleted, making it possible for readers to conjecture from the context what had been deleted. At least the fact that something had been deleted by censorship was obvious to anyone. That being the case, writers could remain aloof from the censorship, never compromising what they wanted to write. It was up to the authorities to delete whatever they wished to delete.

In case of the GHQ censorship, in which no trace of censorship was allowed to be obvious, however, authors were requested to alter the entire work. That is, the fundamental structure of the work itself had to be altered, because, otherwise, consistency could not be maintained. In other words, writers were no longer able to write along their original ideas. If authors, then, refused to write at all, it would deprive them of their bread and butter, and newspapers and publishers would be deprived of their works. This was tantamount to coercing authors and editors to remodel their ideas. As the Japanese side grew accustomed to this method, its effect became profound and persistent.

Chapter 14 of John Dower's *Embracing Defeat* is devoted to the issue of censorship. At its outset, Dower said, "the Japanese quickly learned to identify the new taboos and to practice self-censorship accordingly. One simply did not challenge ultimate authority and expect to win"[23] and concludes the chapter with the following observation:

> ... the conquerors worked hard to engineer consensus; and on many critical issues, they made clear that the better part of political wisdom was silence and conformism. So well did they succeed in reinforcing this consciousness that after they left, and time passed, many non-Japanese including Americans came to regard such attitudes as peculiarly Japanese.[24]

This assessment by Dower appears to concur with Etō Jun's assertion that "the Japanese mentality today has been confined in a limited linguistic space by the censorship by GHQ."

It is true that the postwar Japanese people have become cleverer. Even without corroboration, if it was judged to be politically cleverer to admit forceful requisition of the so-called comfort women, then the Japanese would not hesitate to do so. Recalling the Recruit scandal in Japan in the late 1980s, there certainly was an atmosphere in which it seemed cleverer

---

23  John Dower. *Embracing Defeat: Japan in the Wake of World War II*. (New York & London: W.W. Norton & Company, Inc., 1999. p. 405)
24  Ibid. p.440.

to go along with the public opinion that found the incident wrongful even when what happened was a perfectly legal business transaction. This, too, might have been an aftereffect of the occupation human nature.

It seems reasonable to say that the Japanese in olden days had much more mettle. This seems all the truer in the face of a postwar atmosphere that evaluated Ishibashi Tanzan, a rare man of iron will, as "politically immature."

## Censorship Guidelines Include 30 Items

GHQ's censorship was a large-scale and thorough operation. According to Dower, the central censorship authority alone (excluding numerous local centers) received as many as 26,000 newspaper articles, 3,800 news agency articles, 23,000 radio texts, 4,000 magazines, 1,800 books and pamphlets, and 5,700 other printed materials for mass distribution in a peak month. It is believed that GHQ also unsealed and censored as many as 330 million letters and tapped 800,000 telephone conversations.

How was this gigantic operation possible? Japanese is one of the toughest languages for non-native speakers to master. It would not be an overstatement, perhaps, to say that even American scholars who are regarded to be the best Japanese language experts today would not be able to fully comprehend letters written in the Japanese language of those days.

GHQ required the assistance of native Japanese. According to Etō, as many as 5,076 Japanese individuals were employed by the censorship authority as of March 1947. And they were paid ¥900 to ¥1,200 per month, which was among the highest of the salaries of Japanese employees of GHQ.

The blocked bank account measure adopted in March 1946 to fight hyperinflation did not allow anyone, no matter how rich he might have been, to withdraw more than ¥500 per family per month. A salary of ¥900 to ¥1,200 was, therefore, excellent treatment in those days. All the costs of those Japanese employees were financed by the Japanese government's expenditures for postwar processes—in other words, by revenues from Japanese taxpayers. Thus, GHQ did not set any financial limit whatsoever to collect the most appropriate people.

Even in today's Japan, not too many can translate Japanese into English freely. Considering, on top of that, that the English education during the war was nothing to be proud of, it would have taken men of considerable knowledge with prewar overseas experience to accomplish the task GHQ required of them. According to Etō, those Japanese employees included businessmen with long overseas experience, diplomats, and academics. He went on to say:

> When these people received those high salaries, they automatically became people who belonged to that world of darkness. . . . Many have already died. It has been an open secret in some corners of the country that, among those who were engaged in this work when young, were those who later became governors/mayors of progressive local governments, officials at major corporations, international lawyers, prominent journalists, editors-in-chief of academic journals, and university professors. Needless to say, none of them entered this employment in their CVs.

It can be conjectured that perhaps many of those prewar elites who had been deprived of jobs due to the Purge and other means, launched into this work in order to protect their families and lives. And once they were engaged, their inherent habit of pursuing perfectionism and accomplishing the tasks given them must have gotten the better of them. They must have followed the criteria stipulated by GHQ and picked up each and every problematic sentence and reported it meticulously.

Around the year 1947, all the Japanese people, whether they worked for GHQ or not, were experiencing humiliating destitution. At the same time, it was the year when the next generation of Japanese, those who would later be labeled baby-boomers, was born. Part of this new generation became the *Zenkyōtō* (All-Campus Joint Struggle League) generation in the late 1960s. The league was the core of the student revolt that had held up the immature anti-establishment ideal which had derived from the education during the occupation period. Given the conditions in Japan immediately after the defeat, it would be too harsh to blame their parents' generation for their misconduct. In many cases, it was the lack of imagination and insight on the part of the children concerning their parents' sacrifices to nurture them in destitution and hunger, all the while biting their lips as they endured unbearable humiliations, which led to the misconduct.

Censorship was conducted on a wide range of items. According to an internal document, the censorship guidelines included as many as 30 items. A quick glance at the list makes one realize how extensive its impact must have been on the mentality of the Japanese people in postwar days.

Guidelines (1) through (4) forbade criticism of the occupation policies, criticism of the International Military Tribunal for the Far East (Tokyo Trials), criticism of the U.S. drafting of the Japanese constitution, and the mention of censorship. The aftereffect of not only sealing criticism of the American occupation, the Tokyo Trials, and the new constitution but also glorifying them, which lasted for seven years, cannot be small.

Guidelines (5) through (11) forbade criticism of the Allied countries, including the United States, Britain, the Soviet Union, and China, as well as Korea.

Guideline (12) forbade criticism of the treatment of Japanese in Manchuria. This implies that the atrocities committed at the hands of the Soviet troops had already come to GHQ's attention by that time. What this guideline means is that no criticism of the victors was tolerated.

Guideline (13) forbade criticism of the prewar policies of the Allied countries. Coupled with the approval of the Tokyo Trials, this guideline led to a historical view that everything in prewar Japan was evil and everything in the Allied countries was good.

Guidelines (14) and (15) forbade reference to the possible Third World War and the Cold War.

Using the term "a small time warp," John Dower concludes Chapter 14's section on "Purifying the Victors" as follows:

This mystique of immaculate Allies contributed to the fashioning of a public world that was not merely unreal, but sometimes almost surreal. Isolated from the rest of the world, the defeated Japanese were supposed to ignore the collapse of the victorious wartime alliance, the breakup of national unity in China, the renewed struggles against Western imperialism and colonialism in Asia, the decisive emergence of Cold War tensions, and the beginning of a nuclear arms race. They were placed, as it were, in a small time warp, where the World War II propaganda of the winning side had to be reiterated even as the erstwhile victors engaged in new struggles and polemics.[25]

## A Thorough Reorganization of the Traditional Value System

Throughout the fifty years of debate on national defense and security in postwar Japan, I have always felt it strange that, although the first order of business must be to assess the international situations surrounding Japan and the necessary measures to be worked out, the mainstream of Japan's public opinion seems to deliberately close its eyes and ears to the reality of international relations and chooses to concentrate only on reviewing the domestic situation in Japan concerning the war and particular articles of the Constitution of Japan. When considering Japan's security, this kind of debate inevitably leads to the adoption of primary criteria that emphasize how to restrict the resurrection of militarism and refrain from hurting the feelings of Asians—meaning, the Chinese.

As I have mentioned in my 1983 book *Senryaku Shikō to ha Nanika* (What Constitutes Strategic Thinking?), when I stressed the importance of the expansion of Japan's defense capabilities around 1980 in light of the military situations in the Far East at the time, I came across a scholar of international politics who said, "If Japan cannot make as much defense efforts as the United States expects, its assessment of the military situations in the Far East should not be identical with that of the United States." When I asked for clarification, saying, "Do you mean that Japan should assess the potential threat of the Soviet Union as something Japan's current defense capabilities can meet," he said, to my astonishment, "Yes." It was a geocentric argument, as if to say that world revolves around Japan instead of vice versa.

Although the censorship by GHQ had long been gone by that time, there still was some social restriction, or "censorship," if you will, against such rightwing, reactionary forces as those who called for expansion of the military buildup. The conclusion of the debate had been given as a postulate—that is, that Japan should not expand its military capabilities.

---

25    Ibid. p.425.

If the Soviet military threat were objectively assessed to have increased, however, the given conclusion would become inconsistent. Hence, the assessment itself should be modified. What a miserable decay of mentality! I wonder if this, too, is a part of the aftereffect of the occupation.

This should be exactly what Dower called the "time warp" and what Etō Jun described as the "queerly closed [linguistic] space." And Etō's attribution of this state to GHQ censorship during the occupation period, which might at first glance appear to be a jump in logic, may well be right on the mark.

The remaining guidelines from (16) through (20) forbade defense of the Greater East Asia War; use of such terms as Divine Desent Nation, militarism, and nationalism; and positive evaluation of the Greater East Asia Co-prosperity Sphere. According to the idea of war propaganda, which had been the conventional wisdom of Americans in those days, these were all vices that derived from Japan's past history and tradition. Hence, Etō's conclusion: "As is apparent at a glance, what is intended here is a thorough reorganization of the traditional value system that the Japanese have nurtured since ancient times." Whether such had been the original intention of GHQ or not, the actual effect of the censorship was exactly as Etō expounded.

Additionally, the reporting of such facts as the miserable living conditions in postwar Japan, starvation, and the black market, as well as interactions between the occupation forces and Japanese women, was also regulated. In fact, it was only after the occupation was terminated that Japanese citizens got to see photos of the catastrophes in Hiroshima and Nagasaki with their own eyes.

> Vegetable garden in the midst of a fire-devastated area
> Is beaten by a heavy rain

This is a *haiku* poem depicting typical scenery in those days. But even such an innocent and simple description was banned because "it contained elements that could go against the interests of the United States." Comic strips by Kondō Hidezō and Sugiura Yukio depicting an occupation force soldier and a Japanese woman being together were also forbidden to be published.

Such literary giants as Dazai Osamu, Tanizaki Jun'ichirō, and Kawabata Yasunari were also victimized by the censorship. Even such classics as Tolstoy's *War and Peace* and the autobiography of Uchimura Kanzō became the target of censorship, and some segments of those books were ordered to be deleted at the time of reprinting.

It was exactly how George Orwell had envisioned the totalitarian society of the future. And to think that all of this profound, immeasurable damage to the Japanese mentality was done by mid-level American administrators at GHQ, who were not altogether well-cultured persons, makes everything all the more deplorable.

In retrospect, Japan under GHQ's regulation of freedom of speech was such a closed society that one may wonder whether such a thing is really permissible in a modern society. Today, with the advancement of the Internet, some believe that it is no longer viable to exercise control over people's thoughts. But only a few decades ago, when the possibility of the entire world becoming socialist could not be altogether denied, it was a convincing argument that a modern society was where the development of the radio and newspapers allowed the state authority to regulate citizens' thought. That was what happened in Germany under the Nazis and in the Soviet Union. The same situation still remains in China and North Korea. The George Orwellian world was a portrayal of this state of a closed society, stemming from Orwell's own deep sense of despair toward the future of mankind. Japan under occupation was the embodiment of just that.

# 11

# Change of the Tide

*—Japan's Shift from a "Sea of Red Flags"*
*to the Road to Reconstruction—*

## Atmosphere Akin to the Night before a Revolution

Nineteen forty-six (21st Year of Shōwa), the year following Japan's defeat, was like the night before a communist revolution. Yoshida Shigeru reminisced that "It would be no exaggeration to say that I formed the first Yoshida cabinet surrounded by red flags and revolutionary songs." In fact, wherever he went to deliver a speech, he was always so physically obstructed by members of the communist party that he could not move freely without the protection of armed U.S. MP escorts.

In those days, nothing in Japan could check the menace of the communist party and the labor unions. Matters reached such an extent that the violent and destructive conduct of union members during labor unrest was not regarded as a criminal offense.

On October 10, 1945, members of the Japan Communist Party, including Tokuda Kyūichi and Shiga Yoshio, who had been imprisoned for eighteen years, were released. The party resumed publication of its organ, *Akahata* (Red Flag), the first issue of which praised the liberation of the Japanese people by the occupation forces and pledged the party's cooperation with GHQ. In January 1946, Nosaka Sanzō, founder of the Japan Communist

Party, returned to Japan from his self-imposed exile in China to the welcoming cheers of the mass media. Nosaka declared it to be "a Japan Communist Party loved by the people."

Since prewar days, the Communist Party had always been accompanied by dark images of the gruesome power struggles within the party and resultant lynches. When the Soviet Union was dissolved in 1991, all the dark realities of Communism were disclosed, including the miseries in the USSR during the Stalin days and the Great Cultural Revolution in China. This, in turn, made us realize that in their prewar image of communism, the Japanese people had actually perceived correctly, at least to a certain extent, the true nature of communism. Immediately after the defeat, however, the Japanese mass media posited an argument that the image of communism was distorted by propaganda during the era of militarism and that communism was an irresistible current leading to a new society. Even though the Japanese people still remained suspicious of communism, they felt it risky to openly oppose the Japan Communist Party, seeing as it was under the protection of GHQ, with which it maintained cooperative relations.

Even such a man of higher education as Hayashi Kentarō, the Shōwa historian who later became president of the University of Tokyo, had to reminisce later as follows:

> People were happy to witness what appeared to be fascism being overthrown by U.S.-Soviet cooperation, and they were convinced of rapprochement between the two camps. And I thought that released Japan Communist Party members giving cheers for MacArthur in front of GHQ headquarters and Nosaka Sanzō's declaration that the Japan Communist Party would be loved by the Japanese people were signs indicating the evolution of communism.

Looking back, Hayashi confessed that people in Japan, including himself, were infested with overoptimistic dogmatism.

Meanwhile, labor unions showed remarkable growth in Japan. After the Shidehara cabinet's Labor Union Law—which even GHQ could find no fault with due to its highly progressive content—was promulgated toward the end of 1945, the number of labor union members jumped in one month by one million from 380,000, reaching 5.6 million by the end of 1946 and peaking at 6.7 million in 1948. This was more than 50 percent of all non-agricultural laborers.

John Dower, author of *Embracing Defeat: Japan in the Wake of World War II*, observed that behind this rapid growth of labor unions in Japan was a vacuum left by patriotic labor organizations, which had been organized during the war as a part of the all-out war effort. The leftwing movements filled this vacuum.

It is a universal phenomenon observed all over the world that a war brings a more egalitarian society and more democratic politics in postwar days. Thus, had it not been for the occupation by the Allied powers, perhaps Japan would have experienced a similar postwar development. More than that, as we will see later in this chapter, Japan's inclination toward the left might have been further accelerated without the absolute power of the occupation forces to check it.

The main reason behind the growth of labor unions in postwar Japan must have been the hardship people were facing to merely survive. In the midst of creeping starvation and aggravating inflation, workers' requests for higher wages and fewer dismissals had a ring of desperation. In labor movements in those days, it was not unusual for workers to torment employers with hostile questions and threats. Some unions even resorted to such radical conduct as taking over the management of companies in the name of production management.

Hayashi was originally a Marxist, and he admitted that his Marxist conviction was not easily shaken. Nevertheless, he reminisced that, in the end, he had become quite doubtful of the Japan Communist Party. Hayashi said:

> I gradually began to feel that I could no longer go along with the realities of the Japan Communist Party . . . Realistically speaking, would it really benefit people to subject employers to a kangaroo court when production as a whole had dropped radically due to the defeat in the war? Would it not be necessary, instead, to restore the Japanese economy by boosting production?

The greatest problem, or rather the eternal problem, in dealing with the communist party is its ability to penetrate any organization, even if its members are not a majority in that organization, and, in time, seize the initiative in the organization.

While this is a communist tactic that everyone knows, there is hardly any quotable evidence or documentation. Being a secret operation, naturally there should not be any evidence of it. All that remains are fragmentary testimonies of those who have been outmaneuvered by the communists. For instance, a member of an organization is abruptly called to participate in a conference. When he sits at the conference table, he finds few friends around the table. Seats are occupied predominantly by members of the communist party. Unable to contact friends outside the conference room, the person finds he has no way to stop or moderate the procedure, which is being pursued seamlessly as if on a premeditated scenario.

This kind of operation is enforceable only for an organization with the capacity to carry out an operational plan based on an accurate assessment of situations. This strategy complies with the Leninism that claims that the end justifies the means. It is not easy for any outsider to meet this challenge, especially when one is caught off guard.

Under circumstances that resemble the eve of a revolution, especially, such a threat as "There is no knowing what will happen to you once a people's government is accomplished" was particularly effective in encouraging non-party members to take a wait-and-see attitude. It was this attitude that allowed the Communist Party to control two-thirds of labor unions in Japan.

Prime Minister Yoshida Shigeru dared to resist this menace of communism. In his New Year address of 1947, Yoshida called the leftwing forces "lawless elements" that "hold demonstrations on the street day-in and day-out in the name of a labor offensive, paying no heed to heightened social anxiety they are causing." Yoshida found this conducts "unexpected and regrettable."

Yoshida's comment was more provocative than the anti-communist declaration of Hatoyama Ichirō, who was purged for his view. Unlike Hatoyama, though, Yoshida had a calculation behind his statement. For one thing, he was convinced through his contact with GHQ leadership that GHQ would not leave the situation unattended for long. While there was no knowing when GHQ would actually intervene, Yoshida's statement seemed to have the effect of provoking the Japan Communist Party to take a step toward confrontation. Observing the unanimous chorus of harsh criticism for Yoshida's statement among the mass media, the Communists appeared to decide that the time was ripe to stand up and revolt.

Thus, labor unions at government- and state-owned enterprises, which boasted a membership of some 2.6 million, decided to hold a no-time-limit strike on February 1, 1947, to demand better treatment of workers. If carried out as planned, the strike would precipitate an emergency situation where even railroads and mail services were suspended indefinitely. It is said that the atmosphere in Japan in those days could be compared to Russia during the revolution on the eve of the formation of the Alexander Kerensky cabinet of the Russian Provisional Government. A rumor has it that even a list of prospective members of the incoming "people's cabinet" was prepared. The list included such names as Matsumoto Jiichirō as prime minister, Tokuda Kyūichi as interior minister, Nosaka Sanzō as foreign minister cum education minister, as well as Shiga Yoshio as chief cabinet secretary. It would have been a typical interim cabinet on the eve of a revolution, with all the key power positions monopolized by communist party members. The exception would have been "Prime Minister" Matsumoto, who was popularly perceived as a leader of the Buraku Liberation Movement rather than as a socialist.

In his memoir, Yoshida called this February 1 strike "premeditated political conduct by Communists." While it was not possible to prove what the true intention of the Communist Party had been, it seemed beyond any reasonable doubt that this general strike was under the influence and leadership of the party. After all, party members had monopolized the key positions in each labor union even though union chairmanships were assigned to more moderate figures.

The February 1 strike, however, proved to be the peak of the communist-led revolutionary mood. The tide of change caused by GHQ's intervention swallowed the Communist movement in no time.

It was at this point that GHQ decided to intervene. First, GHQ instructed the Japanese government to prepare a compromise proposal to the labor unions' demands and make it public. Subsequently, GHQ summoned Ii Yashirō, chairman of the joint struggle committee who had expressed discontentment with the government proposal, to its headquarters. Ii was threatened at gunpoint and persuaded to sign the announcement of the cancellation of the strike. Even though Ii protested, saying, "This kind of coercion is undemocratic," such a naïve argument was of no avail. In the end, Ii announced cancellation of the strike in a radio speech, his voice thick with tears.

In a defeated and occupied country, even leaders of labor unions had to grudgingly yield to the pressure of the occupier, just like Shidehara Kijūrō had had to a year earlier.

In contrast to Shidehara, who had no other choice in order to protect the emperor, which was an absolute must for him, the worst that could have happened to Ii had he resisted GHQ's order would have been nothing more than forced labor in Okinawa. It might be said that Ii was much more vulnerable to GHQ's authority than Shidehara.

Admittedly, it must have been objectively impossible for Ii to resist GHQ's pressure. While the communist party had led the plan for the general strike thus far with its strategies and tactics, there was no knowing whether participating labor unions would follow the party's lead if Ii refused GHQ's order and carried out the strike. After all, it would have become a general strike that could gravely affect the life of the entire nation. And because the Japanese people had the good common sense to shy away from a general strike unsanctioned by GHQ, the mounting tide for revolution ebbed overnight.

## Conflict of Opinions within GHQ

It was around this time that changes in the international situation started also affecting U.S. occupation policies.

As early as March 1946, Winston Churchill had started using the term "iron curtain"—the use of which continued for the next half century—to warn of the threat of the Soviet advance into Eastern Europe. While Churchill opposed the iron curtain, he was, at that time, a mere private harbinger who was ahead of his time. Consultations between Britain, the United States, and the Soviet Union on the aftermath of the war in Europe had run aground one after another. Gradually, the confrontation between the western and eastern camps had become decisively apparent. In March 1947, the United States announced the Truman Doctrine to start overseas assistance to block countries from being communized.

While Japan itself was still in what John Dower termed a "time warp" (see Chapter 10)—that is, an extension of World War II—confrontation between the contending views had already begun to be seen within GHQ.

As we saw in Chapter 4 of this volume, American foreign policy had always been characterized by a conflict between idealism and realism. The idealist faction viewed all of Japan's past as evil and deemed it the U.S. mission to fundamentally remake Japan on the basis of the American model. This was, essentially, a mere continuation of the line of thinking during World War II that had been strongly advocated by Chief Courtney Whitney and Deputy Chief Charles Kades of GHQ's Government Section.

There existed another school of thought with a more realistic inclination that argued that Japan's strategic value, including its economic and military powers, must be utilized in anticipation of the imminent confrontation with emerging Soviet threats. This school was convinced that the key issue for future U.S. foreign policy would be the communist threat—and this was proven right in the sense that the communist threat preoccupied the minds of American policymakers for the next half a century. This school was represented by MacArthur's Chief of Intelligence Charles Willoughby and Commanding General of the Eighth Army Robert Eichelberger.

In the realists' eyes, what Kades and his associates were doing must have appeared highly immature—as if they did not know what they were doing . From the realists' viewpoint, Kades' group was not only weakening Japan, a country that would be a great asset to the United States in winning a cold war, through dissolution of the zaibatsu and the Purge but also nullifying its military and public order capabilities.

This intra-GHQ strife lasted for another two years after the abortive February 1 strike until the resignation of a crestfallen Kades. During those two years, Kades' Government Section continued to exercise an overwhelming influence over Japan's politics.

After banning the February 1 strike, MacArthur wrote to Yoshida on February 6 that time was ripe for a general election. This prompted Yoshida to promise MacArthur in his February 10 reply that a general election would be conducted as the first order of business of the new Japan under the new constitution.

There are few documents explaining why MacArthur sent this February 6 letter to Yoshida. Perhaps, having banned a strike, a trump card he should have never played, MacArthur found it necessary to put matters back on the right track. In anticipation of the U.S. presidential election the next year, he also found it wise to attend to expected criticisms from the liberal camp. It was in consideration of these factors that MacArthur dismissed the officer in charge of labor relations at the time of the February 1 strike and named James Killen to head GHQ's Labor Division. Killen was strongly supported by American labor unions.

Although the Yoshida cabinet accomplished enactment of a new constitution, the Japanese economy in those days was in such wretched condition that it would never be well managed no matter who took the helm. And in the realm of politics, the Yoshida cabinet found itself in quite a difficult predicament. If left unattended, Japanese politics might have gone bankrupt, which, together with the intervention into the February 1 strike, could well have been attributed to the alleged failure of the occupation policies. Against this background, MacArthur might have decided that a general election to seek the judgment of the Japanese people could give him a political breakthrough.

In any event, the prime minister's prerogative to dissolve the Diet was still in the hands of GHQ at that time.

When the general election was held on April 25, 1947, the Socialist Party of Japan (*Nippon Shakaitō*) became the number one party, winning 143 seats. Yoshida's *Jiyūtō* (Liberal Party) came in second with 131 seats and *Minshutō* (Democratic Party) followed with 124 seats.


## Yoshida's Strategic Move to Facilitate Longtime Rule

In the face of this defeat, Yoshida decided against forming a coalition government and stepped down. He did so despite opposition from some in the *Jiyūtō* who sought to cling to power. In my view, it was the best political judgment that Yoshida made in his long political career.

Even though the Socialist Party became the largest political party in the first general election, it still remained a minority in the Diet as a whole. As such, it could not be expected to accomplish much. Nor was it endowed with people rich in the administrative experience needed at a time when the Japanese economy was swamped with all kinds of problems. Because there was no doubt that the Socialist Party would fail as the government party, the correct move was for Yoshida to relinquish the position of power for a while and wait for the new regime to self-destruct.

As it turned out, things advanced exactly as Yoshida must have predicted. It would not be an overstatement to say that this politically correct judgment was the origin of Yoshida's long rule after the Second Yoshida Cabinet. And seeing as the two years when Yoshida chose to lie low coincided with the period of the GHQ Government Section's last fruitless resistances—that is, its arbitrary interference in Japanese politics—Japan would not have been able to do anything on its own initiative had Yoshida remained prime minister.

What Yoshida did was nothing new in Japan's politics, and it was something that anyone could have conceived. In fact, both Itō Hirobumi at the time of formation of the *Wai-Han* cabinet (the first Ōkuma cabinet) in 1898 and Yamagata Aritomo at the time of the formation of Japan's first party cabinet by Itō Hirobumi in 1900 chose to force responsibilities on regimes that were grossly underprepared and wait for their self-destruction. In Yoshida's day, however, once one let go of power, one could be liable to a joint purge by GHQ and the Japanese government. Moreover, given the general destitution in Japan in the wake of the defeat, politicians must have had a strong, instinctive desire to stay in power at any cost. Yoshida, therefore, must have been either unselfish enough to step down despite the apparent pitfalls or he could afford to do so psychologically and materially.

The socialist government that was born in Japan as the result of the first general election under the new constitution was what the New Dealers of GHQ's Government Section had long hoped for. The next two years witnessed collusion between GHQ's Government Section and the socialist middle-of-the-road coalition government. During that time, the power-drunk Government Section overdid itself, hurting the occupation policy's reputation and digging the New Dealers' own grave.

From the beginning, Kades poked his nose into the formation of Katayama Tetsu's socialist cabinet, expressing his opposition to the appointment of Hirano Rikizō as agriculture minister. While the official reason for Kades' reservation was that Hirano had been a leader of farmers' organizations during the war days, it is believed that the true reason was Hirano's close association with Yoshida and Willoughby. Katayama's pleading, including in a personal letter, notwithstanding, the Government Section decided to expel Hirano from the cabinet. This decision was overturned by the Japanese side's maneuver via Willoughby, and Hirano was appointed agricultural minister. Finding Hirano to be in mutual sympathy with Yoshida, Kades before long succeeded in pressuring Katayama to dismiss Hirano.

This interference brought disastrous results. Losing the support of 40 members of the Hirano faction, which belonged to the rightwing of the Social Democratic Party, tipped the intra-party balance toward the leftwing faction. The Katayama cabinet found it challenging to control the party. In the end, even the leftwing faction of the party declared its non-cooperation with the Katayama cabinet. This delivered the final blow to the ill-fated government.

When a cabinet collapses, it is a principle of constitutional democracy for the second party to form a new cabinet. Thus, at this point, the reins should have been passed on to the second party, i.e., the *Jiyūtō* under Yoshida. Stubbornly determined not to let Yoshida form a second cabinet, however, the Government Section "suggested" that Ashida Hitoshi should form a new government. Unable to turn down GHQ's "suggestion," the House of Representatives voted in Ashida as the new chief of the cabinet.

Because at the time the orthodox argument that the second party, *Jiyūtō* in this case, should form the government was strongly supported by public opinion, the newly born Ashida cabinet had to make a highly unpopular start. This, too, can be regarded as another stepping stone for the imminent long rule by Yoshida.

Ashida Hitoshi himself was a diplomat with good education and insight as well as a disciplined liberalist. Judging from his words and deeds in the Diet during the war, his written works, and the wisdom that he had displayed as chairman of the Diet's special committee on constitutional amendment, he was endowed with a superior analytical mind and higher degree of insight than Yoshida Shigeru. Needless to say, some politicians are lucky, while some others are not so lucky. In light of Yoshida, who remained extraordinarily lucky throughout his career, it just might not be fair to assess a politician's capacity only on the basis of what he has accomplished.

To speak plainly, it may be said that Ashida was more a cultured and learned man than a politician. This is apparent from the single fact that Ashida was without a sworn friend to help him or a cabinet member that would do anything for him even after he became the head of the government. Moreover, he was under an unfortunate objective circumstance. When there was no political issue that could unite political will (such as the promulgation of the new constitution in the case of the first Yoshida cabinet and the peace treaty in the case of the second Yoshida cabinet), when the Japanese economy was in such shambles that it did not matter who managed it, and when it was as clear as day that any government of the time would be a puppet of the Government Section, there was no way for Ashida to muster whatever political power he might have had.

The direct cause of the fall of the Ashida cabinet was the so-called Showa Electric scandal in which two of Ashida's cabinet members were accused of corruption. In the end, Ashida was proven innocent and the scale of the scandal was not actually very large. But it is believed that behind this scandal might have been a scheme to oust Kades engineered by GHQ's Intelligence G-2 section under Willoughby, who was fed up with the Government Section's conduct. There was no way for outsiders to know how true this speculation was because it was essentially an internal power struggle within GHQ. Nevertheless, bits and pieces of hearsay were enough to verify the rumor.

It had been known that Hinohara Setsuzō, President of Showa Electric, had lavishly entertained government leaders, bureaucrats, and, particularly, GHQ's Government Section officers. Knowing this, the G-2 section had intended to condemn the unethical conduct of Kades and members of the Ashida cabinet.

Former police personnel reminisced that an MP of the occupation forces one day gave a strict order to the Metropolitan Police Department to take a photo of Kades rendezvousing with Viscountess Torio. A policeman succeeded in taking a photo of the two kissing, but he was spotted by them when he accidentally made a noise. Furious, Kades engineered the demotion of the members of the Metropolitan Police Department involved in this operation. This episode sounds like a typical incident under colonial rule.

Even after the downfall of Ashida due to the Showa Electric Scandal, Kades would not give up trying to block Yoshida's comeback to the premiership. Even though formation of the *Minshujiyūtō* (Democratic

Liberal Party in March 1948 through the merger of the *Jiyūtō* and members who defected from the *Minshutō*) cabinet became inevitable after the demise of the Ashida cabinet, Kades suggested again that, instead of Yoshida, who was president of the *Minshujiyūtō*, the party's secretary-general Yamazaki Takeshi should be prime minister. Hearing this wish of GHQ, some within the political parties including *Minshujiyūtō*, began to show signs of accommodating the suggestion. Yoshida himself resisted this movement, saying, "If MacArthur forces us to appoint Yamazaki to prime minister, I will concur. In return, however, I will make full use of my freedom of speech to let the world know of this. But, before that, I shall visit MacArthur personally and confirm his true intention myself."

At this point, Yamazaki with good grace resigned as a member of the Diet, making it impossible for the parties to vote for Yamazaki instead of Yoshida in the House of Representatives. Consequently, the House elected Yoshida to form a single-party minority cabinet with only 185 votes.

## The Government Section's Futile Struggle and the "Conspiracy Dissolution"

At this point, Kades' maneuver to block the formation of the second Yoshida cabinet ended in failure. Kades' anti-Yoshida engineering, nevertheless, still continued.

Although Yoshida formed his second cabinet, his was still a minority government. Among the Japanese people, who had been disappointed by the incompetence of the Katayama and Ashida cabinets, support for Yoshida's *Minshujiyūtō* remained overwhelmingly high. The orthodox political process at this point would be to dissolve the Diet as soon as possible and secure a stable majority through a general election. This was indeed what any political party in power had done without fail during the Taishō Democracy era before the war.

In those cases, the opposition was naturally against the dissolution of the Diet. Some in the opposition brought out a queer legal argument that the prime minister's prerogative under the new constitution to unilaterally dissolve the Diet was questionable, and the Government Section decided to ride with this argument.

To begin with, a prime minister's prerogative to dissolve the Diet is, together with the opposition's right to submit a no-confidence motion, a cornerstone of the checks and balances in parliamentary politics. While, today, a similar argument questioning this prerogative of the prime minister is utterly unthinkable, at that time the new constitution had just been promulgated and arguments, including this one, were still heard.

The opposition's strange arguments and the Government Section's intervention notwithstanding, Yoshida was determined to dissolve the Diet. Learning how determined Yoshida was, Government Section Chief Courtney Whitney paid Yoshida a personal visit and presented a compromise proposal. Whitney proposed that the Diet should pass the bill on public servants' salaries and budget first, after which the Diet would be dissolved by letting the Socialist Party's no-confidence motion pass rather than by invoking the controversial prime minister's prerogative. This was the substance of what came to be called the "conspiracy dissolution."

When things came this far, what the Government Section was doing was a futile struggle to demonstrate GHQ's right to interfere. The only thing it accomplished was to leave the impression that the occupation authority was unjustly abusing its authority and interfering with Japanese politics.

In the general election in January 1949 following this "conspiracy dissolution," Yoshida Shigeru's *Minshujiyūtō* won a landslide victory, winning an absolute majority of 264 seats.

Kades headed for Washington, D.C., toward the end of 1948. Although it was believed that the purpose of his trip was to convince authorities in Washington that the goals of the occupation would not have been accomplished had the situation been left unattended, Kades resigned when he realized his attempt had no chance to succeed. Kades never returned to Japan.

It was the final victory for Yoshida over Kades. More than that, the landslide victory in the general election provided a foundation to Yoshida's long political career: later Yoshida would be called "one-man" for the way he made important decisions by himself. Many of the *Minshujiyūtō* party members whom Yoshida had inherited from Hatoyama Ichirō's *Jiyūtō* earlier were expelled. Instead, Yoshida made a number of notable high-ranking bureaucrats run for the general election. After winning seats, these politicians became the core of Yoshida's personal network nicknamed the "Yoshida School." Originally, Yoshida had become prime minister only to fill in for the purged Hatoyama, but now Yoshida had built his own power base. This became one of the remote causes for the complications when Hatoyama was allowed to return to politics.

## Occupation of Japan Was One Failure after Another

While New Dealers in GHQ's Government Section continued to try to interfere with Japanese politics in the two years between the cancellation of the February 1 strike in 1947 and the formation of the third Yoshida cabinet in 1949, U.S. foreign policy experienced a drastic change due to the intensification of the Cold War.

The main engines of the changes in U.S. foreign policy were the Department of War, which had to face the Cold War squarely; the Department of Defense, which was newly established in 1949 integrating the Departments of the Navy and Army; and the State Department's Policy Planning Office under the leadership of George Kennan, who had drafted America's initial policy of "containment" toward the Soviet Union at the beginning of the Cold War. But this change met strong resistance from the liberals and the New Dealers in GHQ. It would be no exaggeration to say that it was actually the non-governmental Japan lobby that made the United States change its policy toward Japan.

Of the most prominent among Japan lobbies in the United States was the American Council on Japan (ACJ) at which Joseph Grew served as honorary chairman. This council was founded in March 1948 by Harry Kern, the foreign editor of *Newsweek*, Eugene Dooman, Compton Pakenham, and James Kauffman.

Dooman, one of the most prominent Japan experts in the United States, had long been a right-hand man to Grew since prewar days. Pakenham had had friends among prominent Japanese leaders since prewar days and, at Kern's request, served as resident advisor to *Newsweek* in Tokyo during the occupation period.

Hearing criticisms of GHQ's policies, particularly apprehensions about GHQ's noninterference with the Japan Communist Party, from such Japanese dignitaries as Makino Nobuaki, Suzuki Kantarō, and Nomura Kichisaburō, Pekenham wrote to Kern in July 1946 that there was no doubt that the entire occupation of Japan had been one failure after another.

Subsequently, Pakenham contributed an article to *Newsweek* denouncing the occupation policies regarding Japan. Sensitive to American public opinion as a possible candidate for the next presidential election, MacArthur declared Pakenham to be an "undesirable personality." But Charles Willoughby assured Pakenham that, had he written the article himself, it would be exactly the same word for word.

Kauffman rubbed salt in the wound inflicted by Pakenham. Kauffman was a lawyer whose clients included major American corporations, and the purpose of his visit to Japan in August 1947 was to examine business possibilities in Japan. During his stay, he got hold of the Far Eastern Commission's classified document FEC-230 on the dissolution of the zaibatsu. Kauffman criticized the document relentlessly, saying,

> This proposed act would only rip the whole of Japanese industry to pieces and indulge labor unions, making it impossible for American businessmen to profit in the Japanese market. And it would, in turn, deprive Japan of its potential as the bastion in the Far East against communism.

It is said that this criticism by Kaufmann had a grave impact on authorities in Washington because it was a criticism from the standpoint of American business, which no one in the United States could oppose. Kaufmann found fault with occupation policies that had been pursued out of inertia and in complete disregard for actual American interests based on arguments for punishing Japan on the extension of World War II and on the New Dealers' argument for restructuring Japan. Moreover, Kaufmann also pointed out the risk of the occupation policies causing disastrous consequences for U.S. Cold War policy.

It was this criticism by Kaufmann that affected the activities of William Draper of the Department of the Army. Draper provided the turning point of U.S. policies toward Japan. Draper had originally been a prominent banker/businessman on Wall Street. After World War II, he served as chief of the Economic Division, Allied Control Council for Germany, and, subsequently, he was appointed Undersecretary of War in August 1947. Upon his appointment, Draper visited Japan to observe first hand that "Japan's economic and financial institutions were on the brink of collapse, which had become a threat to U.S. accomplishment of its multiple objectives." When he returned to the United States in October, he reported to the then Secretary of Defense James Forrestal that what Kaufmann had written about the U.S. occupation policies was highly accurate.

Convinced that this was a political conspiracy connected to the presidential election, MacArthur adamantly rejected Draper's report and made Kades the spearhead of his counterargument.

Nevertheless, Washington's attitude had been so hardened by that time that it was already impossible to change it. In fact, the Department of the Army concluded in November that FEC230 would be reviewed and reinterpreted from the viewpoint of "promotion of early resurrection of the Japanese economy."

A December issue of *Newsweek* carried an editorial chaacterizing Occupation policy as "far to left of anything now tolerated in America," and Senator William Noland fiercely attacked FEC230 in the Senate chamber. In March 1948, George Kennan, Director of the State Department's Policy Planning Staff, visited Japan and advised GHQ that economic rehabilitation of Japan should be the top priority of the occupation policy. Kennan also said that GHQ should refrain from forcing the existing reforms on Japan any further and, instead, should relax existing reform programs.

Subsequently, Kern became a target of hatred in the mass media and in leftwing elements in Japan because Japan at that time was still in the midst of an era in which anyone who had been close to high society in prewar Japan was bound to be labeled a conservative reactionary element, and particularly because Kern's major contact in Japan was Kishi Nobusuke whom, in the post-occupation period, *Zengakuren* (All-Japan Federation of Students' Self-Governing Associations) generation quite meaninglessly targeted with hatred. Thus, an image of Kern as an evil backstage manipulator has been fixed in the Japanese mind. That image was reinforced further by Kern's involvement in the Douglas Grumman scandal in 1978.

Yet Kern and his associates' contribution to the shift in GHQ's occupation policy toward reconstruction of the Japanese economy cannot be overstated.

Those who remember how things were in Japan in 1947 through 1949 must recall what a miserable time it was.

Figures presented in the *Sengo Keizai 10-nen Shi* (10-year History of the Postwar Economy) compiled by the Ministry of International Trade and Industry in 1954 clearly illustrate the hardship that the Japanese people had to suffer in those days. Using 1924–1926 as the base year, indices of how much daily commodities was supplied were 58 in 1946, which was quite understandable; 65 in 1947, and only 69 in 1948, indicating a highly sluggish recovery. Ratios of earned income to actual expenses per month per household were 70 percent to 80 percent in 1947 and 1948, showing negative earnings. Although the margin of deficit grew slimmer gradually year by year, *Sengo Keizai 10-nen Shi* attributes this phenomenon to the so-called *takenoko-seikatsu* (a poverty-stricken life maintained only by selling one's belongings one by one) instead of an increase in earned income. In other words, this narrowing of the gap revealed that people were running out of things to sell or that their state of destitution was worsening.

As society became increasingly stabilized, people found it embarrassing to wear rags as they had in the immediate postwar days. This forced them to spend more for education, transportation, and other necessities. Yet income remained stagnant. Thus Japanese families were forced to suffer from what appeared to be endless destitution. Politicians in those days were totally devoid of autonomous initiatives, waiting as they were on Kades' nod. This situation contributed to people's sense of despair. As long as GHQ persisted with retaliation through the reform of Japan, it was only natural that the Japanese economy could not find any way out.

In a short while, the Japanese economy became liberated from this stifling atmosphere due to the eruption of the Korean War and the accompanying military demand. As a matter of fact, around that time, GHQ's occupation policy had already converted to emphasizing economic rehabilitation more with the goal of improving people's livelihood. To put it plainly, the entire nation of Japan benefitted from efforts made by the Japan lobby in the United States, including Kern.

The leftwing element in Japan, or, rather, intellectuals in Japan in general, were of the opinion, however, that, instead of allowing such a benefit as an improved economy, GHQ should have destroyed the prewar regime more thoroughly and converted Japan to a socialistic country. I understand John Dower still believes this. But, when confronted with the question of whether further continuation of the political and economic deadlock was really preferable, I am convinced few would answer in the affirmative.

This perverted psychology of the Japanese in the immediate postwar days to turn hostile eyes on those Americans who are sympathetic to Japan still lingers on.

After World War II, numerous Americans visited Japan and were amazed by the extremely high level of Japan's technical capabilities as well as its people's sincerity. These people wished to pursue U.S. world policy hand in hand with Japan as a partner. Americans who are mindful of the U.S. national interest and value Japan as a partner naturally hope for strengthening of the U.S.-Japan alliance relations and expansion of Japan's defense capability.

Because the communists' greatest goal is to make Japan easy to conquer when the time comes, they mobilize all leftwing forces at hand to block the upgrading of this bilateral partnership. Needless to say, communists would not admit in their propaganda that their goal is to make Japan easily conquerable. Instead, they appeal to pacifism and anti-military sentiment in postwar Japan. Consequently, all the leftwing elements, or so-called progressive-minded intellectuals, in Japan have opposed the U.S.-Japan Security Treaty and the Self-Defense Forces. As it turns out, this coincides with the slogan of the communist bloc.

Here emerged a perverted pattern where the words and deeds of pro-Japan Americans were regarded with hostility by Japan's leftwing elements and mass media. This pattern has persisted until today.

## Shift in Occupation Policy

In the end, the Republican Party nominated Thomas Dewey as the party's presidential candidate for the 1948 election, against MacArthur's expectation that he would be nominated. This promoted the shift in GHQ's occupation policy in two ways. For one thing, it made it easy for Washington to pursue a change in the occupation policy against MacArthur's authority. Second, having his personal political ambition cut off, MacArthur himself no longer had to cater to liberal public opinion.

Various GHQ reform programs reached a turning point, at which time the occupation policy was quickly redirected toward the correction of past excesses. Of all the reform programs, dissolution of the zaibatsu (financial combines) and local decentralization of the police forces were two meaningless measures that could only weaken the Japanese economy and administration. Naturally, it was decided that both programs would be revised.

It had been a fixed notion on the part of the Allied countries since the wartime that the zaibatsu and major Japanese corporations had been behind Japan's militarism and expansionism. Thus, GHQ had started tackling the dissolution of the zaibatsu immediately after Japan became occupied. In June 1946, 18 zaibatsu families were expelled, followed by five directives to dissolve 83 companies between September 1946 and September 1947. GHQ issued a separate directive specifically to dissolve Mitsubishi Corporation and Mitsui & Co., Ltd. In July 1947, the Japanese government put in force the Anti-Trust Law to prevent the zaibatsu from resurrecting.

Although further deliberations were continued on enactment of the Excessive Economic Power Deconcentration Law, after the above-mentioned Kaufmann article was carried by *Newsweek*, the U.S. Department of State announced withdrawal of its support for FEC230 in March 1948. In 1949, the Anti-Trust Law was revised, which made it possible for former zaibatsu to regroup.

In terms of war reparation, following the policy to prevent Japan from reviving as a heavy industrial power laid out in Edwin Pauley's *Report on Japanese Reparations to the President of the United States* (Pauley Report) of April 1946, industrial facilities that had survived air raids were dismantled. By May 1949, $40 million worth of facilities and equipment were turned over to China, the Philippines, Britain, and the Netherlands.

MacArthur had been against heavy reparations from the beginning. After the Strike Mission dispatched by the Department of the Army in 1947 proposed revising the Pauley Report, MacArthur made the following announcement in March 1948:

We should completely abandon the idea of demanding more reparations from Japan. By having its assets confiscated in Manchuria, Korea, and northern China, Japan has already paid reparations of more than $5 million. Except for facilities that are exclusively for military use, every one of the industrial machines, factories, and facilities remaining in Japan today is absolutely essential for the country's recovery.

At the same time, as the Cold War commenced, the need for assistance to Japan's reconstruction naturally increased. While the Garioa (Government Appropriation for Relief in Occupied Areas)-Eroa (Economic Rehabilitation in Occupied Areas) fund, for instance, had originally been designed for humanitarian purposes to protect occupied areas from famine and diseases, it increasingly came to be appropriated to assist economic reconstruction. The Garioa fund eventually amounted to $1.8 billion. It was inevitable, then, that Americans began to criticize that Japan's reparations were actually financed by the United States. The situation eventually led to the abolishment of the reparation program in 1949.

Because concentration of police power was believed to have supported Japan's militaristic regime before and during the war, decentralization had been thoroughly pursued to the extent that any city/town with a population larger than 5,000 was to maintain and manage its own municipal police. In such a small land as Japan, however, municipal police in each city/town found it inconvenient to investigate crimes across municipal borders, not to mention crimes encompassing wide areas, and in time each municipality found the financial burden overwhelming. Thus, when municipalities were given the right in 1951 to decline having their own police, more than 80 percent of municipalities actually surrendered their municipal police through citizen referenda within a few months.

The Purge also underwent a major transformation.

By that time the Japanese government had received requests from numerous private companies for at least temporary reinstatement of the purged executives because their absence had damaged the companies' businesses. Against this background, Yoshida, in public statements issued after the formation of the second Yoshida cabinet in 1948, had requested reinstatement of the people essential for Japan's economic reconstruction.

Subsequently, as a result of negotiations with GHQ, a committee to judge petitions for the reinstatement of purge designates was launched. After deliberating for a year and a half, the committee succeeded in reinstating some 10,000 out of some 200,000 who had been purged. In 1951, as the signing of the peace treaty became imminent, another review of the purged was conducted. This resulted in reinstatement of almost all the rest of the purged (except 18,000) by November. When the peace treaty was enacted, the remaining 18,000 were also reinstated.

The spearhead of the Purge was directed this time at the Japan Communist Party. In January 1950, Cominform (Communist Information Bureau) criticized the parliamentary pacifism line of the Japan Communist Party under chairman Nosaka Sanzō. At that, Nosaka instructed party members to confront occupation authorities head-on.

The first clash between the occupation forces and the Japan Communist Party took place on May 30, 1950, during an outdoor convention of the latter. After the clash, GHQ ordered the purge of 41 executive members of the communist party and its party organ *Akahata*. By the time the Purge was lifted after the signing of the peace treaty, an additional 61 members of the communist party had been purged. Party leaders either went underground or sought asylum overseas.

Because the North Atlantic Treaty Organization (NATO) was formed in Europe in 1949, the East-West confrontation became the basic structure of international relations for the next half a century. In the Far East, the Communist Party of China controlled the entire Chinese continent and in 1949, the same year as NATO's origin, declared the foundation of the People's Republic of China on October 1. The wave of the East-West confrontation had gradually advanced into the Far East—and this would culminate in the eruption of the Korea War in July 1950.

Roughly speaking, reforms in Japan during the occupation fall into three categories.

One was the kind of reform that a country of Japan's historical background and cultural standard would have accomplished sooner or later along with the political and social evolutions of advanced countries had it not been for the occupation. This included freedom of speech and association, women's suffrage, workers' rights, and land reform. GHQ, naturally, liked the rest of the world to think these accomplishments were not possible without its guidance, and this thinking still finds its place in American as well as some Japanese historical views. As I have verified related facts in the past chapters in this volume, however, all of these reforms were actually accomplished at the initiative of the Prince Higashikuni and Shidehara cabinets that were permeated with the liberal tradition alive since the time of Taishō Democracy. Their implementation did not require the absolute power of the occupation forces, either. They were all enacted and implemented under the Meiji Constitution and, after the implementation, they smoothly took hold among the Japanese people and have remained unchanged since then.

Some in Japan, however, labeled this category "reforms in anticipation of GHQ's intention." Considering the highly liberal convictions of the members of the Shidehara cabinet, this was a mean and totally groundless accusation that was disrespectful of the cabinet members. To begin with, no one could have even dreamed of GHQ proposing such a new constitution when the Shidehara cabinet was steadily pursuing various liberalization measures.

The second category of reforms had no root in Japan's history or tradition but was simply something that fell abruptly from the sky. Examples include dissolution of the *zaibatsu*, the municipal police, and the Purge. Reforms in this category naturally perished after the termination of the occupation.

And, finally, there were reforms, again without any root in Japan's history or tradition, which have remained intact until today despite people's lack of confidence in their flawlessness and the differences in opinion among the Japanese people regarding them. These reforms were, specifically, the issue of limitations on Japan's rearmament derived from Article 9 of the constitution and the issue of education based on the Fundamental Law of Education and the 6-3 system of education.

It would not be too inaccurate to say that Japan's defeat and the occupation are not completely over until the two issues in this last category are settled for good.

CHAPTER
# 12

# End of the Occupation

## —*The Paradox of Rearmament*—

## Peace Negotiations Shelved

The Occupation of Japan by the Allied powers lasted for seven long years.

In the modern history of wars among sovereign nations, there has been no other case of a postwar occupation of the defeated lasting so long. This exceptionally long occupation deeply scarred Japanese traditions, culture, and ways of thinking. Those scars continue to last until today. Particularly, the divisive debate on the U.S.-Japan security pact, which has tormented Japan for more than half a century since the war ended, originated in this period. The period that this chapter covers was both an ending and a beginning for Japan: the last years of the occupation as well as the start of decades of postwar turmoil.

A long occupation had not been the design from the beginning. It was due principally to the eruption of the Cold War.

As a matter of fact, in March 1947, about a year and a half into the occupation period, MacArthur said in a speech, "If possible, I wish to see the signing of the peace treaty and termination of the military occupation within a year." I think I can relate to MacArthur's wish. The Diet finished deliberations on the new constitution in 1946; it was promulgated in December and waiting to go into force in May 1947. While the February 1 Strike was prevented, prospects for the Japanese economy still remained bleak with no sign of improvement. Leaders of the occupation forces were not confident about their ability to manage the Japanese economy and, in fact, they had not been expected to do so. Thus, MacArthur said in his speech, "The occupation of Japan has already passed the stage of demilitarization and democratization is about to be completed." On the basis of this perception, MacArthur continued to say that the remaining issue of economic recovery was "beyond the occupation forces' capacity" and expressed his hope for an early conclusion of the peace negotiations with Japan so that it could regain its independence and rejoin the international economy.

Looking back, I must say it was truly fortunate for Japan that the peace treaty was not signed at that time however. Had the peace been attained then, Japan would have had to suffer from a punitive treaty resembling what had been imposed on Germany after World War I.

The draft treaty prepared by the United States by that time was called the Byrnes draft, after Secretary of State James F. Byrnes. It prohibited Japan from possessing armed forces and any type of aircraft, whether military or civilian, and restricted industries and merchant marines that could be turned to military use. It also stipulated that representatives of member countries of the Far Eastern Commission, which was to keep watch on Japan for 25 years, would be stationed in Japan. Although MacArthur at first criticized the Byrnes draft as being "too harsh," he grudgingly concurred with it when pressured with the possibility of a delay in signing of the peace treaty.

Totally unaware of the contents of the Byrnes draft, Foreign Minister Ashida Hitoshi listed Japan's conditions for a peace treaty in a memorandum that he handed to GHQ in July 1947. GHQ in turn rejected the memorandum saying, "Japan is in a position to be coerced to accept a peace treaty, not in a position to demand conditions." Japan was in a much severer position at that time than the Japanese people had imagined.

What was fortunate for Japan, as it turned out, was that this coincided with a period when negotiations on the aftermath of World War II among the United States, Britain, and the Soviet Union were deadlocked time after time, with Soviet Foreign Minister Vyacheslav Molotov saying nothing but "Nyet." Regarding the peace treaty with Japan, the United States at one point even presented a compromise proposal extending the surveillance period in the Byrnes draft from 25 years to 40 years. This proposal failed to facilitate an agreement, and the peace treaty with Japan was shelved for the time being.

Subsequent developments can be summarized as a gradual transition from "security from Japan" by curbing Japan's restoration to "security for Japan" so that Japan could be saved from falling into communist hands.

Among GHQ officers, it was Lieutenant General Robert Eichelberger who doubted MacArthur's argument for an early conclusion of the peace treaty with Japan. Eichelberger was Commanding General of the Eighth Army and the man who had highly praised the bravery of the Japanese soldiers during the war. He was a typical military man who openly expressed his wish to "lead a battalion of Japanese soldiers in a battle."

It is believed that Eichelberger was very much worried about an invasion by Soviet troops from Sakhalin and the Kuril Islands after the withdrawal of the U.S. troops in the case of an early peace settlement. In contrast to MacArthur's intimidatingly dignified headquarters at GHQ, Eichelberger's headquarters in Yokohama was very accessible. Various Japanese dignitaries frequented Eichelberger's headquarters with ease.

It was Ashida, one of those who frequented Eichelberger's office, who handed Eichelberger what was to be known later as the Ashida memorandum in September 1947. This letter was a first step toward the U.S.-Japan Security Treaty, as noted by Ashida's contemporary, Yoshida, later.

In this memo, Ashida displayed his usual logical thinking. First, Ashida brought up two future scenarios—that is, the scenario in which the United States and the Soviet Union collaborated and the United Nations functioned well and the scenario in which such was not the case. The first scenario was really a dummy to make the argument flawless. Ashida's principal concern, of course, was the second and worse scenario.

And as a means to defend Japan should the second scenario materialize, Ashida argued that while (1) the stationing of U.S. military forces in Japan for "security for Japan" might contribute to Japan's security in its own right, (2) the signing of a special treaty between the United States and Japan to ensure Japan's independence (not security but independence) by entrusting Japan's defense to the United States would be the best solution.

Looking at the so-called Ashida revisions to Article 9, which I introduced earlier in Chapter 7, and this Ashida memo, one cannot help but be struck by how outstandingly smart Ashida was. The Ashida letter, in fact, exhausted all the issues in the subsequent debates on the U.S.-Japan security pact.

While being fully aware of the futility of saying "what if . . ." in history, I'd like to make this point. If it had been Eichelberger (who was once slated to succeed MacArthur) and Ashida, instead of MacArthur (with his authoritarian fixation) and Yoshida (who was highly illogical), who had led Japanese politics during the occupation, the turmoil in Japanese thought and speech for more than half a century after the war undoubtedly would have been avoided.

Perhaps the Japanese military would have restored its tradition and glory. And Japan and the United States would have established partner relations based on mutual trust and respect as genuine equals during the Cold War that lasted for half a century. In other words, it might have been possible for Japan and the United States to achieve a relationship that was akin to the U.S.-U.K. relationship after the British-American wars in the 18th and 19th centuries. The influences of one war perish when another war erupts. Because Japan fought the Cold War together with the United States and won it, both countries should have put the defeat in the Pacific War behind them. But, in actuality, both countries are still obsessed with the defeat and the occupation. This is due to pacifism in postwar Japan, which has obstructed the two countries from mutually perceiving Japan as a formal partner of the United States during the Cold War.

In 1948, East-West relations were at a highly volatile state, provoked by such incidents as the Czechoslovak coup d'état and the Berlin Blockade. Facing this situation, Eichelberger, who believed that the 43,000-strong occupation force (including 20,000 non-combatants) could by no means counter a Soviet invasion, drafted a proposal in March to organize a Japanese army of three to five divisions. Eichelberger went so far as to form a presentable plan in consultation with principal U.S. military leaders, including Charles Willoughby. Eichelberger had to withdraw the plan, however, when he met the explosive rage of MacArthur, who opposed the rearmament of Japan.

One line of reasoning that MacArthur resorted to at that time was assessment of situations. Because Chiang Kai-shek was then still fighting strongly against the Communist forces in mainland China and it was not very likely that Soviet troops would advance into southern Korea, MacArthur even said to his subordinates, "Japan is much safer now than the United States. You can all bring your families here."

MacArthur's assessments of situations, however, were often proven erroneous. From the beginning, in fact, his were more justifications of his policy of occupation based on Article 9 of the postwar Constitution in order to contain any idea to topple his policy than objective assessments of a particular situation. An isolated dogmatic person is often liable to this fallacy.

That same month of March, MacArthur had a discussion with George Kennan and William Draper, who were visiting Japan at that time. As introduced earlier, both Kennan and Draper were of the view that Japan should have its own defense capability in order to make it independent politically and economically. Against their arguments, MacArthur made a long speech about the international situation, just like when he argued with Eichelberger earlier, and raised the following five reasons why he completely opposed the rearmament of Japan:

(1) Rearmament would be a violation of the sacred international contract with the United States. It would generate massive protests from Asian countries fearful of Japan's re-militarization;
(2) Rearmament would hamper GHQ's authority vis-à-vis Japan;
(3) Because Japan had lost its overseas colonies, rearmament would only make Japan a fifth-class military power with inadequate resources to resist a Soviet threat;
(4) Japan's economic capacity would not withstand the burden of military expenditures; and
(5) Because the Japanese people fully support the renunciation of war, they would not desire to rearm their country unless so coerced.

Although the above are more justifications of existing policies than objective analyses, they nevertheless were consistent themes of MacArthur's subsequent remarks and they were faithfully reflected in Yoshida's statements, too.

# No Rearmament of Japan

But it was not only Europe that experienced drastic changes. Asia, too, shifted greatly. In China, Communist forces conquered former Manchuria toward the end of 1948 and triumphantly entered Beijing at year-end. In 1949, the Communists seized Nanjing, Shanghai, and Guangdong. The People's Republic of China was established in October that year.

Under these circumstances, an early conclusion of a peace with an unarmed Japan as MacArthur had envisioned had already become utterly unrealistic. The NSC13/2 that was adopted at the October 9, 1948, conference of the National Security Council, which was also attended by President Harry Truman, decided on the continued stationing of U.S forces in Japan and the indefinite postponement of a peace treaty with Japan.

Entering 1949, the influence and power of GHQ's Government Section declined markedly. In February, the third Yoshida cabinet was formed, marking the beginning of the long rule of Yoshida or, according to the leftist mass media, the era of the "reverse course." Concerning the issue of the rearmament of Japan, however, MacArthur remained unchanged and so did Yoshida. At this point, thus, there emerged a discrepancy between Washington's macroscopic strategy and the MacArthur-Yoshida line.

According to Hata Ikuhiko, a Shōwa-Heisei historian who has written extensively about the situation in Japan in those days, for Washington, "The issue of the occupation of Japan was, in a nutshell, nothing but the issue of how to handle MacArthur." In one conference after another, the argument went round and round in circles—but the issue was, simply, who was to bell the cat, i.e., MacArthur. While all the U.S. government high officials departed for Tokyo with great enthusiasm for persuading MacArthur, each and every one returned having failed to do so. For instance, Secretary of the Army Kenneth Royall visited Japan in February 1949 only to pledge to MacArthur that the United States would not rearm Japan.

Seeing how determined MacArthur was, Yoshida could not change his attitude, either. Although popular belief says that it was Yoshida who rejected the American demand for Japan's rearmament, at least by this time it was MacArthur who singlehandedly blocked the U.S. attempts .

Coming to their wits' end, some in Washington argued for the dismissal of MacArthur, while others argued for abandoning Japan because the United States could not defend a Japan that lacked the capability for its own self-defense. In light of the U.S. government's decision in March 1948 to withdraw U.S. troops from Korea, it was quite plausible that a similar measure would be taken regarding Japan.

## Paving the Way for a U.S.-Japan Security Pact

In 1949, the Japanese government was forced to adopt a financial and monetary contraction policy (the Dodge Line) drafted by Joseph Dodge, the financial advisor to the Supreme Commander for the Allied Powers. In 1950, in anticipation of the House of Councilors election in June, Finance Minister Ikeda Hayato considered paying a visit to the United States as a cabinet member to appeal the need to relax the stringent financial/monetary policies.

On the eve of his departure, Ikeda called on Yoshida and asked for his view on the peace settlement issue, which was being actively debated among the Japanese people by then. It was during this visit that Yoshida for the first time shared with Ikeda his schematic plan for a peace treaty and instructed him to sound out U.S. intentions while in Washington.

To quote Ikeda, Yoshida was of the view that:

> Japan hopes for an early conclusion of a peace treaty. After the signing of a peace treaty, the United States would find it necessary to station its armed forces in Japan for the sake of the security of Japan and Asia. If the U.S. government finds it difficult to propose this, the Japanese government is willing to request the continued presence of the U.S. forces in Japan.

Thus, the wish of the Japanese side was officially conveyed via Ikeda to the authorities in Washington for the first time. There is no knowing, however, what MacArthur had in mind or what kind of tacit understanding there was between MacArthur and Yoshida.

The only thing that was clear to everyone was that there was no criticism from the occupation authority on this offer from the Japanese side.

To begin with, it was the position of the occupation forces that the financial/monetary policies, which were the original objectives of Ikeda's trip, were what the Japanese side was given or instructed by GHQ in consultation with the occupation forces. Therefore, the Japanese government would not be allowed to negotiate directly with authorities in Washington on this matter.

In fact, after Ikeda returned to Japan, GHQ threatened him with a letter that said,

> The finance minister of Japan must obey the orders of the occupation forces. He is simply not in a position to negotiate relaxation of the Dodge Line directly with the authority in the U.S. government. Furthermore, it would be disrespectful of the occupation forces to use this negotiation in the political campaign for the coming House of Councilors election. If you dare to do so, you should expect difficulties in your future relations with GHQ.

This was such naked interference that Miyazawa Kiichi, secretary to Ikeda at that time, who received the letter felt like saying, "What on earth are they talking about, goddammit," temporarily forgetting his manners.

When GHQ became so furious about economic policies, talking about the peace treaty issue must have struck it as conduct that grossly exceeded the authority given to the Japanese government. Nevertheless, GHQ made no reference to this issue.

Perhaps Yoshida might have calculated that MacArthur would not oppose the Japanese offer on the continued stationing of the U.S. military in Japan. He might even have heard from MacArthur directly.

One possible background to this development might be Yoshida's abrupt recognition of Japan's right of self-defense in his January 22, 1950, policy speech three months earlier.

As I have already introduced in Chapter 7, in the June 1946 Diet session, Yoshida declared that Japan had "renounced war as an exercise of the right of self-defense" and continued to say, "it would be harmful to recognize that . . . a war to exercise a nation's legitimate right of self-defense is justifiable." His commitment to the renunciation of war remained consistent throughout subsequent years. Even in his November 1949 policy speech, Yoshida said,

The only way to ensure Japan's security would be to become, ahead of other countries in the world, an unarmed nation by renouncing war as solemnly declared in the new constitution, removing all armaments, and relying on the world's peace-loving public opinion.

One can see this was perfectly consistent with remarks by MacArthur in those days.

Yoshida's tone, however, changed abruptly in his January 1950 policy speech:

To thoroughly renounce war does not mean the renunciation of the right of self-defense at all. As long as Japan persists with the policy of democracy and pacifism and as long as the entire nation is determined to act on these principles, Japan can gain the trust of those democratic countries that cherish democracy. It is this mutual trust that ensures Japan's security. And it is for this mutual trust that I wish to invite international cooperation to discuss how Japan's security should be in order to promote the mutual interests of democratic countries.

Naturally, this speech was harshly criticized by the left wing as a drastic change of Yoshida's attitude. They claimed that, by shamelessly stating that Japan had the right of self-defense, Yoshida rescinded his own promise. After all, they complained, it was Yoshida who had earlier denied Japan's right of self-defense saying, "Many modern wars were fought in the name of self-defense. So was the Manchurian Incident as well as the Greater East Asia War."

From the point of legal arguments, as far as Article 9 was concerned, the so-called Ashida revision had indeed occurred. Moreover, the Japanese government had also made a modification through the question Ashida raised and the response by Kanamori Tokujirō, minister in charge of constitutional amendments, at the August 1946 session of the Special Committee on Constitutional Amendments, which took place after Yoshida's statement in June 1946. However, seeing as Yoshida himself had made no modification to his public stance vis-à-vis Article 9 and had continued to make parliamentary statements with similar nuances, he could well be criticized for rescinding his own promise.

Setting these legal arguments aside, this January 1950 remark by Yoshida had a fundamental implication that would provoke protests from the left wing. Because the constitution of Japan denies Japan's right of self-defense on the assumption that Japan can rely on other countries' goodwill for its survival, to entrust to the United States Japan's protection from invasion by a country with malicious intent would constitute a contradiction.

In a nutshell, Yoshida said in his January 1950 remark that, even if Japan did not have its own armaments, it could be protected by the United States as a form of an exercise of the right of self-defense. This was exactly how Ashida had interpreted the constitution and, in retrospect, it paved the way for the signing of the U.S.-Japan Security Treaty.

And Yoshida changed a portion of the wording in the constitution in his remarks. This change was so subtle that many readers would miss it. But its implication was rather significant. Instead of "the peace-loving peoples of the world" as is written in the preamble of the constitution, Yoshida said, "democratic countries that cherish democracy." Simply put, Yoshida was saying that, as long as Japan obeyed MacArthur's instructions and remained thoroughly unarmed, it could be protected through mutual trust with the peace-loving, democratic United States. And Yoshida concluded his remarks with the expression, "I wish to invite international coopera-tion," hinting at the signing of a peace treaty and a security pact.

## It Has to Be the Japanese Spontaneous Initiative, No Matter What

Another notable thing about this January 1950 speech by Yoshida was the striking similarity of its interpretation of the right of self-defense with that in MacArthur's New Year message that same year. Toward the end of MacArthur's lengthy message, there was a paragraph that said:

> Although some snigger at Japan's renunciation of war as a fantasy, you should not let them mislead you. It is done on the initiative of the Japanese people based on the supreme ethical ideal. There can-not be any constitutional article that is more fundamentally healthy and practical than this. Needless to say, no matter what reasoning is applied, Japan's renunciation of war should not be interpreted as a

complete denial of its legitimate right of self-defense against unprovoked assault, which is inherent to any sovereign nation. But this is indeed a proud declaration by a nation that has been defeated by arms of its confidence in international ethics that does not resort to arms and in the final victory of justice.

While GHQ had been aware that it could not deny Japan's right of self-defense since the time of the Ashida revision, this was the first time it clearly admitted it. Thus, it can be said that Yoshida's January policy speech coincided perfectly with MacArthur's New Year message three weeks earlier.

When Japan had the right of self-defense and yet remained unarmed, the only logical conclusion would be for Japan to be protected by U.S. forces. This shows that by January 1950 MacArthur and Yoshida shared the same perception.

While it might not be entirely impossible to conjecture that the thinking of the two men happened to coincide by chance and that they spoke out without any consultation between themselves, that is not how a diplomat's mind works. The more convinced one is that the two perceptions are identical across the national boundary, the more carefully he should look into the background. All told, it would be more natural to conjecture that there must have been some communication between the two.

In any event, the U.S.-Japan Security Treaty was to be concluded shortly, taking the form of a Japanese initiative to request the continued stationing of U.S. forces in Japan.

Around this time, so-called intellectuals with progressive ideas in Japan started arguing openly for concluding a comprehensive peace treaty that would also include the People's Republic of China and the Soviet Union. There must have been a mechanism through which the Kremlin's policy against the U.S.-Japan peace treaty would be reflected in public opinion in Japan via a channel connecting the Communist Party of the Soviet Union, the Communist Party of Japan (CPJ), CPJ's advance organs, and intellectuals with progressive ideas. While it is, almost by definition, impossible to determine evidence of this kind of operation, it seems beyond doubt that all the communist forces concerned at that time did everything they were supposed to do to influence the debate.

Leftwing-affiliated commentary magazines, including the monthly *Sekai* (World), advocated Japan's neutrality in the Cold War and clarified their position that they were against a peace treaty only with the United States excluding China and the Soviet Union.

A peace treaty with a U.S.-Japan security pact attached even indirectly such as Yoshida envisioned could by no means satisfy communist countries. The comprehensive peace treaty that the communists envisioned was nothing but an attempt to destroy Yoshida's peace treaty scheme to ensure Japan's security as a member of the free world.

At the graduation ceremony in March 1950, President Nambara Shigeru of the University of Tokyo called for a comprehensive peace treaty. This had been his pet theory. Two months later at the party convention of the *Jiyūtō* in May, Yoshida attacked Nambara directly, calling him a distorter of learning trying to curry favor with the public.

In the same month of May, John Foster Dulles was put in charge of U.S. peace negotiations with Japan. Born into a prominent family with both his grandfather and uncle having served as secretary of state, Dulles was at one time a Republican Senator from New York before President Truman, a Democrat, appointed him to this position as a symbol of bipartisan diplomacy.

Thirty years before in 1918, President Woodrow Wilson had appointed Dulles as legal counsel to the U.S. delegation to the Versailles Peace Conference. Yoshida Shigeru also participated in this conference as secretary to Japan's chief delegate Makino Nobuaki. It might have been what Dulles had witnessed in this conference in terms of the cruel and retaliatory peace settlement with Germany, which later facilitated the rise of the Nazis, that made him oppose putting restrictions on Japan's economic capacity and reparations.

With the ultimate goal of developing Japan into a full-fledged member of the Western camp, Dulles was contemplating the establishment of a formidable police force to restrict indirect invasions and the signing of a security treaty separate from the peace treaty as necessary measures. While reparations were implemented, albeit on a limited scale, due to the insistence of the Philippines and several other countries, other than that the peace negotiations were carried out more or less in line with Dulles' initial plan.

Arriving in Tokyo on June 21, 1950—four days before the Korean War broke out—Dulles met not only MacArthur, Japan's political leaders, and heads of political parties but also representatives of businesses and labor unions to hear their respective views.

Talking to those individuals, Dulles became bewildered by the vague ideas they expressed on the security of their own country. They said such things as, "We place high hopes on the United Nations" or "We would protect peace with Article 9 of our constitution." Three years after the promulgation of the new constitution, during which the stringent control of freedom of speech by the occupation forces blocked the entry of other perspectives, the Japanese views on their own security had degenerated that much.

There also are numerous testimonies to the strong leftist inclination even at the Ministry of Foreign Affairs at that time. For instance, when foreign ministry officials submitted a draft peace treaty to Yoshida in October 1950, Yoshida sent it back with a note in big letters saying, "This looks like a speech by the opposition parties. Useless discussion that is not worth even a thought." But the same Yoshida himself developed his own defense of pacifism as expressed to the visiting Dulles. If these episodes quoted here indeed represented the starting point of the view on Japan's security among the Japanese people in general, no wonder turmoil followed in Japanese thinking on security subsequently as the country faced the reality of the international situation under the Cold War.

The situation took a sudden turn with the eruption of the Korean War.

To fill the vacuum caused by the U.S. forces stationed in Japan having to be deployed to the Korean Peninsula hastily, MacArthur instructed that a 75,000-man-strong National Police Reserve be established and that the Maritime Safety Agency, created in 1948 to patrol and protect the coasts, be reinforced by 8,000 personnel.

While it is hard to believe that Yoshida had not anticipated that these movements would eventually lead to the rearmament of Japan, he officially declared that these measures were to maintain public order and were totally unrelated to rearmament.

As a matter of fact, Major General Charles Willoughby, MacArthur's chief of intelligence, had for some time brought together colonel-class former Japanese officers, such as Hattori Takushirō and Horiba Kazuo, in order to compile a history of the Pacific War. Willoughby's quiet aim was to rebuild a Japanese army. When Willoughby decided to take advantage of the eruption of the Korean War to pursue rebuilding the Japanese army using the group of former military men he had handpicked as a nucleus, Yoshida directly appealed to MacArthur to stop this plan. When organizing the National Police Reserve, Yoshida staffed its executive posts solely with ex-police officers, rejecting former military personnel.

One historical view attributes this decision to Yoshida's loathing for the military, which fits very well with Yoshida's anti-military myth. There is, however, no evidence to prove that Yoshida disliked military men in general. On the contrary, he showed positive goodwill toward old acquaintances in the military and, subsequently, to young officers of the Self-Defense Forces, established in 1954. Perhaps his stance was more attributable to his fussy and hard-nosed disposition, which made him dislike personnel arrangements that were determined without his knowledge.


## Obstacles to Be Overcome or Just Excuses?

The Dulles mission to formally negotiate peace with Japan arrived in Japan in January 1951. This was just the time when the United Nations forces were trying to reorganize the battlefront south of Seoul after having advanced deep into North Korea beyond the 38th parallel north only to be routed by the sudden intervention of the Chinese "volunteer" army. Against voices that demanded that peace negotiations with Japan be left on the back burner in such an emergency situation, Dulles retorted that, because of the eruption of the Korean War, conclusion of peace with Japan must be hastened all the more so that the Western camp would have an additional partner. Because of Dulles' policy to trust Japan and make it an effective partner of the United States in international politics, he was another American who became the target of hostility from the leftwing and intellectuals with progressive ideas in Japan who regarded him as an advocate of the rearmament of Japan.

During the first Yoshida-Dulles meeting, Yoshida said, "We wish to regain Japan's independence at the earliest time, and I would like you to work out a treaty that Japan can accept without hurting its self-respect." At the same time, he said, "Among reforms promoted by GHQ are those that ignore Japan's situation and obstruct Japan's self-reliance, including abolishment of the Japanese *ie* (family) system and restrictions on business organizations [which presumably meant dissolution of the zaibatsu]." Yoshida stressed his hope that these "reforms" would be revised by GHQ while the occupation forces were still stationed in Japan. There were a number of reforms imposed by GHQ that Yoshida had found unacceptable.

In the course of discussion, Dulles asked, "When Japan regains its independence and becomes a member of the Western camp, what contribution does it aim to make to the strengthening of the free-world camp?" To this, Yoshida said, "If you are asking if Japan has an intention to rearm, I would say it is a question that should be raised after Japan regains its independence. It is premature, therefore, to ask now what kind of contribution Japan intends to make." Yoshida went on to argue the case for why Japan could not rearm from economic and political, both domestic and international, perspectives.

When the time came to meet with MacArthur, the two men headed for GHQ headquarters together. During this meeting, MacArthur sided with Yoshida when he said,

> What the free world world asks from today's Japan should not be its military capability. It is actually impossible to do so. Because Japan possesses the capacity to produce military equipment as well as manpower, we should provide materials to fully utilize Japan's production capabilities so as to make great contributions to the strengthening of the free-world camp.

Prior to this meeting, it is believed that Yoshida had asked for MacArthur's help regarding the negotiations with Dulles. Even without Yoshida's pleading, however, it was obvious from MacArthur's previous exchanges with Washington that MacArthur had been determined to oppose Japan's rearmament. Had MacArthur sided with Dulles, citing the change in the situation due to the eruption of the Korean War, would Yoshida have resisted the duo? Because the successful signing of the peace treaty was at stake, Yoshida probably would not have been able to oppose them even if he had wanted to. On the contrary, I believe it would be only natural if he had concurred with MacArthur.

Some call the policy to minimize military buildup so as to concentrate on economic growth the "Yoshida Doctrine." However, Yoshida was a worldly person who couldn't be further from a doctrine. In fact, MacArthur's disposition was much more prone to advance a doctrine. Thus, it might be far more accurate to call it a MacArthur Doctrine rather than a Yoshida Doctrine.

There is a myth about Yoshida Shigeru—that is to say, that he was a statesman who rejected the American demand for Japan's rearmament and let Japan concentrate on economic reconstruction. This myth is the product of the antiwar ideology in postwar Japan. Close scrutiny of Yoshida's words and deeds would reveal, however, that all Yoshida actually did was to faithfully study MacArthur's thinking and expressions and concentrate on paying close attention not to go against him.

When Yoshida resisted Dulles's demand for Japan's rearmament during the peace treaty negotiations, he presented a united front with MacArthur. Given the politics and public opinion in Japan, the situation did not allow Yoshida to make any sudden shifts. Thus, Yoshida just maintained what he had been saying and doing by force of habit. Meanwhile, many have testified that, behind the scenes, Yoshida had secretly hoped for the rearmament of Japan.

The basic structure of the peace treaty with Japan was more or less completed during Dulles's visit to Japan (January 25 through February 11, 1951) before MacArthur's dismissal in April.

Meanwhile, as far as Japan's rearmament was concerned, the MacArthur-Yoshida viewpoint and that of the U.S. government represented by Dulles did not converge.

One time, Dulles asked Yoshida if what he enumerated as obstacles to rearmament were simply obstacles to be overcome or just excuses for doing nothing. This, too, is a question that has been asked repeatedly by Americans who placed high hopes on Japan and wished Japan to play certain roles over the past half century-plus. On the need for Japan to contribute more to its defense, whenever the Japanese side explains that the Japanese people's awareness has not become mature enough yet, Americans respond with such questions as "If you really have a will to rearm Japan, why don't you go ahead and do it and then persuade the Japanese people of its virtue?" or "Are you not going to change the Japanese people's awareness by conducting activities to enlighten them? Or are you blaming the Japanese people for your own lack of determination?" Most of the time, the Japanese reaction to these questions is silence and inaction. Thus, this reaction or lack thereof by the Japanese has disappointed hundreds of Americans who are favorable to Japan and led them to other options, e.g. closer U.S.-China relations. This has been one typical pattern in postwar U.S.-Japan relations.

Sakamoto Kazuya, professor of international politics at Osaka University, said,

> If Yoshida had said from the beginning that Japan could do this and that toward its rearmament, albeit "very slowly," the discussion could have been a little more fruitful for Dulles. According to the record of the discussion on the American side, however, Yoshida did not give away "any kind of hint" at specifically what kind of contributions Japan could make. Unexpectedly failing to get at the crux of the matter at the first meeting with Yoshida, Dulles was extremely frustrated.

This was, indeed, the first manifestation of what was to become the typical scene at postwar U.S.-Japan summit meetings.

Being a diplomat, Yoshida was aware that his attitude made Dulles very frustrated. Thus, on February 3, believing that, "It would be presumptuous to expect a successful negotiation toward the peace agreement without making any disclosure of our intent on Japan's defense efforts," Yoshida instructed his subordinates to present a proposal to establish a 50,000-strong National Safety Force to the U.S. side. Because amending the Constitution to enable the rearmament of Japan would be an "extremely delicate and challenging" matter at that time, however, it was decided that this National Safety Force "should be perceived as a policing capability to maintain public order until the Japanese people feel like possessing military capabilities after signing the peace treaty and returning to the international community."

Yoshida's urge to do something is quite understandable. The most important thing was to accomplish the signing of a peace treaty as soon as possible. When amending the constitution had already become as difficult as it is today after more than half a century since its promulgation, there would have been no knowing when Japan could become independent if constitutional amendment had been made a condition for a peace treaty. In this particular case, instead of nagging about Yoshida's opportunistic attitude, we should understand that he had no other options. His explanation, "until the Japanese people feel like possessing military capabilities after signing the peace treaty," was not a mere excuse. In fact, it was the only response that Japan could offer at that time. From his reference to being "presumptuous," though, it was clear that Yoshida's opposition to the rearmament of Japan did not come from his philosophy or political conviction.

Even after this proposal from Yoshida, the U.S. side did not give up the expectation that Japan would someday rearm in the future. Because it was clearly written in the Introduction of the Security Treaty between the United States and Japan of 1951 that "The United States of America . . . in the expectation, . . . that Japan will itself increasingly assume responsibility for its own defense . . . ," this has become the basic stance of the United States. This stance remained consistently unchanged during the half-century-long Cold War. Meanwhile, Japan has continued to expand its defense capability without amending the constitution, barely maintaining logical coherency with the constitution, at least formally, by making full use of parliamentary statements. As a result, Japan has come to possess a world-class military capability in order to counter to an actual threat from the Soviet Union. These Japanese government efforts to make continued military expansion seem coherent, when accumulated like a scab, have caused the present-day disarray in the security debate, particularly in the face of rapidly growing Chinese military power.

## MacArthur's Dismissal

MacArthur was relieved of his command on April 11, 1951.

The direct cause of his dismissal was what was interpreted as his insubordination. When the war situation on the Korean Peninsula turned favorable to the United Nations Forces in March 1951, the U.S. government instructed MacArthur to make preparations for an armistice along the 38th parallel north. MacArthur deliberately resisted the instruction and made a formal announcement to argue for continuation of the war, saying, "To accomplish the goals of the war, negotiation with the opponent would be useless."

From the beginning, MacArthur had made a series of misjudgments about the Korean War. He did not believe in the possibility of the war, to begin with, and even after it erupted, he denied the possibility of China's intervention. After China participated in the war, MacArthur repeatedly advised air raids on Manchuria and mobilization of the Republic of China (Taiwan) Armed Forces, grossly underestimating the adverse effect of hardline measures against China. At the conference that decided on the dismissal of MacArthur, Secretary of Defense George Marshall and others said, "MacArthur should have been relieved of his command two years earlier."

In a nutshell, behind MacArthur's dismissal was his ill-naturedness that surfaced conspicuously toward the end of the occupation period. More specifically, MacArthur's arbitrary assessment of situations, or, more accurately, his inclination to arbitrarily assess situations, which must be judged objectively, to fit his own agenda, his self-righteousness that rejected any advice from others, and his narrow-mindedness to avert interference from others became more prominent.

It is true that this arbitrary assessment of situations and arbitrary conduct enabled MacArthur to protect the emperor system of Japan and accomplish the successful occupation of Japan. Yet his persistence with the pacifism line that he had imposed on Japan, in total neglect of the more realist views of the United States represented by Kennan through Dulles, led to the disarray in the defense debate in Japan over the next half century. From the viewpoint of the Japanese people, who had been totally passive during the occupation period, unable to decide anything themselves, we are tempted to question his responsibility.

Nevertheless, it is true that the entire nation was saddened by the news of MacArthur's dismissal.

In his April 14 farewell letter, Yoshida Shigeru praised MacArthur's accomplishments during the occupation and added, "The entire nation of Japan, from the Emperor to people on the street, are saddened by your departure . . ." Although some even started a fundraising drive to erect a statue of MacArthur in Japan, the project became crippled, partly because of MacArthur's speech to the U.S. Congress after he returned to the United States in which he described the Japanese as a "nation of 12-year-olds."

In the same speech, however, MacArthur also said, "Japan started the war as an act of self-defense to protect its resource-poor country [against economic blockade]." He was another one of the last generation of Americans who had experienced the Russo-Japanese War and knew the flow of the subsequent history of Japan first hand.

The last service for Japan that Yoshida wished from MacArthur while he still retained his absolute power and before the signing of the peace treaty was to revise and, if necessary, repeal over-earnest reforms imposed by GHQ. Thus, on April 9, only two days before MacArthur's dismissal, Yoshida wrote a lengthy letter requesting revision and/or repeal of the National Civil Service Law, the Local Autonomy Law, the Civil Law (particularly articles pertaining to the family system), the Police Act, the Education Act (particularly articles pertaining to the 6-3 system), the Criminal Procedure Code, and the Antimonopoly Act. Judging from the above list of targeted reforms, it is not hard to imagine that reviewing those measures would have been the last task for which Yoshida would have been engaged in the full use of mutual trust with MacArthur had the latter remained in his position.

But the occupation was terminated before Yoshida received MacArthur's reply to this letter.

The peace treaty with Japan was signed in San Francisco on September 8, 1951, followed by the U.S.-Japan security pact signed on the same day in a different location.

In the course of the negotiations for the peace treaty, almost the only problem that required a delicate adjustment of intentions between the two sides was that of security. Other than that, while there were a few areas of minor adjustments including territory, reparation, and relations with the Kuomintang government on Taiwan, the two sides were able to reach agreements mostly along the lines advocated by the U.S. side. Thus, after an agreement was reached about the security issue, the bilateral negotiations proceeded without faltering.

At the signing ceremony convened on September 8 in the opera house in San Francisco, Yoshida recited his speech accepting the treaty. The text of his speech had undergone prior consultation with the U.S. side. In the speech, Yoshida said, "This is a fair and unprecedentedly magnanimous treaty."

Actually, Yoshida did not recite all the speech text. He later reminisced that, "I had to grudgingly put up with reciting the speech text." During the course of his speech, Yoshida started speaking rapidly and, eventually, skipped a passage. When asked about this, Yoshida allegedly said, "Although I was reciting the text earnestly in the beginning, when I realized that most people in the audience would not understand Japanese, it became unimportant for me to recite the text faithfully. That's why I skipped a few lines."

Had it been a speech into which Yoshida had put his heart and soul, skipping a few lines would have been utterly unthinkable.

And this was the last, humiliating performance for Japan as it put an end to the occupation period.

Thus, the occupation concluded. What was waiting for Japan after this were days and years of coping with such burdens as the loss of traditional values and the schism in public opinion over the national security issue that had emerged during the seven years of the occupation.

# The Distorted "History Issue" in Postwar Japan

*—Japan's Self-Generated Masochistic View of History—*

## History of the Anglo-Saxons, the Winners

More than 70 years have passed since Japan's defeat in World War II, but the so-called history issue with China and Korea has not yet been settled.

What is peculiar about this issue is that even though it is an international issue, its origins lead solely to Japan. In fact, this way of seeing history is called the "masochistic view of history" in Japan.

To be sure, holding a critical view of one's past conduct became some what of a global phenomenon in the late 20th century that was not confined to Japan alone. There was the rise of "revisionism," which in the United Kingdom cast a critical eye on the slave trade with West Africa and the United States criticized the appropriation of land from Native Americans. Nevertheless, these movements only occupied a small portion of the public opinion in those Western countries and, unlike the Japanese case, did not really affect the countries' attitudes toward their foreign policies.

In the case of Germany, the Holocaust was not a matter of historical interpretation. There is an abundance of undeniable evidence on both the intention and the means to pursue the Nazi Jewish policy. For Germans, this makes the Holocaust a historical fact that defies any alternative interpretation. There is no room for getting mired in masochistic views of their history.

It goes without saying that the masochistic historical view held by the Japanese is one of the aftermaths of Japan's defeat in World War II. In fact, Japan's defeat did not end with the surrender by acceptance of the Potsdam Declaration on August 15, 1945. In the previous chapters of this book, I presented hard historical facts on this matter. But let me summarize them here again, in order to explain this unusual phenomenon.

In modern international society, when a war comes to a certain point, a cease-fire agreement is signed. That is followed by conclusion of a peace treaty, under which conditions the war is terminated.

That was what the Japanese leaders envisioned when they decided to surrender. They thought, since they had proposed the surrender by accepting the conditions stipulated by the Potsdam Declaration, that they could reconstruct the country in due time after having met those conditions. This was the path that past loser nations had taken in modern times. In fact, Shidehara Kijūrō, former foreign minister and prime minister, always had in mind the precedent of the French capitulation in 1871.

In retrospect, one of the reasons this formula did not work for Japan was that since World War I, war had transformed into "total war," or an operation involving an entire nation. Prior to that, a war was, in extreme terms, a confrontation between militaries that ordinary citizens had nothing to do with. A total war, in contrast, requires the cooperation of the entire nation. And in order to secure the all-out cooperation of its citizens, a state needs to convince its people that the enemy is the devil incarnate while it itself is a champion of righteousness.

Although it simply is not possible for one side to be absolutely just and the other side to be absolutely evil, people tend to believe in this dichotomy at a war's climax or immediately after a peace settlement. Because the loser, then, is the devil incarnate, the winner is allowed to mete out whatever treatment it sees fit to the loser. In short, the winner is allowed to impose tyrannical rule over the loser.

Moreover, judgments by the winner remain as history, while the arguments of the loser are erased from the surface of history. Anglo-Saxons, particularly, are good at writing history. It would not be an overstatement to say that almost all coherent history books on many great nations with long, glorious traditions of their own were written by Anglo-Saxons, except those on China and Japan, both of which had uniquely distinct civilizations of their own. Edward Gibbon, who wrote the voluminous *The*

*History of the Decline and Fall of the Roman Empire,* is a good example.

Thus, it is the Anglo-Saxon view of history that will remain as orthodox histories of World Wars I and II.

## The U.S. and the Ideology of Unconditional Surrender

Another reason U.S. occupation policy for Japan neglected the international custom of modern times was the precedent created by the occupation of Germany. There was no cease-fire agreement or peace treaty in the case of Germany. Allied forces invaded the whole of Germany and made the country an occupied territory without a government of its own. This precedent was applied to Japan in its entirety even though Japan had accepted the Potsdam Declaration and received the occupation forces in a marvelously disciplined manner.

President Franklin Roosevelt consistently insisted on the unconditional surrender of Japan. In contrast, Winston Churchill, a sympathizer of Japanese tradition who had been deeply moved by the bravery shown by the Japanese military on Iwo-Jima and Okinawa, proposed that Japan be granted an honorable way out of the war. But Roosevelt stuck to his insistence, saying that after the attack on Pearl Harbor, Japan had no honor to protect.

After Roosevelt passed away, his successor, Harry Truman, ceased to insist on an unconditional surrender. Truman instead proposed a surrender based on the Potsdam Declaration, which Japan accepted.

Nevertheless, the ideology of unconditional surrender, a legacy of the Roosevelt days, lingered tenaciously within the U.S. government. The ideology found expression in what Professor Iokibe Makoto described as the "most uncivilized of all the documents" which the U.S. Department of State sent to the Supreme Commander for the Allied Powers in Japan twenty days after Japan's surrender. This document says, ". . . Our relations do not rest on a contractual basis, but on an unconditioned surrender. . . Control of Japan shall be exercised through the Japanese Government to the extent that such an arrangement produces satisfactory results. . ." The United States maintained this policy throughout the seven-year occupation of Japan. In other words, what Judge Radhabinod Pal of the International Military Tribunal for the Far East described as a "denial of the development of civilizations in the past few centuries that divide the ancient times when the defeated was completely annihilated and our own time" became a fait accompli.

Small consolation, or rather the only consolation, was that it was the U.S. military that occupied Japan instead of the Mongols, who had swept across the Eurasian continent leaving behind heaps on heaps of human skeletons, or the Russians, who had recently terrorized Berlin and Manchuria. From the viewpoint of legal theory, Japan was put in the same situation as an occupation under an uncivilized country. The only difference was that the occupation forces were Americans, not Mongol or Russians. And yet, the colonial bureaucrat-like behavior of the likes of Charles Kades, deputy chief of GHQ's Government Section, is still remembered with abhorrence by the Japanese.

The origin of the masochistic view of history, which is seen among the Japanese people even today, can be traced to the earlier days of the occupation administration.

Among the occupation policies, the Japanese side showed no resistance to such policies as the restoration of freedom and democracy. Most of the policies, in fact, were resurrections of policies that the Japanese had already instituted with their own hands during the Taishō Democracy. During the long period of war, any country has to intensify governmental control over its people, thus making the system more inflexible. Japan was no exception. But this tight governmental control of people is automatically abolished when a war ends—and this was exactly what happened in Japan.

Freedom of speech and freedom of association, for instance, were restored by the Higashikuni Naruhiko cabinet immediately after the war ended and before the arrival of the occupation forces. Movements toward woman suffrage, labor laws, and agrarian reform had already been initiated in Japan during Taishō Democracy. All GHQ had to do concerning these reforms was to ride on the coattails of the Japanese initiatives, with hardly any modification.

The only area that the Japanese side had not anticipated was the Constitution of Japan. In fact, this document, which was nothing more than a translation from the draft that had been prepared hastily in only a week due to special circumstances within GHQ, still remains incompatible with the reality of Japan as an independent nation.

As I elaborated in Chapter 10 of this volume, the masochistic view of history is attributable more to the brainwashing of the Japanese people during the early period of the occupation than to the laws and institutions of the occupation administration.

Military occupation of Japan lasted for seven years, which was an appallingly long time. This means that without exception those Japanese citizens who were in leadership positions in their 60s at the start of the 21st century (those born between 1930 and 1940) had all experienced these seven years of occupation during their formative years.

Moreover, the effect of the occupation is not confined to this particular generation. The occupation profoundly affected the formation of the personality of a wide range of individuals who are socially active today. This is because the leftwing, Marxist elements in Japan preserved early U.S. occupation policies for more than half a century until today—after the United States itself abandoned them promptly.

When Japan surrendered, the first thing the United States did was to physically disarm the Japanese military. Subsequently, it imposed strict restrictions on freedom of speech. These restrictions were clear violations of the freedom of speech guaranteed by the Potsdam Declaration ("The Japanese government shall remove all obstacles to the revival and strengthening of democratic tendencies among the Japanese people, freedom of speech, of religion, and of thought. Respect for fundamental human rights shall be established"), of the new constitution of Japan that the Americans had drafted, and of the U.S. Constitution. With these restrictions, GHQ aimed to convince the people that their country's past history was evil, and eradicate in people's minds any incentive to defend their country. *This* is the very origin of the history issue for Japan.

Meanwhile, the international situation changed. The Soviet Union emerged as a new threat. And this new threat led to dispute within the U.S. government between strategists in the heart of Washington including, most notably, George Kennan, who wanted Japan to contribute militarily as a member of the Western bloc, and Douglas MacArthur, who persisted with the early occupation polices.

The real problem, however, was the Japanese people themselves rather than MacArthur. The Japanese who had been brainwashed during the occupation were no longer the Japanese of the past. When Secretary of State John Foster Dulles visited Japan in the early 1950s to negotiate the peace treaty with Japan and make Japan a partner in the Western camp, he was amazed to find how pacifistic the Japanese had become.

## Earlier Occupation Policies Amplified by the Left Wing in Japan

This peculiar phenomenon was caused by the earlier occupation policies of the United States being preserved and amplified by the Japanese left-wing element for over half a century after the end of the occupation.

Why, then, did the Japanese left wing want to do that? The reason was simple. The goal of the earlier American occupation policies was perfectly identical to that of the leftists. It was the left wing's goal to make Japan easily subjugated by the Communist bloc when it needed to be so. In order to accomplish this goal, it was necessary to deprive Japan of all of its material, mental, and legal capabilities to wage a war—identical with the early American occupation policy. And the Japanese left-wing elements fully—or maybe more than fully—succeeded to this mission from the occupation forces.

The two main forces of the Japanese leftists in those days were, of course, the Japan Socialist Party and the Japanese Communist Party. The Japan Socialist Party held power only twice—the Katayama Tetsu cabinet (May 24, 1947 through March 10, 1948) and the Murayama Tomiichi cabinet (June 30, 1994 through January 11, 1996)—and both times as a member of a coalition government. The Japan Socialist Party has never become a majority party single-handedly. Meanwhile, it was labor unions, particularly those in the fields of education, publishing, and newspaper media, that took the earlier occupation policies of the United States under their protection, representing the interests of the Communist countries.

In 1949, the Communist Party of China succeeded in putting all of China under its control. In 1950, the North Korean army invaded South Korean territory, starting the Korean War. As East Asia became a major arena of confrontation between the Western, liberal camp and the Communist bloc, labor unions intensified their pro-communist activities. The Japan Teachers' Union, for instance, adopted the slogan, "Never send our children to the battlefield again. Japanese youths, you should never hold a gun again," at its central committee meeting convened in January 1951.

Defining Japan as a bastion for countering communism, MacArthur instructed that the National Police Reserve be founded. The National Police Reserve later grew into the Self-Defense Force of Japan, paving a path for the rearmament of Japan. MacArthur also started preparations for the signing of the U.S.-Japan Security Treaty, which would enable continued stationing of U.S. military bases in Japan.

In response, the Japan Teachers' Union declared, "On the basis of the grand principle of the Constitution of Japan, which renounces all military means whatsoever, we adamantly oppose the provision of Japan's territory to any foreign country for the use of military bases, which could become a factor to lead Japan into a war."

The Japanese government began to pursue educational policies that included restoration of the *Hinomaru*, the national flag of Japan; *Kimigayo*, the Japanese national anthem; and moral education. It did this in anticipation of the restoration of national sovereignty following the termination of the occupation.

Against these government initiatives, the Japan Teachers' Union decided to oppose the compulsory raising of the national flag and singing of the national anthem after 1950 (25th Year of Shōwa). It was under the Obuchi Keizō cabinet in 1999, more than fifty years after Japan's defeat, that a law was finally passed to officially recognize the Hinomaru as the national flag and *Kimigayo* as the national anthem. Resistance of many types had to be overcome in enacting thee laws. But that was hardly the end of the issue. Immediately after the passing of this law, various chapters of the Japan Teachers' Union brought suits claiming the illegality of the legislation one after another, and it was only in 2011 that the matter was legally settled finally with a decision at the Supreme Court. Thus, it took 60 long years after the defeat in the war before the Japanese national anthem began to be sung routinely in schools all over Japan. This fact was a manifestation of the rampancy of antinationalism in Japan—something that was unthinkable, not only in the United States and Britain but, in fact, any other country in the world.

In postwar Japanese politics, this type of leftist antinationalism, or, more specifically, movements against constitutional reform, the expansion of national defense capabilities, and the alliance with the United States, reached their apex during the so-called campaign against the Japan-U.S. Security Treaty in and around 1960 and 1970.

The security pact of 1960 was an attempt to revise the older treaty, a treaty concluded simultaneously with the San Francisco Treaty at the termination of the occupation and with some elements of an unequal treaty, to a new one that was more suitable for an independent nation. Thus, it was a cause that nobody could oppose theoretically. The left-wing element in Japan, representing the interests of the communist bloc at that time, nevertheless initiated a massive opposition campaign against the revision of the security treaty because they were against the continuation of the U.S.-Japan alliance itself.

Students became the actual vanguard of the anti-treaty movement. This was, indeed, a season of student riots all over the world.

In neighboring Republic of Korea, Syngman Rhee, the first president of the republic, was forced to resign in 1960. In the latter half of the 1960s, the anti–Vietnam War movement was rampant in the United States, while in France, events erupted in May 1968 that later forced President Charles de Gaulle to step down. These upheavals during the 1960s had all started with student riots. It was indeed the season of student movements.

Because these movements were initiated and led by students, the logic behind them was necessarily immature and full of contradictions and inconsistencies. It was exactly as Henry Kissinger severely complained about the anti–Vietnam War movement in the United States.

While these movements could be categorically summarized as an outlet of youthful passions, they nevertheless gave birth to the anti–Vietnam War generation in the United States, the Generation of 1968 in France, and the *Zengakuren* (All-Japan Federation of Students' Self-Governing Associations) in 1960 and *Zenkyōtō* (All-Campus Joint Struggle League) in 1970 generations in Japan. These generations still remain the source of anti-establishment thinking seen even among contemporary leaders in these countries. In the case of Japan, the influences of these generations have lingered in subsequent generations due to slanted education that continued to be provided by teachers' unions.

In fact, the leftist, anti-establishment movements were on the ebb after the anti–U.S.-Japan Security Pact movement in 1970. In the general election toward the end of 1969, which was conducted after riot police forcefully removed students occupying the Yasuda Auditorium at the University of Tokyo, the Liberal Democratic Party won a landslide victory of 300 seats—which clearly revealed the direction of public opinion in Japan. Expo '70 was opened in Osaka the next year, putting the entire nation in a festive mood. Against this background, the anti-establishment movement and the leftist movement went almost completely underground.

## In the 1970s, "End of War" Period No Longer

Here I wish to call readers' attention to the fact that, for the next decade, there was absolutely no international dispute over the so-called history issue. This goes to show that the postwar period for Japan was already over in the 1970s.

Memories of a war are bound to fade away in one generation. One generation after the Battle of Waterloo in 1815 was the period called "reaction" in France, in which Napoleon Bonaparte was a war criminal, exiled in Saint Helena and denounced severely as a mere vulgar aggressor from Corsica. The 18th- and 19th-century Spanish painter Francisco de Goya produced a number of paintings that thoroughly portrayed the brutalities of Napoleon's army in Spain. In terms of their graphic impact, these paintings deserve to be called the 19th century version of the Nanjing Massacre Memorial Hall in China.

But a full generation later after the Battle of Waterloo, a state funeral was held for Napoleon in France in 1840, and his remains was enshrined at *Les Invalides* in Paris. Napoleon was resurrected in French people's minds as a hero who had glorified France, a historical view that still lingers in France today. One may recall the episode of Marius Pontmercy, a character in Victor Hugo's *Les Misérables*, who converted himself from a republican to a Bonapartist after he was awakened by Napoleon's glory.

Today, the "history issue" is said to be a problem that Japan has left unsettled for seventy years since World War II. But, as we saw earlier in this section, it had already become something of the past in the 1970s.

Singling out the one year of 1980, I was seconded from the Ministry of Foreign Affairs to the Defense Agency. Representing the Agency, I replied to questions in the Diet more than three hundred times around that year; Japan's "history issue" during the Greater East Asia War was never taken up even once. This can be verified by reviewing the minutes of Diet sessions.

Whenever I subsequently encountered politicians, critics, and scholars from the United States, Europe, Korea, and China who argued in international conferences that Japan had failed to settle the "history issue" or apologize enough, I made it a rule to ask them, "If in the single year of 1980 any of you ever spoke a word to the effect that Japan had not settled the war, show me the evidence." Up until now, nobody has produced counterevidence yet.

This goes to show that, like the other historical examples above, the memory of the Greater East Asia War already belonged to the past once a full generation had passed after the end of the war. It was by the hands of the later generation Japanese that this issue was given a chance to resurrect.

While this was a fact, nobody has yet analyzed why the Japanese had to revive the issue. Allow me, here, to share with readers my own personal hypothesis as follows: The anti-establishment leftist movements in Japan had come to a dead end in 1970 as the result of the failure of the anti-U.S.-Japan Security Pact riot. Because students who joined the riot had a hard time finding employment in ordinary companies because their names were on the police dossier, many of them entered the world of journalism. And these former riot students came to the frontline of newspapers and news agencies ten years later. In my view, this is what was behind the resurrection of the "history issue." A similar thing can be said about other former student radicals who remained in universities after graduation and became scholars without becoming employed by private companies. In other words, the revival of the "history issue" was, in my judgment, retaliation by the Zenkyōtō generation. And the "history issue" was first deployed outside Japan because it was not able to inspire support within Japan.

As a matter of fact, all subsequent outbursts of the "history issue" overseas were without exception triggered by Japanese themselves.

The origin of the series of "history issue" outbursts was the 1982 controversy over the screening of textbooks. It was first reported by a Japanese private TV network that the Ministry of Education had instructed that the words "invasion of the Imperial Japanese Army into north China" in a high school history textbook be rephrased to read "advance into north China." Soon, however, this report was found to be erroneous. The textbook in question had used the phrasing "advance into north China" from the beginning. Nevertheless, this erroneous reporting was taken up by a lot of other media and it spread widely, leading to a diplomatic issue when the

Chinese and Korean governments protested.

In response, the Japanese government, fully aware that the incident was triggered by erroneous reporting, decided to settle the controversy by issuing a statement by Chief Cabinet Secretary Miyazawa Kiichi. As a result, a standard was established that Japanese textbooks should "pay due consideration to the handling of modern and contemporary historical events involving neighboring Asian countries from the viewpoint of international cooperation," paving the way for Japan's neighbors to interfere with Japanese textbooks.

The Yasukuni Shrine controversy is a typical example of a "historical issue" that is not an unsettled issue at all. Until Prime Minister Nakasone Yasuhiro visited the shrine in 1985, postwar prime ministers of Japan had visited the shrine sixty times. And no visit had stirred an international controversy. Some may remember, however, that when Prime Minister Miki Takeo visited Yasukuni Shrine on August 15, 1975, the anniversary of the day Japan had surrendered 30 years earlier, he was asked whether the visit was a private one or an official one as prime minister. Miki stressed that he was visiting the shrine in a private capacity. The National Diet in the fall of the same year debated whether the Emperor's visit to Yasukuni Shrine could be a private visit. One can only imagine what went on inside the Imperial Household Agency after that because no documentation is available. However, it is not hard to imagine that the Agency decided to discontinue the Emperor's visits and dispatch an imperial envoy instead in order to prevent the Emperor from being involved in any political controversy whatsoever.

It is obvious that suspension of Prime Minister Nakasone's visits to the shrine after 1985 was engineered by Japanese hands. The daily *Asahi Shimbun* had started a campaign against Nakasone's visits before his last visit in 1985 and had succeeded in inviting criticism of the visit from the Chinese government for the first time. The Japan Socialist Party's mission to China that year also requested China's intervention in the Yasukuni Shrine issue. These and other Japan-initiated movements made Nakasone decide not to visit Yasukuni Shrine again during his tenure.

This was the genesis of foreign intervention in the controversy over visits to Yasukuni Shrine. Since then some Western media started to report on the Japanese prime ministers' visits to Yasukuni Shrine as some kind of symbol of Japan's turn to the right. This is a phenomenon that had never been seen for forty years after Japan's defeat until 1985.

Today, enshrinement of Class A war criminals in Yasukuni Shrine constitutes one major reason behind opposition to the prime minister's visit to the Shrine. But it should be recalled that, when Class A war criminals were enshrined there in 1978, there was no international repercussion whatsoever. And Yasukuni continued to be visited by Japanese prime ministers— nine times by Suzuki Zenko, who begun his career as a member of the Socialist Party, and ten times by Nakasone.

Thus, Japanese mass media succeeded in luring interference from abroad into the textbook issue in 1982 and the Yasukuni Shrine controversy in 1985. This state of affairs functioned as a fuse for the future international explosion of these issues. The turning point arrived toward the end of the 1980s.

## Settlement of Japan-Korea-China Historic Issue Is Possible

In Korea in 1988, Roh Tae-Woo became the sixth president of the Republic of Korea. Under Roh, freedom of speech was promoted. While a thorough anti-Japanese education had been given in Korean schools since the days of President Syngman Rhee, decades of Korean governments had continued to restrict free speech that could obstruct the country's foreign policies.

However, due to this newly won freedom of speech under the Roh government, coupled with maneuverings by Japanese mass media to lure anti-Japanese comments from Koreans, severe criticism of Japan erupted all at once to the extent that those who did not criticize Japan were instantly labeled unpatriotic.

The fierceness of anti-Japanese criticism in Korea in those days was of equal, if not greater, intensity as under the current Park Geun-hye administration. An old Korean friend of mine in those days said to me, "Don't ask me about my country's views of Japan. If you do, I must criticize Japan. Otherwise, I cannot protect myself." It was during this period of fierce anti-Japanese criticism in Korea that even a few Japanese people who had defended Korea and Korean students studying in Japan against the predominantly pro–North Korea intellectual climate, including my friend the late Professor Satō Seizaburō, had to experience a sense of despair about the Republic of Korea.

It should be noted, however, that Korea's anti-Japan criticism at that time was temporarily subdued. When President Kim Dae-jung visited Japan in 1998, he accepted the Japanese official apologies, declaring, "I will be personally responsible for restricting the Korean government from bringing up the past issue again." President Kim strictly kept his promise and, for the subsequent two years, no criticism on Japan was heard from Korean top government leaders or cabinet members until the rekindling of the textbook issue. This issue was triggered by publication of the history textbook compiled by the Japanese Society for History Textbook Reform. This episode is proof that the history issue between Japan and Korea can be and, indeed, has been settled, at least temporarily.

In the case of China, the greatest turning point was the Tiananmen Square Incident in 1989. The Chinese government at that time chose to suppress student movements for freedom and democratization and replaced Premier Zhao Ziyang, who was sympathetic with the student movements, with the more hardline Jiang Zeming. It also advocated patriotism so that it could take over the democratization movement.

Patriotism is a natural presence in any nation, and it can universally flare up wherever the government encourages it, as shown in prewar Japan and Germany. And the Chinese government's attempt to chase off the democratization movement with patriotism worked 100 percent. Former student leaders, who had been released from imprisonment a few years after the Tiananmen Square Incident, experienced despair when their suggestion to restart the democratization movement met with the following reaction from former comrades: "It is no longer time for such a thing. It is time to recover Taiwan and avenge 100 years of humiliation." Many such former student leaders, who must be in their late 40s if they were, say, twenty years old at the time of the Tiananmen Square Incident, fled to the United States and Japan, in despair of China today.

In 1995, which coincided with the 100th anniversary of the end of the First Sino-Japanese War and the 50th anniversary of the defeat of Japan, the Chinese government gave a boost to the patriotic movement. It was around this year that a number of anti-Japanese monuments were raised in various regions in China and anti-Japanese propaganda was escalated.

It is believed that engineering by the Japanese leftwing element had been behind the construction of these anti-Japanese monuments since the early 1980s. Tanabe Makoto, a one-time chairman of the Japan Socialist Party, suggested that China should raise a monument of the Nanjing Massacre. When the Chinese side showed hesitation, Tanabe donated \30 million to the Nanjing City Government from the coffer of the General Council of Trade Unions of Japan (Sohyo) in 1983. The donation was made as a fund for building, but the actual construction would have cost only \8.7 million; the remaining balance was a donation to the top echelon of the Communist Party of China.

When Deng Xiaoping visited Nanjing in February 1985, he used a calligraphy brush to write the name of the memorial building, The Memorial Hall of the Victims of the Nanjing Massacre by Japanese Invaders. Construction of the memorial began immediately after Deng's visit. The memorial opened on August 15, 1985, the 40th anniversary of the end of the war.

Subsequently, the anti-Japanese movement in China escalated further, leading to the enactment of a law promoting patriotic education and launching bases for patriotic education all over China. All schools in China were required to comply with this law.

Today, patriotic education has been increasingly reinforced as a tool of President Xi Jinping's anti-liberalism, anti-democratization drive.


## Comfort Women Issue Brought up by the Japanese Side

The comfort women issue is a typical example of an international controversy over Japanese conduct started by the Japanese themselves. The surfacing of the issue is attributed to a publicity stunt by a hitherto unknown Japanese commentator.

In his book, *Watashi no Sensō Hanzai* (My War Crimes) published in 1983, Yoshida Seiji testified that two hundred women on Jeju Island had been kidnapped as comfort women for Japanese soldiers. The book was translated into Korean in 1989. That same year, a Korean reporter for a local newspaper on Jeju Island introduced in his article the testimony of an 85-year-old female resident of Jeju's Seongsanpo village. The woman said, "While it would have been big news if as many as fifteen women were kidnapped from my village of only 250 households, I don't recall any such incident." Based on this and other testimonies, this Korean reporter argued that Yoshida's book "lacked supporting testimonies" and that the "forced recruitment of comfort women" on Jeju Island that Yoshida had written about was a groundless allegation. The reporter concluded that Yoshida's assertion was a complete fabrication.

This reporting was further backed up by Kim Pong-ok, a Jeju local historian, who criticized Yoshida's testimony based on years of investigative research, saying, "I have found it [Yoshida's allegation] groundless. I would say Yoshida's book is a product of frivolous salesmanship, revealing the immorality of the Japanese."

These criticisms from the Korean side, however, remained unknown to the Japanese until they were introduced in Japanese newspapers and magazines by historian Hata Ikuhiko in 1992. Hata quoted the testimonies gathered by the Korean reporter. Until then, Yoshida's allegation of forced recruitment of comfort women by the Japanese had retained life as a historical fact to the extent that it flared anti-Japan criticism in Korea and obstructed bilateral relations.

The Japanese government at that time was under Prime Minister Miyazawa Kiichi, one of the most liberal administrations of the postwar Liberal Democratic governments. In an attempt to somehow appease Korean displeasure and normalize Korean-Japanese relations, the Miyazawa cabinet released official statements by two of its Chief Cabinet Secretaries, Katō Kōichi and Kōno Yōhei. At that time, it appeared that the Korean side was willing to settle the issue without demanding compensation for former comfort women when and if the Japanese side showed some kind of intention to apologize.

A product of the mutual compromise thus reached was the so-called Kōno Statement. While recognizing that there was no evidence of the forced recruitment of Korean comfort women by Japanese authorities, the Japanese side also realized that settlement of the issue would not be possible without an admittance of official wrongdoing. Thus, the wording of the Kōno Statement was highly ambiguous. It said, "[Although] the recruitment of the comfort women was conducted mainly by private recruiters, . . . their recruitment, transfer, control, etc., were conducted generally against their will . . ."

Since it is only natural for any organizational or group action to have some restrictions on its freedom, at a glance this statement appeared to be a harmless enough document. Nevertheless, it came to be regarded as evidence of Japanese recognition of the forceful recruitment of comfort women and was used as such for a long time to come. This was an example of a measure based on shallow thinking to temporarily fend off criticism leaving the source of a problem remaining for subsequent decades.

This issue of comfort women subsequently developed into a wider, international controversy. Again, it was the Japanese, or Japanese Americans, who triggered the escalation. In 1992, the Japan Federation of Bar Associations, which had traditionally shown a leftist tendency, started lobbying the United Nations, in hopes of prompting the United Nations Commission on Human Rights to promote international recognition of comfort women for the Japanese military as sex slaves. As a result, comfort women for the Japanese military was explicitly described as "military sexual slavery" in the Report of the Special Rapporteur on violence against women by Ms. Radhika Coomaraswamy and submitted in accordance with Commission on Human Rights resolution 1995/85 (Coomaraswamy Report), published in 1996.

In 2007, Japanese-American member of the U.S. Congress Mike Honda proposed United States House of Representatives House Resolution 121, which stated that "Japan should formally acknowledge, apologize, and accept historical responsibility in a clear and unequivocal manner" regarding the institution of comfort women in World War II. The resolution argued that the Kōno Statement acknowledged the participation of the Japanese authorities in said institution.

At this point, Japan was in a decisively disadvantageous position. While, at first, the issue had been whether the military was involved in the forced recruitment, as time went by, management of brothels by the military itself came to be regarded as a violation of human rights. Although the institution and management of bordellos for soldiers has been a common practice among the militaries of the world, including of the United States, in order to avoid sexual violence against outsiders, Japan had no chance of winning international understanding on this issue when the management itself of such institutions became sinful.[26]

---

26  The *Asahi Shimbun*, whose reporting on Korean comfort women had played a decisive role in the compilation of Radhika Coomaraswamy's report on violence against women for the U.N. Human Rights Commission, admits errors in past "comfort women" stories. According to the August 5, 2014, edition of the *Japan Times*:

The same article continues to say that, "[Although Prime Minister Abe had] suggested he might revise or retract the key government apology to the women issued by Chief Cabinet Secretary Yohei Kono in 1993, . . . Abe has upheld the Kono statement, which admitted that the Japanese authorities and military were 'directly or indirectly, involved in the establishment and management of the comfort stations and the transfer of comfort women'."

Reacting to this admission of groundlessness of Yoshida's claims by the *Asahi Shimbun*, the October 16, 2014, edition of the *Japan Times* reports:

> The government has asked the author of a U.N. report that accused Japan of wartime military sexual slavery to amend the document, the top government spokesman said Thursday. It wants Radhika Coomaraswamy, former Special Rapporteur on violence against women at the U.N. Human Rights Commission, to revise the document she wrote in 1996 in light of the "comfort women" reports recently retracted by the daily *Asahi Shimbun*, Chief Cabinet Secretary Yoshihide Suga told a news conference.
>
> In September, Coomaraswamy told Kyodo News that she had no intention of correcting her report, saying her findings were mainly

---

The *Asahi Shimbun* admitted Tuesday to serious errors in many articles on the "comfort women" issue, retracting all stories going back decades that quoted a Japanese man who claimed he kidnapped about 200 Korean women and forced them to work at wartime Japanese military brothels. The correction came more than 20 years after the *Sankei Shimbun* based on studies by noted historian Ikuhiko Hata first pointed out apparent errors in the man's account in April 1992. Hata and the *Sankei* said there was no evidence supporting the account of Seiji Yoshida, who claimed he conducted something akin to "human hunting" by rounding up about 200 women on Jeju-do Island in present-day South Korea. All local residents interviewed by Hata denied Yoshida's claims. Mainstream historians have now agreed that his statements were false.

In April and May this year, the *Asahi* dispatched reporters to the island and interviewed about 40 elderly residents and concluded that Yoshida's accounts "are false." As far as the present-day Korean Peninsula is concerned, the Asahi, like most mainstream Japanese historians, maintained that no hard evidence had been found to show the Japanese military was directly involved in recruiting women to the brothel system against their will.

based on testimony by former comfort women, and Yoshida's account was "only one piece of evidence."

Efforts have been made to settle this and other "history issues."

At a summit talk between China and Japan in 2006, it was decided that a joint historical study should be conducted by prominent scholars representing the two countries. The resultant Japan-China Joint History Research Committee met four times. It published its final report in 2010. The report succeeded in maintaining the semblance of an academic document, allowing the inclusion of both Chinese and Japanese arguments where no agreement was reached between the two.

In contrast, the Japan–South Korea Joint History Research Project that was conducted from 2002 through 2005 failed to produce an academically significant report. One reason was the Korean side's refusal even to peruse source materials that the Japanese side presented.

## Anti-Government Movement by the Japanese Themselves

How can this issue be settled?

The problem is there is no historical precedent to this issue. Even the aftereffect of the Napoleonic wars that had stormed all of Europe subsided after a generation passed. In contrast, in the case of Japan, the controversy quieted down within a generation of the end of the war, only to be dug up ten years later by Japanese hands to persist even today, seventy years after the end of the war.

Japan's case is also unique in the sense that all the controversies have originated from anti-government movements of the Japanese themselves.

There is no guarantee, either, that even though the problem originated in Japan, it would be automatically settled once anti-establishment movements in Japan subside. In China and South Korea, criticism of Japan on the grounds of the history issues has already become widespread public opinion, no matter whether it was originally triggered by anti-government movements in Japan or not.

Further reflection, however, would make us realize that, even though this is indeed an international controversy, it is not an issue that involves a shift in the balance of power among nations—which is an axis of international affairs. Rather, the issue involves the national sentiments of concerned parties, and its influence is confined to such formalities as the convening of summit meetings, which have no bearing on the basic national interests of the concerned parties.

International relations today are full of unsolved issues, including environmental issues and population problems, as well as the issue of sustaining economic expansion and improving the standard of living for all. These issues call for international cooperation. The world cannot afford to be caught up by the memory of the history in the first half of the 20th century any longer, particularly when the "history" is purposely misrepresented.

Of all these international issues, what has been particularly important traditionally is how to maintain international peace in the face of the changing balance of power among nations. Once this issue surfaces, it will eclipse all other issues.

China's recent rise is seen by some as a shift of the balance of power in the world that is comparable to the ascension of Germany in the early 19th century. I personally do not think that China has come that far. China's military power is still far from being a threat to the primacy of the United States. The United States, therefore, can still afford to take a liberal and tolerant approach toward China.

I suspect that problems such as the "history issue" will persist until the balance of power in the world undergoes a radical change.

# REFERENCES

Abe Shin'nosuke (1954). *Gendai Seijika-ron* (Discussing Contemporary Statesmen). Tokyo: Bungei Shunjūsha.

Arai Hisashi (1953). *Nikkyōso Undō-shi* (History of Japan Teachers' Union's Activities). Tokyo: Nippon Shuppan Kyōdō.

Asahi Shimbun Hōtei Kishadan, eds. (1962). *Tokyo Saiban* (International Military Tribunal for the Far East). Tokyo: Asahi Shimbunsha.

Asahi Shimbun Rōdō Kumiai, ed. (1982). *Asahi Shimbun Rōdō Kumiai-shi* (History of the Asahi Shimbun's Labor Union). Tokyo: Asahi Shimbun Rōdō Kumiai.

Bisson, Thomas A. (1983). *Bisson Nippon Senryō Kaisōroku* (Reform Years in Japan 1945–47: An Occupation Memoir), translated by Nakamura Masanori. Tokyo: Sanseidō.

Bungei Shunju, ed. (2000). "Dawā Intabyū" (Interview with John Dower) in monthly *Bungei Shunjū*. June 2000.

Dōdai Keizai Konwa-kai, ed. (1995). *Kindai Nihon Sensō-shi* (Military History of Modern Japan). Tokyo: Dōdai Keizai Konwa-kai.

Dower, John (1999). *Embracing Defeat: Japan in the Wake of World War II* New York: W.W. Norton & Company.

—(1991). *Yoshida Shigeru to Sono Jidai* (Empire and Aftermath: Yoshida Shigeru and the Japanese Experience, 1878–1954), translated by Ōkubo Genji. Tokyo: Chūō Kōron-sha.

Etō Jun (1995). *Senryō Shiroku* (Record of the History of Occupation). Tokyo: Kōdansha.

—(1989). *Tozasareta Gengo-Kūkan* (Closed Linguistic Space). Tokyo: Bungei Shunjūsha.

Fish, Hamilton (1985). *Nichibei Kaisen no Higeki* (Tragic Start of the U.S.-Japan War), translated by Okazaki Hisahiko. Tokyo: PHP Kenkyūsho.

Gayn, Mark (1998). *Nippon Nikki* (Japan Diary: 1945–1948), translated by Imoto Takeo. Tokyo: Chikuma Shobō.

Hayashi Itsurō (1960). *Haisha* (The Loser). Tokyo: Futami Shobō.

Hayashi Kentarō (1992). *Shōwa-shi to Watashi* (Showa History and I). Tokyo: Bungei Shunjūsha.

Inoki Masamichi (1981). *Hyōden Yoshida Shigeru* (Critical Biography of Yoshida Shigeru). Tokyo: Yomiuri Shimbunsha.

Iokibe Makoto (1985). *Beikoku no Nippon Senryō Seisaku* (U.S. Occupation Policies Regarding Japan). Tokyo: Chūō Kōron-sha.

—(1997). *Senryōki* (Occupation Period). Tokyo: Yomiuri Shimbunsha.

Ishihara Hōki (1999). *Sengo Nippon Chishikijin no Hatsugen Kiseki* (Locus of Remarks by Postwar Japanese Intellectuals). Tokyo: Jiyūsha.

Kasumigasekikai, ed. (2001). *Gekiteki Gaikō* (Dramatic Diplomacy). Tokyo: Seikō Shobō.

Kennan, George F. (1973). *Jōji F. Kenan Kaisōroku* (Memoirs, 1925–1950), translated by Shimizu Toshio. Tokyo: Yomiuri Shimbunsha.

Kiyose Ichiro (1967). *Hiroku Tokyo Saiban* (Secret Record of the Tokyo Trials). Tokyo: Yomiuri Shimbunsha.

Kobori Keiichiro, ed. (1995). *Tokyo Saiban: Nippon no Benmei* (Tokyo Trials: Japanese Vindications). Tokyo: Kōdansha.

—(1996). *Sai-Kenshō: Tokyo Saiban* (Reviewing the Tokyo Trials). Tokyo: PHP Kenkyūsho.

—(1997). *Tokyo Saiban no Noroi* (Curse of the Tokyo Trials). Tokyo: PHP Kenkyūsho.

Kojima Noboru (1971). *Tokyo Saiban* (International Military Tribunal for the Far East). Tokyo: Chūō Kōron-sha.

MacArthur, Douglas (1964). *Makkāsā Kaisōroku* (Douglas MacArthur Reminisces), translated by Tsushima Kazuo. Tokyo: Asahi Shimbunsha.

Masuda Hiroshi (1996). *Kōshoku Tsuihō* (The Purge). Tokyo: University of Tokyo Press.

Mears, Helen (1948). *Mirror for Americans, Japan.* Boston: Houghton Mifflin.

Nippon Kyōsantō, ed. (1982). *Nippon Kyōsantō no 60-nen* (60 Years of the Japan Communist Party). Tokyo: Nippon Kyōsantō.

Nippon Kyōshokuin Kumiai, ed. (1980). *Sengo Kyōiku Saiban-shi* (History of Postwar Education-Related Trials). Tokyo: Nippon Kyōshokuin Kumiai.

—(1989). *Nikkyōso 40-nen Shi* (40-year History of the Japan Teachers' Union). Tokyo: Rōdō Kyōiku Sentā.

Nippon Tosho Sentā, ed. (1996). *GHQ Nippon Senryō-shi—Kōshoku Tsuihō* (History of the Occupation of Japan by GHQ—The Purge). Tokyo: Nippon Tosho Sentā.

Nishi Osamu (1999). *Nippon-koku Kenpō wo Kangaeru* (Pondering the Constitution of Japan). Tokyo: Bungei Shunjūsha.

Reischauer, Edwin O. (1987). *Raishawā Jiden* (My Life between Japan and America), translated by Tokuoka Takao. Tokyo: Bungei Shunjūsha.

Röling, Bernard & Antonio Cassese (1996). *Rērinku Hanji no Tokyo Saiban—Rekishiteki Shōgen to Tenbō* (The Tokyo Trial and Beyond: Reflections of Peacemonger), translated by Kosuge Nobuko. Tokyo: Shinyōsha.

Sakakibara Natsu (2000). *Makkāsā Gensui to Showa Ten'nō* (General MacArthur and Emperor Showa). Tokyo: Shūeisha.

Sato Isao (1947). *Kenpō Kaisei no Katei* (Process of Constitutional Amendment). Tokyo: Nippon Hyōronsha.

Schonberger, Howard (1989). *Aftermath of War: Americans and the Remaking of Japan, 1945–1952.* Kent: Kent State University Press.

Seki Yoshihiko (1998). *Watashi to Minshu-Shakaishugi* (Democratic Socialism and Me). Tokyo: Kindai Bungeisha.

Sherwood, Robert (1957). *Rūzuberuto to Hopukinsu* (Roosevelt and Hopkins: An Intimate History), translated by Murakami Mitsuhiko. Tokyo: Misuzu Shobō.

Shidehara Heiwa Zaidan (1955). *Shidehara Kijūrō*. Tokyo: Shidehara Heiwa Zaidan.

Shidehara Kijūrō (1951). *Gaikō 50-nen* (50 Years of Diplomacy). Tokyo: Yomiuri Shimbun-sha.

Shigemitsu Mamoru (1952). *Shōwa no Dōran* (Showa: A Time of Upheaval). Tokyo: Chūō Kōron-sha.

— (1986–88). *Shigemitsu Mamoru Shuki* (Personal Accounts by Shigemitsu Mamoru). Tokyo: Chūō Koronsha.

Shikanai Nobutaka & Sakurada Takeshi (1973). *Ima Akasu Sengo Hishi* (Secret History of the Postwar Days that Can Be Disclosed Now). Tokyo: Sankei Shimbunsha.

Shimomura Kainan (1950). *Shūsen Hishi* (Secret History of the End of War). Tokyo: Kōdansha.

Shisō no Kagaku, ed. (1978). *Nippon Senryō-gun* (Japan Occupation Forces). Tokyo: Tokuma Shoten.

Sodei Rinjirō (1985). *Haikei Makkāsā Gensui Sama* (Dear Your Excellency General MacArthur). Tokyo: Dai-nichi Shobō.

—ed. and translated (2000). *Yoshida Shigeru Makkāsā Ōfuku Shokanshū* (Collected Correspondences between Yoshida Shigeru and MacArthur). Tokyo: Hōsei Daigaku Shuppankyoku.

Tōgō Shigenori (1985). *Jidai no Ichimen: Tōgō Shigenori Gaikō Shuki* (An Aspect of the Times: Diplomatic Memoranda by Tōgō Shigenori). Tokyo: Hara Shobō.

Tokyo Daigaku Shakai Kagaku Kenkyūsho, ed. (1975). *Sengo Kaikaku 6—Nōchi Kaikaku* (Postwar Reforms 6—Land Reform). Tokyo: University of Tokyo Press.

Tokyo Saiban Kenkyūkai (1984). *Paru Hanketsusho* (Judge Pal's Judgment Documents). Tokyo: Kōdansha.

Tokyo Saiban Shiryō Kankōkai, ed. (1995). *Tokyo Saiban Kyakka Miteishutsu Bengogawa Shiryō* (Compilation of Defense Counsels' Evidence that Was Rejected and Unadopted by the International Military Tribunal for the Far East). Tokyo: Kokusho Kankōkai.

Truman, Harry (1992). *Torūman Kaisōroku* (Truman Memoir), translated by Horie Yoshitaka. Tokyo: Kōbunsha.

Tsūsanshō Kanbō Chōsaka, ed. (1954). *Sengo Keizai 10-nen Shi* (10-year History of the Postwar Japanese Economy). Tokyo: Ministry of International Trade and Industry.

Ujita Naoyoshi (1985). *Shidehara Kijūrō*. Tokyo: Jiji Tsūshinsha

Watanabe Takeshi (1966). *Senryōka no Nippon Zaisei Oboegaki* (Notes on Financial Policies in Occupied Japan).

Yoshida Shigeru (1958). *Kaisō 10-nen* (10-years in Reminiscence). Tokyo: Shinchōsha.

—(1967). *Nippon wo Ketteishita 100-nen* (100 Years That Determined Japan's Fate). Tokyo: Nippon Keizai Shimbunsha.

—(1962). *Ōiso Zuiso* (Essays from Oiso). Tokyo: Sekikasha.

# APPENDIX
# Chronogical Table of Outstanding Events in the Period Covered by the Current Volume

| Year | Japanese Era year | Age of Person in Events Column | Events in Person's Life | Domesitic/Overseas Incidents |
|------|------|------|------|------|
| 1878 | Meiji 11 | 1 | Yoshida Shigeru born in Tokyo on September 22 to the family of Takenouchi Tsuna, one of the leaders of the Jiyūtō's Tosa faction, as the fifth son. | Ōkubo Toshimichi assassinated. |
| 1880 | Meiji 13 | 3 | Shigeru adopted by Yoshida Kenzō, a friend of Takenouchi, in August. | |
| 1889 | Meiji 22 | 11 | After graduating from Ota Elementary School, Yokohama, Shigeru enters the boarding school Kōyo Gijuku, a private junior high school in Fujisawa, at the recommendation of Nakajima Nobuyuki, the then governor of Kanagawa prefecture who later became the first president of the House of Representatives. | Promulgation of the Constitution of the Empire of Japan and the Imperial Household Law . |
| | | | Shigeru's stepfather, Yoshida Kenzō, passes away at the young age of 40, leaving an immense legacy, including a huge mansion in Ōiso, to Shigeru. | |
| 1894 | Meiji 27 | 16 | Shigeru graduates from Kōyo Gijuku and enters Nippon Junior High School in Azabu, Tokyo. | Donghak Peasant Revolution in Korea. |
| | | | | Japan declares war against Qing China (First Sino-Japanese War). |
| 1895 | Meiji 28 | 17 | Shigeru transfers to the Higher Commercial School (present-day Hitotsubashi University) only to be transferred again to the Seisoku Normal Junior High School in three months. | Treaty of Shimonoseki signed. |
| | | | | Triple Intervention by Germany, France, and Russia, leading to return of the Liaodong Peninsula to Qing China. |

| Year | Japanese Era year | Age of Person in Events Column | Events in Person's Life | Domesitic/Overseas Incidents |
|---|---|---|---|---|
| 1896 | Meiji 29 | 18 | Shigeru enters the Tokyo Academy of Physics (present-day Tokyo University of Science). | The Yamagata-Lobanov Agreement on Korean affairs signed. |
| 1897 | Meiji 30 | 19 | Shigeru transfers to Grade 6 of Gakushūin Junior High School. | |
| 1901 | Meiji 34 | 23 | Shigeru graduates from Gakushūin High School and enters Gakushūin University. | |
| 1902 | Meiji 35 | 24 | | The Anglo-Japanese Alliance signed. |
| 1904 | Meiji 37 | 26 | Shigeru transfers to Faculty of Law, Tokyo Imperial University, due to closing of the university section of Gakushūin. | Russo-Japanese War (until 1905). |
| 1905 | Meiji 38 | 27 | | Treaty of Portsmouth signed between Japan and Russia |
| 1906 | Meiji 39 | 28 | Shigeru graduates from Department of Political Science, Faculty of Law, Tokyo Imperial University. Shigeru passes the Foreign Service Examination with the 7th highest score of the eleven successful examinees, which includes Hirota Kōki. | The South Manchuria Railway Co. Ltd. established. |
| | | | Shigeru appointed assistant consul in November. | |
| 1907 | Meiji 40 | 29 | Shigeru stationed in Mukden, China, in February. | French-Japanese agreement on Vietnam signed. |
| 1908 | Meiji 41st | 30 | Shigeru stationed in London in November. | |
| 1909 | Meiji 42nd | 31 | Shigeru marries in March to Yukiko, 19-year-old eldest daughter of Makino Nobuaki, Privy Councilor, who is the second son of Ōkubo Toshimichi. | Itō Hirobumi, President of the Privy Council, assassinated by Korean nationalist/independence activist An Jung-geun at the Harbin Railway Station. |
| | | | Shigeru stationed in Italy in December. | |
| 1910 | Meiji 43 | 32 | Shigeru's eldest daughter, Sakurako, born in June. | Japan-Korea Treaty (on Japan's annexation of Korea) signed. Terauchi Masaki appointed the first Governor-General of Korea |
| 1911 | Meiji 44 | 33 | | Xinhai Revolution (in Qing). |

| Year | Japanese Era year | Age of Person in Events Column | Events in Person's Life | Domesitic/Overseas Incidents |
|---|---|---|---|---|
| 1912 | Meiji 45 | 34 | Shigeru's first son, Ken'ichi, born in April. | Fall of Qing and foundation of the Republic of China. |
| | Taishō 1 | 35 | Shigeru appointed Japanese Consul in Andong cum secretary to Governor-General Terauchi in August. | Emperor Meiji passes away at the age of 61, followed to the grave by General Nogi Maresuke and his wife. |
| 1914 | Taishō 3 | 36 | Shigeru's second daughter, Kōko, born in January but passes away in July 1915. | Siemens Scandal. |
| | | | | World War I erupts (until 1918). |
| 1915 | Taishō 4 | 37 | Shigeru's third daughter, Kazuko, born in May. | The Twenty-One Demands. |
| | | | | Enthronement of Emperor Taishō. |
| 1916 | Taishō 5 | 38 | | Yuan Shikai passes away. |
| 1917 | Taishō 6 | 39 | Shigeru appointed Acting Director of Document Division, Minister's Secretariat, Ministry of Foreign Affairs, in July. | The October Revolution in Russia. |
| | | | Shigeru's second son, Masao, born in August. | |
| 1918 | Taishō 7 | 40 | Shigeru appointed Japanese Consul in Jinan cum Government Section of Tsingtau Garrison in February. | Japanese troops dispatched to Siberia (until 1920). |
| | | | | Rice Riots in Toyama prefecture/Terauchi Masaki cabinet steps down. |
| | | | | Hara Takashi cabinet, the first party cabinet in Japan, formed. |
| 1919 | Taishō 8 | 41 | Shigeru attends Paris Peace Conference as an assistant to the Japanese chief delegate, Makino Nobuchika. | Paris Peace Conference. |
| | | | | Treaty of Versalles (creation of the League of Nations, territorial restrictions on Germany, war reparations imposed on Germany) signed. |
| | | | | The March 1st Movement (Manse Demonstrations) in Korea. |
| | | | | The May Fourth Movement in China. |
| | | | | Weimar Constitution promulgated in Germany. |

| Year | Japanese Era year | Age of Person in Events Column | Events in Person's Life | Domesitic/Overseas Incidents |
|------|------|------|------|------|
| 1920 | Taishō 9 | 42 | Shigeru appointed First Secretary at Japanese Embassy in London in September. | The League of Nations established. |
| | | | | 1920 California Alien Land Law passes in California. |
| 1921 | Taishō 10 | 43 | Crown Prince Hirohito (later Emperor Shōwa) tours European countries. | The Washington Conference (1921-22). |
| | | | | Prime Minister Hara Takashi assassinated. |
| | | | | Japan-Britain-France-U.S. four-country treaty in the Pacific signed and the Anglo-Japanese Alliance is invalidated. |
| 1922 | Taishō 11 | 44 | Shigeru's biological father, Takeuchi Tsuna, passes away in January at the age of 82. | The Washington Conference concluded (Washington Naval Treaty to limit naval construction, Nine-Power Treaty on the sovereignty and territorial integrity of China, treaty on China's tariffs, and several other treaties signed). |
| | | | Shigeru appointed Consul-General at Tianjin in March. | |
| 1923 | Taishō 12 | 45 | | Great Kantō Earthquake. |
| 1924 | Taishō 13 | 46 | | First United Front between Kuomingtang and the Communist Party of China formed. |
| | | | | Immigration Act of 1924 enacted in the United States. |
| 1925 | Taishō 14th | 47 | Shigeru appointed Consul-General at Mukden in October. | General Election Law and Public Security Preservation Law of 1925 enacted. |
| 1926 | Taishō 15 | 48 | | Emperor Taishō passes away (at the age of 48). Crown Prince Hirohito receives the succession. |
| | Shōwa 1 | | | |
| 1927 | Shōwa 2 | 49 | | Nanjing Incident. |
| | | | | The first dispatch of Japanese troops to Shandong. |

| Year | Japanese Era year | Age of Person in Events Column | Events in Person's Life | Domesitic/Overseas Incidents |
|---|---|---|---|---|
| 1928 | Shōwa 3 | 50 | Shigeru appointed Vice-Minister for Foreign Affairs in the Tanaka Giichi cabinet in July | Zhang Zuolin assassinated by explosion. |
| | | | | First general election carried out. |
| 1929 | Shōwa 4 | 51 | Shigeru continues to serve as Vice-Minister for Foreign Affairs in the Hamaguchi Osachi cabinet to help pursue international cooperative diplomacy under Foreign Minister Shidehara Kijūrō. | The Great Depression triggered by the collapse of U.S. stock market prices. |
| 1930 | Shōwa 5 | 52 | Shigeru appointed Japanese Ambassador to Italy in December. | London Naval Conference among Japan, United States, Britain, France, and Italy. |
| 1931 | Shōwa 6 | 53 | | The Liutiaohu Incident erupts, marking the beginning of the Manchurian Incident. |
| 1932 | Shōwa 7 | 54 | Shigeru returns home from Britain in September. Although recommended by Foreign Minister Uchida Kōsai as Japanese Ambassador to the United States, Shigeru declines and becomes an ambassador in reserve. | The January 28 Incident erupts. |
| | | | Shigeru dispatched to observe Manchukuo and Republic of China as ambassador extraordinary and plenipotentiary. | The Manchu State (Manchukuo) proclaimed. |
| | | | | The May 15 Incident erupts. Prime Minister Inukai assassinated. |
| 1933 | Shōwa 8 | 55 | | Japan withdraws from the League of Nations. |
| 1934 | Shōwa 9 | 56 | Shigeru visits Europe as the first foreign minister's special envoy. | |
| 1935 | Shōwa 10 | 57 | Shigeru retires from Ministry of Foreign Affairs in November. | |
| 1936 | Shōwa 11 | 58 | Hirota Kōki cabinet formed upon resignation of the Okada Keisuke cabinet in March. Although Hirota Shigeru to serve as his foreign minister, it falls through due to Imperial Japanese Army's interference. | The February 26 Incident. |
| | | | Shigeru appointed Japanese Ambassador to Britain in April. | Germany-Japan Anti-Communist Pact signed. |

| Year | Japanese Era year | Age of Person in Events Column | Events in Person's Life | Domesitic/Overseas Incidents |
|------|------|------|------|------|
| 1937 | Shōwa 12 | 59 | | The Marco Polo Bridge Incident erupts, marking the beginning of the Second Sino-Japanese War. |
| 1938 | Shōwa 13 | 60 | Shigeru returns home from Britain in November. | The National Mobilization Law promulgated. |
| 1939 | Shōwa 14 | 61 | Shigeru's dismissal from the foreign ministry at his own request in March. | Britain and France declare war on Germany, marking the beginning of World War II. |
| 1940 | Shōwa 15 | 62 | | The Tripartite Pact concluded among Germany, Italy and Japan. |
| 1941 | Shōwa 16 | 63 | Shigeru's wife, Yukiko, passes away of pharyngeal cancer in October. | The Tōjō Hideki cabinet formed. |
| | | | | The Attack on Pearl Harbor, marking the beginning the Greater East Asia War. |
| 1942 | Shōwa 17 | 64 | Shigeru sounds out Kido Kōichi, Lord Keeper of the Privy Seal, on his intention to start peace nego-tiations. | Imperial Japanese Navy defeated in the Battle of Midway. |
| | | | | Imperial Japanese Army decides to withdraw from Guadalcanal. |
| 1943 | Shōwa 18 | 65 | | Admiral Yamamoto Isoroku of the Imperial Japanese Navy killed. |
| | | | | The Japanese garrison on Attu island conducts suicidal attack and is annihilated. |
| 1944 | Shōwa 19 | 66 | | Invasion of Normandy by the Allied forces. |
| | | | | Fall of Saipan and Guam. |
| | | | | Kamikazae suicide attacks launched. |
| 1945 | Shōwa 20 | 67 | Shigeru advises Konoe Fumimaro on his memorial to the Emperor in February. | Fall of Iwo-Jima/Bombing of Tokyo commenced. |
| | | | Shigeru detained for forty days by the Imperial Japanese Army mili-tary police, which detects Konoe's plan to submit his memorial to the Emperor in April for release in June. | Franklin D. Roosevelt passes away. |

| Year | Japanese Era year | Age of Person in Events Column | Events in Person's Life | Domesitic/Overseas Incidents |
|------|------|------|------|------|
| 1945 | Shōwa 20 | 67 | Shigeru appointed foreign minister in the Prince Higashikuni Naruhiko cabinet in September. | Benito Mussolini executed and Adolf Hitler commits suicide, heralding Italian and German surrender to the Allied forces. |
| | | | Shigeru continues to serve as foreign minister in the Shidehara Kijūrō cabinet in October. | Fall of Okinawa. |
| | | | | Atomic bombs dropped on Hiroshima and Nagasaki. The Soviet Union declares war on Japan. |
| | | | | Japan accepts the Potsdam Declaration and surrenders unconditionally to the Allies, ending World War II. |
| | | | | MacArthur's arrival at Atsugi airbase followed by the signing of the instrument of surrender on board *USS Missouri*. |
| | | | | Censorship by GHQ commenced. |
| | | | | Emperor Shōwa visits MacArthur at GHQ. |
| | | | | Dissolution of zaibatsu and the first land reform implemented. |
| | | | | Konoe Fumimaro commits suicide by poisons. |
| 1946 | Shōwa 21 | 68 | Shigeru appointed president of Jiyūtō upon the purge of Hatoyama Ichirō and prime minister of Japan in May (First Yoshida cabinet, coalition between Jiyūtō and Shimpotō, with Shigeru serving concurrently as foreign minister and the first and second minister of veterans affairs). | Renunciation of divinity by Emperor. |
| | | | Constitution of Japan promulgated in November. | The first Purge implemented. |
| | | | | Emperor Shōwa's tour of inspection commenced. |
| | | | | Minister of State Matsumoto Jōji submits a draft constitution to the Emperor. |

| Year | Japanese Era year | Age of Person in Events Column | Events in Person's Life | Domesitic/Overseas Incidents |
|---|---|---|---|---|
| 1946 | Shōwa 21 | 68 | | MacArthur instructs Major General Courtney Whiteney, chief of GHQ's government section, to prepare its own draft constitution, along the lines of which Japan's cabinet meeting decides to amend Japan's constitution. |
| | | | | International Military Tribunal for the Far East commenced. |
| | | | | The second Purge implemented. |
| 1947 | Shōwa 22 | 69 | Shigeru calls militant labor unions "lawless elements" in an NHK radio program, stirring a controversy. | The February 1 General Strike banned. |
| | | | Public Office Election Act amended in February. | The Japanese Constitution goes into effect. |
| | | | Shigeru runs for House of Representatives from his biological father's district (Kōchi Prefecture) in April General Election and is elected. | Katayama Tetsu, chairman of the Socialist Party, forms a coalition government with Minshutō and Kokumin Kyōdōtō. |
| | | | Shigeru decides against forming a coalition government with the socialist party, which wins the election, and steps down in May. | |
| 1948 | Shōwa 23 | 70 | Shigaru elected to president of the newly founded Minshu-Jiyūtō in March. | The Katayama Tetsu cabinet resigns. |
| | | | The second Yoshida cabinet formed (a single-party, minority government) in October. | Ashida Hitoshi cabinet formed (a tri-party coalition government among Socialist Party, Minshutō, and Kokumin Kyōdōtō). |
| | | | Socialist Party's nonconfidence motion passes the Diet and the House of Representatives is dissolved in December (the so-called conspiracy dissolution). | Ashida cabinet forced to step down due to the Showa Electric scandal. |
| | | | | Decisions of the Tokyo Trial read and seven defendents including Tōjō Hideki executed by hanging. |

| Year | Japanese Era year | Age of Person in Events Column | Events in Person's Life | Domesitic/Overseas Incidents |
|------|------|------|------|------|
| 1949 | Shōwa 24 | 71 | Minshu-Jiyūtō wins a landslide victory in the January general election. | China's People's Liberation Army triumphantly enters Beijing. |
| | | | The third Yoshida cabinet formed in February. | Soviet Union announces its possession of nuclear bombs. |
| | | | The Japanese government forced to adopt a financial and monetary contraction policy (the Dodge Line) in March. | Shimoyama Incident and Mitaka Incident. |
| | | | | People's Republic of China established. |
| 1950 | Shōwa 25 | 72 | Minshu-Jiyūtō merges with pro-coalition Minshutō members to launch Jiyūtō in April with Shigeru selected to be its president. | MacArthur makes an announcement that does not deny Japan's right to self-defense. |
| | | | Shigeru criticizes President Nambara Shigeru of the University of Tokyo who advocated the comprehensive peace treaty argument in May, calling him a distorter of learning. | Storm of McCarthyism blows all over the United States. |
| | | | 24 members of the executive committee of the Japan Communist Party purged in June by MacArthur's instruction. | The Korean War (1950-53) erupts. |
| | | | | National Police Reserve launched. |
| | | | | The Chinese Army participates in the Korean War. North Korean and Chinese Armies advance southward beyond the 38th parallel north. |
| 1951 | Shōwa 26 | 73 | Shigeru meets John Foster Dulles, special envoy for peace negotiation with Japan, in January and refuses the latter's request Japan rearm. | MacArthur relieved of his post by President Truman. |
| | | | Shigeru participates in 52-nation San Francisco peace conference in September as Japan's chief delegate and signs the Treaty of San Francisco, which the Soviet Union, Czechoslovakia, and Poland abstain from signing. Shigeru also signs the U.S.-Japan Security Treaty, allowing continued stationing of the U.S. military forces in Japan. | U.S. GARIOA emergency aid to Japan terminated. The first Purge lifted. |

| Year | Japanese Era year | Age of Person in Events Column | Events in Person's Life | Domesitic/Overseas Incidents |
|---|---|---|---|---|
| 1951 | Shōwa 26 | 73 | The Treaty of San Francisco and the U.S.-Japan Security Treaty pass the House of Representatives in November. | The Socialist Party split between the Leftist Socialist Party and the Rightist Socialist Party. |
| 1952 | Shōwa 27 | 74 | GHQ abolished in April. | Coastal Safety Force founded. |
| | | | House of Representative dissolved in August (Sudden Dissolution). | Reinstatement of the last group of the Purged. |
| | | | First general election after the signing of Peace Treaty in October, in which Jiyūtō wins the majority, leading to formation of the fourth Yoshida cabinet. | San Francisco Peace Treaty comes into effect. |
| | | | | Bloody May Day incident. |
| | | | | Japan joins International Monetary Fund and the World Bank. |
| | | | | National Police Force reorganized to National Safety Force. |
| 1953 | Shōwa 28 | 75 | Shigeru calls Nishimura Eiichi, a member of the Rightist Socialist Party who interpellates at Budget Committee of House of Representatives, an idiot in February. | NHK television broadcasting commenced. |
| | | | Motion for disciplinary measures and, subsequently, motion of no-confidence against Prime Minister Yoshida pass the Diet, leading to dissolution of the House of Representatives in March ("You Idiot" Dissolution). | Stalin passes away. |
| | | | The fifth Yoshida cabinet formed in May (Jiyūtō single-party minority government). | Korean Armistice Agreement signed in Panmunjom. |
| | | | | Soviet Union announces its possession of hydrogen bombs. |
| 1954 | Shōwa 29 | 76 | Shipbuilding Scandal in February. | Japanese fishing boat, *Daigo Fukuryūmaru*, exposed to and contaminated by nuclear fallout from the U.S. Castle Bravo thermonuclear device test on Bikini Atoll. |

| Year | Japanese Era year | Age of Person in Events Column | Events in Person's Life | Domesitic/Overseas Incidents |
|------|------|------|------|------|
| 1954 | Shōwa 29 | 76 | Shigeru instructs Justice Minister Inukai Takeshi to exercise his authority to block the arrest of Satō Eisaku, Secretary-General of Jiyūtō, against prosecutors' request to arrest him in April, when multiple members of the party are arrested. | Japanese Defense Agency and Self-Defense Forces established. |
| | | | House of Representatives' Audit Committee passes a denunciation motion against Shigeru in September, when Shigeru takes off to tour five European/U.S. countries, which is, de facto, the prelude to Shigeru's retirement. | The Geneva Accord to restore peace in Indochina signed, stipulating the independence of Cambodia and Laos and withdrawal of French troops from the peninsula. |
| | | | Nippon Minshutō founded in November. In the same month, Jiyūtō decides on Shigeru's honorable retreat and appointment of Ogata Taketora to its presidency. | |
| | | | The fifth Yoshida cabinet resigns in December to be replaced by the newly formed Hatoyama Ichirō Minshutō cabinet. | |
| 1955 | Shōwa 30 | 77 | The Second Hatoyama cabinet formed in March. | The Rightist Socialist Party and the Leftist Socialist Party merge to form the Japan Socialist Party. |
| | | | The Liberal Democratic Party established in a merger between Jiyūtō and Nippon Minshutō in November, consolidating the so-called 1955 System, from which Shigeru abstains. | Japan's application to join the United Nations vetoed by Soviet Union. |
| | | | | Economic White Paper announces that Japan should no longer be termed postwar. |
| 1956 | Shōwa 31 | 78 | The Ishibashi Tanzan cabinet formed in December. | Soviet-Japan Joint Declaration signed. |
| | | | | Japan joins the United Nations |
| 1957 | Shōwa 32 | 79 | The Kishi Nobusuke cabinet formed in February. | Soviet Union successfully launches the first artificial earth satellite, Sputnik 1. |
| | | | Shigeru publishes the four-volume Kaisō 10-nen (10 Years in Recollection). | |

| Year | Japanese Era year | Age of Person in Events Column | Events in Person's Life | Domesitic/Overseas Incidents |
|------|------|------|------|------|
| 1958 | Shōwa 33 | 80 | The second Kishi cabinet formed in June. | |
| 1959 | Shōwa 34 | 81 | | Cuban Revolution. |
| | | | | Crown Prince Naruhito's wedding. |
| 1960 | Shōwa 35 | 82 | The first Ikeda Hayato cabinet formed in July. | Revised U.S.-Japan Security Treaty signed. |
| | | | | Anti-U.S.-Japan Security Pact riot and Mitsui Miike Coal Miners' strike erupt. |
| 1961 | Shōwa 36 | 83 | The Ikeda cabinet reshuffled in July. | The Berlin Wall constructed by East Germany. |
| 1963 | Shōwa 38 | 85 | Shigeru resigns from the House of Representatives. | President John F. Kennedy assassinated in Dallas, Texas. |
| 1964 | Shōwa 39 | 86 | Shigeru goes to the U.S. to attend MacArthur's funeral in April. | Douglas MacArthur passes away at the age of 84. |
| | | | Shigeru awarded the Grand Cordon of the Supreme Order of the Chrysanthemum in May. | The 1964 Summer Olympics held in Tokyo. |
| 1967 | Shōwa 42 | 89 | Shigeru passes away at his Oiso residence on October 20 from cardiac infarction. | |
| | | | The first postwar state funeral held for Shigeru at Nippon Budōkan on October 31 for which Prime Minister Satō Eisaku serves as the master of ceremonies. | |

# INDEX

Fundamental Law of Education 238

（英文版）吉田茂とその時代
*Yoshida Shigeru and His Time*

2019年3月29日　第1刷発行

著　者　　岡崎久彦
訳　者　　野田牧人
発行所　　一般財団法人出版文化産業振興財団
　　　　　〒101-0051 東京都千代田区神田神保町3-12-3
　　　　　電話　03-5211-7282（代）
　　ページ　http://www.jpic.or.jp/
　　　　　大日本印刷株式会社